Competency-Based Teacher Education for English as a Foreign Language

Providing a series of chapters, written by teacher educators in three continents, this edited volume explores the concepts, challenges, possibilities, and implementations of competency-based instruction for developing English competencies in English as a foreign language (EFL) contexts. Recent trends in education have emphasized the need to develop competencies that connect learning with real-life performances. This need has brought about a massive increase in the number of studies and scholarly works devoted to research into competency-based education. However, for teachers and learners of EFL, it is challenging to develop competencies for using a language that does not seem to connect with their real-life scenarios. The chapters apply the concept of competency-based instruction in different EFL contexts and are structured around three themes:

1 Theory: current thoughts on theories of competency-based education
2 Research: empirical research on competency-based teacher education
3 Practice: integrating competency-based instruction into teacher education

This book offers examples of competency-based EFL teacher education through both research and practical applications. In addition to the innovation in competency approaches, the inclusion of language learning in virtual environments offers a valuable resource for scholars, educators, researchers, and all those concerned with current and future education.

Amber Yayin Wang is an Associate Professor in the Department of English at National Taichung University of Education, Taiwan. She has worked on many national projects in English language teacher education for years and published research related to language learning, English teacher education, and TPACK.

Routledge Research in Language Education

The *Routledge Research in Language Education* series provides a platform for established and emerging scholars to present their latest research and discuss key issues in Language Education. This series welcomes books on all areas of language teaching and learning, including but not limited to language education policy and politics, multilingualism, literacy, L1, L2 or foreign language acquisition, curriculum, classroom practice, pedagogy, teaching materials, and language teacher education and development. Books in the series are not limited to the discussion of the teaching and learning of English only.

Books in the series include:

Being and Becoming a TESOL Teacher Educator
Research and Practice
Edited by Rui Yuan and Icy Lee

Education for Sustainable Development in Foreign Language Learning
Content-Based Instruction in College-Level Curricula
Edited by María J. de la Fuente

Competency-Based Teacher Education for English as a Foreign Language
Theory, Research, and Practice
Edited by Amber Yayin Wang

Globalization and English Education in Taiwan
Curriculum, Perceptions, and Pedagogies
I-Chung Ke

Advocacy for Social and Linguistic Justice in TESOL
Nurturing Inclusivity, Equity, and Social Responsibility in English Language Teaching
Edited by Christine E. Poteau and Carter A. Winkle

For more information about the series, please visit www.routledge.com/Routledge-Research-in-Language-Education/book-series/RRLE

Competency-Based Teacher Education for English as a Foreign Language

Theory, Research, and Practice

Edited by Amber Yayin Wang

Routledge
Taylor & Francis Group
LONDON AND NEW YORK

First published 2022
by Routledge
2 Park Square, Milton Park, Abingdon, Oxon OX14 4RN

and by Routledge
605 Third Avenue, New York, NY 10158

Routledge is an imprint of the Taylor & Francis Group, an informa business

British Library Cataloguing-in-Publication Data
A catalogue record for this book is available from the British Library

Library of Congress Cataloging-in-Publication Data
Names: Wang, Amber Yayin, editor.
Title: Competency-based teacher education for English as a foreign language: theory, research, and practice/edited by Amber Yayin Wang.
Description: Abingdon, Oxon; New York, NY: Routledge, 2022. | Series: Routledge research in language education | Includes bibliographical references and index.
Identifiers: LCCN 2021025343 (print) | LCCN 2021025344 (ebook) | ISBN 9781032080727 (hardback) | ISBN 9781032080741 (paperback) | ISBN 9781003212805 (ebook)
Subjects: LCSH: English teachers—Training of—Taiwan. | English language—Study and teaching—Taiwan. | English language—Study and teaching—Foreign speakers.
Classification: LCC PE1068.T3 C66 2022 (print) | LCC PE1068.T3 (ebook) | DDC 428.0071—dc23
LC record available at https://lccn.loc.gov/2021025343
LC ebook record available at https://lccn.loc.gov/2021025344

ISBN: 978-1-032-08072-7 (hbk)
ISBN: 978-1-032-08074-1 (pbk)
ISBN: 978-1-003-21280-5 (ebk)

DOI: 10.4324/9781003212805

Typeset in Galliard
by KnowledgeWorks Global Ltd.

Contents

List of figures

List of tables

Acknowledgments

This book would not have been possible without the assistance of many individuals. On behalf of all authors, I would like to express our gratitude toward all of those who have provided the opportunity for the publication of this manuscript.

We want to thank Routledge for publishing this book, especially Bruce Roberts, Katie Peace, and Kendrick Loo from Taylor & Francis and anonymous reviewers. Katie provided suggestions and support during the process of the proposal review. Her positive attitude, valuable time, and kind assistance are highly appreciated. Kendrick walked us through the process of preparing all the necessary documents. We thank him for his patient and prompt responses. The three anonymous reviewers helped us clarify confusion and encouraged us in many ways.

Special thanks go to those who have helped improve the clarity of the book. Many professors in the field of English language teaching and learning at different universities served as anonymous reviewers to provide positive and constructive comments. We appreciate their precious time and valuable perspectives. In the revision process, we thank Dr. Massoud Moslehpour and Dr. Stacie Moore for their editing suggestions. During the long process of preparing the manuscripts, many other people spent extra time helping with details, including contacting reviewers, formatting, checking references, and other administrative assistance. They are, in alphabetical order, Hsiang-Ling Huang, Shu-Fang Hsieh, Ling-Ling Hsu, Yun-Hui Kuo, Liang-Ying Lu, and Yi-Cheng Lu.

We are grateful to the Ministry of Education (MOE) in Taiwan for supporting teacher educators in forming professional teacher groups. Without the professional teacher group funding by the MOE from 2019–2020, the authors of this book would not have had the chance to discuss and exchange ideas about EFL teacher education, and this book would not have been possible. We are grateful for this valuable support.

Thanks also to all authors of this book for sharing their valuable experiences and observations. All the authors supported the ideas of sharing what we had experimented with and managed to write, revise, and re-revise their chapters despite their tight schedules. It has been my pleasure to work with all the authors in this book.

I would also like to thank my friend and colleague Dr. Sa-hui Fan, who invited scholars from France, Spain, and Brazil to contribute to the book allowing it to be rich in content and perspectives.

Finally, we would like to thank all those who have inspired and supported us during the long journey of writing this book, including our friends and the broader research and scholarly community.

Amber Yayin Wang (editor)

List of abbreviations

3CIT	3 Continents Intercultural Telecollaboration
3R	reduce, recycle, reuse
4C	Content, Communication, Cognition, and Culture
ACTFL	American Council on the Teaching of Foreign Languages
BA	Bachelor of Arts
BPST-II	Basic Phonics Skills Test
BR100L	Beginner Reader 100 Lexile
BR300L	Beginner Reader 300 Lexile
CALL	computer-assisted language learning
CBE	competency-based education
CBLT	competency-based language teaching
CBLTE	competency-based language teacher education
CBTE	competency-based teacher education
CCSS	Common Core State Standards
CEFR	Common European Framework of Reference for Languages
CLIL	content and language integrated learning
CoE	Council of Europe
COVID	coronavirus disease
CVC	consonant-vowel-consonant
DIBELS	Dynamic Indicators of Basic Early Literacy Skills
DU	Deakin University
EFL	English as a foreign language
EFL-TPACK	Technological Pedagogical and Content Knowledge in EFL settings
ELF	English as a Lingua Franca
EJ	Experience Journal
ELT	English Language Teaching
ERIC	Education Resources Information Center
ESD	education for sustainable development
ESL	English as a second language
ESSA	Every Student Succeeds Act
EU	European Union
GCED	global citizenship education

HBTE	humanistic-based teacher education
IAC	identity as a competence
ICC	identity and competencies as complementary
ICT	Information and Communications Technology
ILA	International Literacy Association
K-12	kindergarten through twelfth grade
KARDS	Knowing, Analyzing, Recognizing, Doing, and Seeing
KFC	Kentucky Fried Chicken
L2	second language
TEFL	Teachers of English as a Foreign Language
LNF	Letter Naming Fluency
LTE	Language Teacher Education
LTI	Language Teacher Identity
MA	Master of Arts
MOE	Ministry of Education, Taiwan
MOST	Ministry of Science and Technology, Taiwan
NAER	National Academy for Educational Research, Taiwan
NCATE	National Council for the Accreditation of Teacher Education
NRF	Nonsense Word Reading Fluency
OECD	Organization for Economic Cooperation and Development
PCK	Pedagogical Content Knowledge
PISA	Program for International Student Assessment
pre-K	pre-kindergarten
PSF	Phonemic Segmentation Fluency
SBC	school-based curriculum
SCDA	Sociocultural Discourse Analysis
SDGs	Sustainable Development Goals
SPSS	Statistical Product and Service Solutions
SUP	school-university partnerships
TESOL	Teaching English to Speakers of Other Languages
TESOL MA	Teaching English for Speakers of Other Language Master of Arts
TPACK	Technological Pedagogical and Content Knowledge
TPCK	Technological Pedagogical Content Knowledge
UbD	Understanding by Design
UCLA	University of California, Los Angeles
UK	United Kingdom
UN	United Nations
UNESCO	United Nations Educational, Scientific and Cultural Organization
UNIDO	United Nations Industrial Development Organization
US	United States
USA	United States of America
WRF	Word reading Fluency

Contributors

Patrícia Fabiana Bedran has a PhD in Linguistics, with a focus on Applied Linguistics Language teaching and learning. She is currently Professor at the Department of Education at São Paulo State University (Unesp), São José do Rio Preto campus, where she works in the area of Applied Linguistics—First Language Teaching and in the orientation and supervision of Supervised Curricular Internships in First Language. She also conducts research in the area of mother tongue and foreign language teacher training.

Paloma Castro-Prieto is currently an Associate Professor at the Faculty of Education, University of Valladolid, Spain. Her lines of research are ELT teacher education and the development of plurilingual competences, the intercultural dimension of foreign language education, internationalization of higher education, and intercultural telecollaboration or virtual exchanges.

I-An Chen completed her PhD in education at University of Massachusetts Amherst, USA. She is currently an Assistant Professor at the Department of English at National Taichung University of Education, Taiwan. Her research agenda centers on understanding second language literacy development, EFL teachers' professional development, and the discourses of educational reform in Taiwan.

Yilin Chen is a Professor of the Department of English Language, Literature and Linguistics and the director of the Global Foreign Language Education Program at Providence University. Her research expertise lies in bilingual eduction, Shakespeare study, and gender issues in education.

Chin-Wen Chien received her Doctor of Education degree from the University of Washington (Seattle, USA). She is an Associate Professor in the Department of English Instruction at National Tsing Hua University in Taiwan. Her research interests include language education, language teacher education, and curriculum and instruction.

Ya-Chen Chien, a.k.a. Jane Chien, is an Assistant Professor in the Department of Children's English Education at the National Taipei University of Education.

During the past 16 years, she has been engaged in pre-service EFL elementary school teacher training and in providing professional development to in-service teachers. As the Director of the Center for Research on Bilingual Education at NTUE, she has dedicated her work to promoting bilingual education through CLIL, supervising several elementary schools' bilingual programs in the northern part of Taiwan.

Martine Derivry-Plard is currently Professor in applied linguistics at INSPE, Bordeaux University, France. She has been engaged in many European projects of telecollaboration and her research interests include intercultural learning, and telecollaboration in EFL and language teaching as well as plurilingualism and native-speakerism.

Sa-hui Fan received her PhD in Curriculum and Instructions from the University of Texas at Austin and is currently an Assistant Professor at the Department of English at National Taichung University of Education, Taiwan. Her research interests include bilingual education, educational ethnography and telecollaboration in language learning.

Jeffrey Gamble is an Assistant Professor in the Department of Foreign Languages at National Chiayi University in Taiwan. His teaching emphasizes English Teaching pre-service teacher training and in-service English teacher training. His research interests include educational policy for language learning, innovative instructional design, adaptive language instruction, and the role of technology in teaching and learning.

Eric K. Ku is Lecturer in the Department of International Resources at Akita University, Japan. His current research interests include language teacher identity, language teacher education, multimodal composition, and linguistic landscapes.

Rae Ping Lin is an Assistant Professor in the Department of English Language, Literature and Linguistics of Providence University. Her research interests include teacher education, curriculum study, and identity issues in language teaching and learning.

Yeu-Ting Liu is Professor of the Department of English at National Taiwan Normal University. His research focuses on bilingual processing and cognitive development of second/foreign language learners. He is currently one of the principal investigators for the Immersion/CLIL programs sponsored by the Taiwanese Ministry of Education.

Tzyy-Yuh Maa is a primary school teacher of English at Jian-Xing Elementary school in Taiwan. She has completed her MA degree and is currently a doctoral student at National Taichung University of Education. Her research interests include creativity, English writing, and competency-based education.

Ana Cristina Biondo Salomão has a PhD in Linguistics, with focus on Applied Linguistics Language teaching and learning. She is currently Professor at the

Department of Modern Languages of the School of Sciences and Languages of São Paulo State University (Unesp), Araraquara campus, where she coordinates the Teletandem Brasil Project (http://www.teletandembrasil.org/). She is also coordinator of the Brazilian Virtual Exchange (BRaVE) Program at institutional level. She is an accredited lecturer in the Postgraduate Program in Linguistics at the same institution, supervising research at Masters and PhD levels. Her research focus is language teacher education, interculturality and telecollaboration.

Amber Yayin Wang completed her PhD in education at Claremont Graduate University in the United States. She is currently an Associate Professor in the Department of English at National Taichung University of Education, Taiwan. Her research explores EFL teacher education, EFL TPACK, competency-based English instruction, and how teaching influences language learning, critical and creative thinking, and cultural awareness.

Ai Chun Yen is an Associate Professor in the Department of English, National Dong Hwa University, Taiwan. Her research concerns theories of constructivist learning environments and technological applications. Her recent research interests are: (1) competent English-knowing bilingual education; (2) strategic teaching and learning; and (3) literature in language education.

Introduction

Amber Yayin Wang

Beginning

A simple question, *What is competency?* initiated the discussion of this book project. Although countless scholars have answered the question over the past decades, competencies cannot be of a static body of knowledge, skills, and attitudes, particularly when the importance of contextualization is considered. Competencies are dynamic, evolving continuously with different times and contexts (Docking, 1994). When competencies were first incorporated into the most recent curriculum guidelines in Taiwan, the concept of "competency" remained vague to many stakeholders in this environment where English is a foreign language (EFL). As such, many teachers in Taiwan, who had mastered the ability to plan lessons based on existing curricular content, were confused when requested to plan lessons that emphasized the development of competencies. The journey of writing this book began with this question when a group of EFL teacher educators discussed the confusion schoolteachers in Taiwan were facing after the curriculum guidelines were put into practice in 2019. Subsequent discussions, both online and offline, about competencies in 21st-century EFL teaching and learning have led to the development of this book.

Competencies are a significant factor in boosting innovation and competitiveness (EU, 2019; OECD, 2018). Aligning with global education trends (EU, 2018, 2019; OECD, 2014, 2018; UNESCO, 2015; US Department of Education, 2015), the 12-Year Basic Education Curriculum Guidelines in Taiwan (MOE, 2014) feature nine core competencies for the development of lifelong learning. According to the guidelines (MOE, 2014), these core competencies are what "a person should possess to equip him or her for daily life and for tackling future challenges" (p. 5). The guidelines promote competency-based education (CBE), emphasizing the concept that "learning should consider real-life scenarios" (MOE, 2014, p. 5). As with the latest definitions from other educational organizations (e.g., EU, 2019; OECD, 2018; UNESCO, 2015), the word "competency" in the 12-Year Basic Education Curriculum Guidelines (MOE, 2014) does not mean any specific skill, behavior, or task. Instead, competencies refer to holistic learning that can be applied in everyday life to help individuals function effectively in an unknown and uncertain world.

DOI: 10.4324/9781003212805-1

Challenges

CBE has accentuated the importance of connecting school learning with real-world performances (Richards & Rodgers, 2014). CBE in Taiwan was originally introduced as part of a government-subsidized policy (C.-W. Chang, 2018). However, given the challenges faced by EFL teachers in developing competences for a language that is too often not connected with students' real life, it is increasingly important for EFL teacher educators to bridge theory and practice in order to integrate competency-based approaches for teaching and learning.

Given the fact that, in Taiwan, English is not commonly used in daily life, how EFL teachers can design and assess competency-based learning for students in English language instructional settings has become an increasingly salient issue. Many EFL learners might be able to memorize and practice a foreign language but might not be able to authentically use the language for communicative purposes (Forsberg et al., 2019; Ke & Cahyani, 2014). EFL teachers have already struggled to design meaningful activities for students to acquire English language based on existing textbooks and are now overwhelmed by the expectation of integrating competences into their lesson designs and activities. From a CBE perspective, teachers must not only consider students' language learning outcomes and the development of communicative skills, but also strive to create a purpose for EFL learners to "use" English as an authentic language in real-life scenarios. This requires teachers to break the boundaries among subjects and help learners use English "across the curriculum" to apply, analyze, evaluate, and create—transfer what they have learned in the classroom to function effectively in their lives!

As a first step toward empowering EFL teachers in the use of CBE, strategies and perspectives must be gleaned from the wealth of related international literature. CBE has a long history and has been practiced in the United States and Europe for years (Nodine, 2016; Springer, 2020), with many successful interventions available as a reference. While EFL teachers and researchers can learn a great deal from the literature on CBE, it remains challenging, and fundamentally inappropriate, to simply transplant experiences from contexts wherein English is a native language to design interventions in Asian EFL contexts. Moreover, over the course of time, CBE has evolved into a new phase (EU, 2019; OECD, 2018), which requires a deeper consideration of both the world we live in today and local sociocultural and linguistic contextual factors.

Motivation

The confusions, struggles, and challenges that EFL teachers had about competencies were the reasons why we EFL teacher educators started experimenting with CBE in preparing future teachers. This book brings together our practices for change, enabling us to think anew, share strategies, and challenge the status quo. This volume, as a synthesis of our collective explorations and experiments, presents examples of how EFL teacher educators have attempted to support learners in developing competences in using or teaching English in EFL contexts. Although our observations cannot represent all EFL contexts or address the concerns of every EFL teacher, it is our sincere intention to share our experiences, believing that the results of our efforts may enable and inspire other EFL educators to continue experimenting with CBE in their own teaching and learning contexts. While many EFL educators continue to explore ways to incorporate competencies in education, a book that includes the Taiwanese context and the western theoretical heritage can be beneficial for EFL researchers and educators.

Significance

CBE is an international trend in the development processes of all education levels (EU, 2019; Mulder, 2017; OECD, 2018). Despite a rich theoretical heritage and considerable empirical support, calls for more CBE research continue to be made (e.g., CCSSO, 2013; Johnstone & Soares, 2014). According to the literature review conducted in Chapter 1 of this book (Wang & Ma), studies on competency-based teacher education (CBTE) for EFL teacher education are relatively scarce. Many EFL scholars (e.g., C. H. Chang, 2018; Fwu, 2018) also urged for more CBE research in EFL settings. This volume responds to those calls.

The contributors of this book include research-active teacher educators from three continents, providing insights and perspectives from contexts including Taiwan, France, Brazil, Spain, and the Netherlands. For preparing 21st-century competencies, this book offers innovation in competency approaches and language learning in virtual environments. The book represents a Taiwanese perspective on competency-based language teaching and learning, as well as competency-based language teacher education and training at the international level by including different scholars in different contexts. It is our hope that this book will be helpful for EFL teachers, teacher educators, and researchers who endeavor to plan competency-based language teaching and learning.

Organization

This volume aims to provide a research-based and practice-based account of what EFL teacher educators have envisioned and observed in implementing CBTE. This book includes three sections: (1) theory, (2) research, and (3) practice. The theory section sets the tone for this volume, including a review of relevant current literature, an overview of language teacher education, and a perspective on a balanced competency-based framework for language teacher education. The research section includes empirical CBTE studies in Taiwan, centering on methodological and analytical approaches. Finally, the practice section offers practical examples of applying competency-based approaches in EFL teacher education. One thing to note is the use of the words *competency* and *competence* in the book: the two words are interchangeable, though *competency* implies an essential attribute to function well in this rapid-changing world, and competence refers to the ability to do something well in a specific area.

Section I: Theory

This section begins with a chapter reviewing the current CBE literature on EFL teacher education, serving as a foundation for later topics and chapters in the book. Chapter 2 overviews language teacher education and observes its connections to competency-based language education through the lens of socio-cultural theory. Chapter 3 argues the necessity for developing teacher identity in competency-based language teacher education.

Section II: Research

Following the same thread of teacher identity, this section starts with a chapter investigating teacher agency among EFL student teachers. Chapter 5 examines diagnostic reading training for pre-service EFL teachers. Chapter 6 evaluates a CBTE model with the support of school-university partnerships. Finally, with a focus on technology, Chapter 7 explores the development of competency-based repertoires of teachers in intercultural telecollaboration.

Section II: Practice

Chapter 8 describes how telecollaborative environments help develop intercultural communication competencies and intercultural reflexivity among EFL students. Chapter 9 reports the approach of how to prepare EFL student teachers to integrate real-world issues into English instruction. Chapter 10 demonstrates the integration of global competences into pre-service EFL teacher education. Chapter 11 proposes a mind-mapping model to support EFL student teachers in developing their interdisciplinary competencies. Chapter 12 suggests collaborative work in international learning contexts for enhancing pedagogical competences for Content and Language Integrated Learning (CLIL).

Conclusion

As EFL teachers require competencies in diverse areas to assist learners in adapting to changing demands, EFL teacher education is experiencing essential changes. This book does not claim to address all possible issues relating to CBTE for English as a foreign language. However, we aim to provide experiences and open up possibilities for further exploration of the issue of CBE and CBTE in other EFL contexts.

The different approaches in this book can provide valuable lessons and insights for both researchers and practitioners. It is suggested that different readers can use the book in different ways. Readers interested in what CBTE is in the 21st century may start from the very beginning with the theory section.

Researchers and policymakers aiming at the latest empirical CBTE studies may go for any chapter in the research section. EFL teachers and teacher educators looking for direct application may find the practice section helpful. We hope that this book can serve as a stepping-stone for the future exploration of CBTE for EFL.

References

CCSSO (Council of Chief State School Officers). (2013). *Interstate teacher assessment and support consortium (InTASC) standards: Model core teaching standards and learning progressions for teachers 1.0.* https://ccsso.org/sites/default/files/2017-12/2013_INTASC_Learning_Progressions_for_Teachers.pdf

Chang, C. H. (2018). 素養導向的未來師資培育 [Cultivating teachers for core competence orientation]. *School Administrators, 113*, 11–18.

Chang, C.-W. (Ed.). (2018). 面向未來的能力：素養導向教學教戰手冊 *[Future competencies: Handbook for competency-based instruction].* Ministry of Education.

Docking, R. (1994). Competency-based curricula: The big picture. *Prospect, 9*(2), 8–17

EU (European Union). (2018). *Council recommendation on key competences for lifelong learning.* https://eur-lex.europa.eu/legal-content/EN/TXT/PDF/?uri=CELEX:32018H0604(01)&from=EN

EU (European Union). (2019). *Key competences for lifelong learning.* https://op.europa.eu/en/publication-detail/-/publication/297a33c8-a1f3-11e9-9d01-01aa75ed71a1/language-en

Forsberg, J., Mohr, S., & Jansen, S. (2019). "The goal is to enable students to communicate": Communicative competence and target varieties in TEFL practices in Sweden and Germany. *European Journal of Applied Linguistics, 7*(1), 31–60

Fwu, B. J. (2018). 素養導向國教新課綱的師資培育：國立臺灣大學「探究式— 素養導向的師資培育」理想芻議 [Teacher preparation in response to competence-based curriculum reform for K-12 education: National Taiwan university's proposal of inquiry-based and competency-based teacher education]. *Journal of research in education sciences, 63*(4), 59–87

Johnstone, S. M., & Soares, L. (2014). Principles for developing competency-based education programs. *Change: The Magazine of Higher Learning, 46*, 12–19.

Ke, I.-C., & Cahyani, H. (2014). Learning to become users of English as a Lingua Franca (ELF): How EFL online communication affects Taiwanese learners' beliefs of English. *System, 46*, 28–38.

MOE (Ministry of Education, Taiwan). (2014). *Curriculum guidelines of 12-Year basic education.* https://cirn.moe.edu.tw/WebContent/index.aspx?sid=11&mid=9900

Mulder, M. (Ed.). (2017). *Competence-based vocational and professional education: Bridging the worlds of work and education.* Springer International Publishing.

Nodine, T. R. (2016). How did we get here? A brief history of competency-based higher education in the United States. *Competency-based Education, 1*, 5–11.

OECD (Organization for Economic Cooperation and Development). (2014). *Competency framework.* https://www.oecd.org/careers/competency_framework_en.pdf

OECD (Organization for Economic Cooperation and Development). (2018). *The future of education and skills. Education 2030.* https://www.oecd.org/education/2030/E2030%20Position%20Paper%20(05.04.2018).pdf

Richards, J. C., & Rodgers, T. S. (2014). *Approaches and methods in language teaching* (3rd ed.). Cambridge University Press.

Springer, S. B. (2020). Forty years: Where is competency-based education? *Adult Learning*, *31*(2), 54–56

UNESCO (United Nations Educational, Scientific and Cultural Organization). (2015). *UNESCO Competency Framework.* https://en.unesco.org/sites/default/files/Competency%20Framework_E.pdf

US Department of Education. (2015). *Every student succeeds act.* https://www.congress.gov/114/plaws/publ95/PLAW-114publ95.pdf

Section I

Theory

1 Competency-based education

A literature review and its practical considerations for EFL teacher education

Amber Yayin Wang and Tzyy-Yuh Maa

Introduction

In preparing teachers of English as a foreign language (EFL), some challenges have been identified. For instance, teacher training courses are disconnected from the actual teaching field, and they fail to respond to student teachers' needs (Ali et al., 2014; Al-Jaro & Asmawi, 2019; Cabaroglu, 2014). Teacher education reform has therefore been called for to solve these problems, and a growing number of EFL researchers and educators have directed their attention to competency-based education (CBE) (Johnstone & Soares, 2014; Louiza & Sarnou, 2018; Nkwetisama, 2012; Pérez-Llantada, 2011; Vail, 2019). Recent educational reforms worldwide (EU, 2018; MOE, 2014; OECD, 2014, 2018; UNESCO, 2015; US Department of Education, 2015) emphasize "competency" and declare the core competencies that future citizens should possess.

Conventional education has been criticized as having the problem of disconnecting with the modern workplace and real life (Lunce, 2006; Senge, 2000). CBE attempts to address the issues as it stresses real-life performance, fosters intrinsic motivation, and considers diverse needs in learning (Henri et al., 2017; Moon, 2007; Sturgis & Casey, 2018). Mulder (2017) indicated that in America, Australia, and Asia, where CBE has been implemented with prodigious achievement, the reform on the learning content, agenda, and even the qualification of the teachers has started, and an educational paradigm shift is taking place. CBE aims to develop interests and strategies for learning and enhance learner autonomy with an ultimate goal for lifelong learning (Agudo, 2017; Makulova et al., 2015; MOE, 2014). Reflecting on the past 40 years of education, Springer (2020) emphasized the importance of CBE and its positive influence on future education.

With the importance mentioned above, CBE has extensively been implemented and explored in recent years. Following the CBE trend, Taiwan developed a new curriculum, known as the 12-Year Basic Education Curriculum, and has currently put it into operation. According to Anderson (2018) and Timothy (2018), CBE has been put into motion by nearly 90% of the states in the United States. Researchers and educators in diverse contexts have followed the trend and made an effort to reshape and redesign curricula (Eldridge, 2020). Since CBE has

DOI: 10.4324/9781003212805-2

been embraced as a valuable way of learning and teaching, educational reforms in EFL settings have also been initiated. However, as some studies (e.g., Akane, 2019; Kabombwe & Mulenga, 2019; Lai, 2019) indicated, many teachers in various EFL settings are not familiar with how to make the most use of competency-based instruction. To apply CBE properly and prepare EFL teachers for CBE instruction, as Casey (2018) implied, a clear vision is needed.

Objectives

Therefore, this chapter attempts to provide the so-called clear vision for the current progress of CBE research and the existing literature in EFL teacher education. This chapter introduces the background of CBE, reviews CBE studies from 2010 to 2020, and discusses how the literature may shed light on EFL teacher education. The chapter addresses the following questions: (1) What are the underpinnings of CBE? (2) What are the principles for CBE? (3) How do recent studies of CBE inform EFL teacher education?

Method

Based on the above research questions, several databases were selected to identify and assess relevant studies. Primo Central Index, Education Resources Information Center (ERIC), and Google Scholar were used to do the primary search. The initial search key terms were: "competency-based education competency-based learning or CBE," "English as a foreign language or EFL or ESL," and "teacher education or teacher training or teacher preparation." The results yielded 146 citations. The years of publications were set between 2010 and 2020 to find the latest CBE papers, though a portion of significant works published earlier than this period were also selected. The full papers were assessed to select studies that were directly related to CBE. After eliminating duplicates, papers that were not relevant to CBE, and papers that were not peer-reviewed, 63 publications directly related to CBE or EFL teacher education were used for detailed examination. Only 42 journal articles from 2010 to 2020 dealt explicitly with CBE and EFL teacher education.

Underpinnings of competency-based education

Historical origin

CBE has been around for over a half-century, and it has been applied in various contexts. Starting in the 1950s, CBE originated after World War II with the background of military competition between the Soviet Union and the USA (Hodge, 2007). CBE in the 1960s thrived in vocational education because of a large number of adults returning to college (Nodine, 2016). In the 1960s, education transformation was advocated (Makulova et al., 2015), requesting a better teacher training system (Tuxworth, 2005). In the 1970s, teacher education adopted the CBE approach to emphasize performance-based rather than knowledge-based instruction (Burke, 1989; Malan, 2000; Makulova et al., 2015; Nodine, 2016). From 1970 to 1990, different studies to identify professional competencies flourished (Makulova et al., 2015). After 1990, various programs using a competency-based approach at all levels of education appeared (Makulova et al., 2015). When the Every Student Succeeds Act (ESSA) was signed in 2015, CBE became a buzzword again in the education field (Curran & Petersen, 2017). In the 21st century, CBE has been implemented and researched extensively in many different countries.

CBE in the 1970s and in the 21st century shares some similarities, including personalized instruction (Edwards, 1973; Nodine, 2016) and the application of mixed learning media (Cator et al., 2014; Ford, 2014; Hohn & Meinke, 1978). CBE in the 1970s aimed to make higher education more efficient, life and work relevant, and help students develop competencies required by the workforce (Gallagher, 2014) while contemporary CBE focuses on developing life skills that help function in society (Richards & Rodgers, 2014). In addition to the constant emphasis on student outcomes, as Cator et al. (2014) and Ford (2014) observed, CBE in the 21st century created more opportunities for learning efficiency with the advancement of technology, online resources, and adaptive learning technology. CBE in the 21st century allows students to develop life skills, such as critical thinking and lifelong learning (Casey, 2018; MOE, 2014; Mulder, 2017; Sturgis & Casey, 2018).

Theoretical basis

CBE has lasted persistently for more than half a century, so various theories are involved in describing CBE. Originating in the 1960s and flourishing in the 1970s, CBE had been linked with behaviorism, Taylorism, and Fordism to emphasize efficiency (DU, 1994). Later, the impact of essentialism and neoliberalism mixed in around the 1980s, and under the background that quality should surpass efficiency, learning outcomes became the focus (Wu & Chan, 2018). In the 1990s, functional and personal competence approaches started to be included in CBE, aiming at achieving desired outcomes and developing personal characteristics (Cheetham & Chivers, 1996). In the 21st century, pragmatism, constructivism, and learner-centered teaching took shape (Wu & Chan, 2018). Mixed theories led to varied course design feasibilities. As Gallagher (2014) suggested, both behavioral and humanistic elements can exist in CBE courses. Contemporary CBE went beyond the concept of knowledge and skills and instead emphasized metacognitive and higher-order thinking skills (Westera, 2001).

In the 1970s, under the influence of behaviorism, CBE took the concepts of atomism and reductionism and considered that learning targets or skills could be broken down into basic units and be learned bit by bit (Ford, 2014; Wu & Chan, 2018). Nonetheless, teaching is a complex procedure and it does not merely consist of several basic unit tasks. CBE at that time demanded teacher education to measure the competencies a teacher should possess, which was very difficult to specify and list out, leading to the problem of developing assessment criteria (Cangelosi, 1975; Edwards, 1973; Ford, 2014; Gallagher, 2014; Hohn & Meinke, 1978). As Edwards (1973) noted, simplifying the teaching process could overlook the complex nature and theory of teaching and learning. Competency-based teacher education (CBTE) in the 1970s was often associated with mastery testing, but it could only distinguish between incompetent and competent teachers. This type of CBTE required student teachers to meet fixed criteria without encouraging them to reach their potential as future educators. Later, CBE evolved when different theories such as essentialism, neoliberalism, pragmatism, and constructivism mixed in. Based on the observation of Zeichner (1983), different theories were adopted in different teacher training programs, including behaviorist, personalistic, traditional craft, and inquiry-based theories.

CBE theories are holistic (Hoogveld, 2003; Westera, 2001; Wu & Chan, 2018) but can be generally divided into two categories: one is the type used in the United Kingdom and the United States, and another is used in other European countries. CBE in the United Kingdom and the United States take a functional and personal approach, providing standard and proficiency-based educational programs, while CBE in European countries adopts the ethical and meta-competence approach, focusing on interdisciplinary programs and the context in which actions occur (Cheetham & Chivers, 1996; Wu & Chan, 2018). Theory and practice complement each other. The diverse theories provided educators and researchers what they needed to develop their understanding, design, and way to improve CBE. CBE's holistic theory provides varied and abundant profiles for practical use.

Definition

In the long history of CBE, "competency" has been a conceptual word that does not have a widely agreed definition (Butova, 2015; Gervais, 2016; Koenen et al., 2015; Nodine, 2016; Westera, 2001). In the Merriam-Webster Dictionary (2020), "competency" is defined as "competence" or "a specific area of competence," with a note to refer to competence as "possession of sufficient knowledge or skill." According to the European Union (EU, 2010), competency is the ability to use knowledge and skills in work or study situations. In a recently updated definition, Levine and Patrick (2019) mentioned competencies as "knowledge, skills, and dispositions" (p. 3). To emphasize the hidden quality that makes use of knowledge and skills, the United Nations Industrial Development Organization (UNIDO, 2002) referred to competency as the knowledge, skills, and attributes that allow an individual to perform a specific job effectively. The Organization for Economic Cooperation and Development (OECD) (2018) made it clear:

> The concept of competency implies more than just the acquisition of knowledge and skills; it involves the mobilization of knowledge, skills, attitudes and values to meet complex demands. (p. 5)

The word competency nowadays involves knowledge, skills, attitudes, and values, which constitute complex abilities to function effectively in this global village.

With the above definition of the word "competency" in mind, the term CBE becomes clearer. Casey (2018) describes CBE as a system for the nurture of independent learners. The spirit of CBE was to align the world of education with life (Ashworth & Saxton, 1990; Mulder, 2017). Traditional education emphases, such as academic skills, memorization, and comprehension of content, failed to respond to the needs of modern society. That was why Sturgis and Casey (2018) marked that CBE nowadays focuses on foundational and lifelong learning skills, such as social-emotional skills and the ability to transfer knowledge to new contexts.

Principles of competency-based education

Core competencies

Based on the contemporary conceptions about CBE, different educational organizations have proposed different core competencies for education in their respective contexts. For example, OECD (2014), in its competency framework, proposed 15 core competencies, which summarize "the capabilities that are important across all jobs" (p. 2) in three clusters: (1) delivery-related: for achieving results; (2) interpersonal: for developing relationships; and (3) strategic: for planning the future. The Ministry of Education in Taiwan (MOE, 2014) announced nine core competencies grouped into three dimensions: (1) spontaneity: for developing autonomy; (2) communication: for interacting with the world; and (3) social participation: for seeking the common good. Makulova et al. (2015) summarized different perspectives in Russia and Kazakhstan into five sets of professional competencies: (1) cognitive; (2) functional; (3) personal; (4) ethical; and (5) meta-competences. The European Union (EU, 2019) indicated eight key competencies for lifelong learning, including literacy, multilingual, mathematic, digital, personal/social/learning to learn, citizenship, entrepreneurship, and cultural awareness/expression competencies. British Columbia (n.d.) presents three sets of competencies: (1) communication; (2) thinking; and (3) personal/social, and explains that they are "sets of intellectual, personal, social and emotional proficiencies that all students need in order to engage in deep, lifelong learning."

All the above organizations appeared to agree that core competencies are for lifelong learning and for individuals to function independently and interdependently in this ever-changing world. To summarize the above core competencies, at least three sets of competencies are considered crucial: (1) strategies (for being independent); (2) communication (for reaching out to the world); and (3) social abilities (for interdependent needs). These are competencies that are transferable across all curricula. Based on the above overview of core competencies suggested by different organizations, CBE in whatever field would need to address these core competencies.

Features of competency-based education

According to different reviews of the CBE literature (Casey, 2018; Henri et al., 2017; Sturgis et al., 2011), five critical components marked CBE: (1) performance; (2) objectives; (3) assessment; (4) support; and (5) real-life training. Sturgis et al. (2011) also illustrated these components when they proposed five principles for developing high-quality CBE. The following paragraphs elaborate on the five features of CBE in detail.

First, "performance" refers to how students move on to the next level only when they demonstrate evidence for specific competencies (Garrison, 2018; Henri et al., 2017; Levine & Patrick, 2019; Ortlieb & Lu, 2011; Serdenciuc, 2013). Replacing the traditional model of having a seat-time requirement, as Casey (2018) and Henri et al. (2017) noted, student advancements are revealed as demonstrating mastery toward acquired learning contents. The emphasis of CBE on mastery learning and individualized learning has made the learners the center of instruction (Richards & Rodgers, 2014).

Second, identifying meaningful "objectives" is essential in CBE. Unlike the traditional focus on what the teacher teaches or what the school provides (the input), CBE has shifted its focus to learning outcomes (the output) (Richards & Rodgers, 2014). CBE requires a predetermined learning goal and specific learning outcome (Garrison, 2018; Henri et al., 2017; Ortlieb & Lu, 2011; Serdenciuc, 2013). The CBE objectives need to be explicit, observable, measurable, and transferable (Casey, 2018; Sturgis et al., 2011). Gervais (2016) and Akos et al. (2019) reviewed CBE literature in different fields, and both concluded that CBE put emphasis on learning outcomes that meet the objectives.

Third, "assessment" in CBE needs to be an observable performance with explicit assessment criteria (Garrison, 2018; Henri et al., 2017; Ortlieb & Lu, 2011; Serdenciuc, 2013) and, at the same time, meaningful and positive learning experience for students (Sturgis et al., 2011). CBE assessments are authentic with an emphasis on actual demonstration of the targeted competencies. As the planning of CBE starts with outcomes and is followed by acceptable evidence, principles of backward design have often been used to plan its instruction (Fwu, 2018; Richards & Rodgers, 2014; Urofsky & Bobby, 2012). These are the two key components that CBE and the backward design share: (1) meaningful learning outcomes and (2) performance-based assessment.

Fourth, "support" in CBE refers to providing additional individualized support and resources during the learning process. With technology development, abundant learning materials can now be easily accessed by the students to learn at their own pace. This new technology development makes it more possible than ever to achieve individualized and adaptive learning. According to Sturgis et al. (2011), in addition to learning resources, formative assessments and effective feedback are also strong support in CBE.

Fifth, "real-life training" means that CBE training is based on real-life needs, and the training process engages learners in solving problems in real-life scenarios (Gervais, 2016; OECD, 2018). Thus, its learning outcomes need to be knowledge, skills, and dispositions for real-life needs (Sturgis et al., 2011). Addressing real-life needs is a feature that has remained consistent throughout CBE history. As Henri et al. (2017) remarked, it is one of the key factors that distinguishes CBE from other mastery learning approaches.

Recent studies on competency-based teacher education

In an attempt to connect teacher education with the authentic teaching fields, a large amount of research has been devoted to investigating CBTE. Many studies on CBTE appeared in the 1970s, but this section reviews mainly the recent CBE studies. As mentioned in the method section, 42 articles were selected from 2010 to 2020 and analyzed to understand the current status of CBE research, especially CBTE for EFL teachers. Figure 1.1 presents the numbers of related articles published in the years 2010–2020. According to Figure 1.1, less than 10 studies each year in the past decade were found. The highest number of studies (eight articles) appeared in 2018 and 2019. The articles in 2020 were not found because related articles in 2020 have not been collected in the databases at the time of the search. It looked like studies on CBTE related to EFL teachers were rare but had been increasing in the recent two years.

The citations in this study manifest various national perspectives. The research areas in the 42 studies included Asia (*N*=13, 30.95%), Europe (*N*=10, 23.81%), America (*N*=9, 21.43%), Africa (*N*=6, 14.29%), and the Middle East (*N*=4, 9.52%). Figure 1.2 indicates the number of studies in each area. In Asia, six studies were done in Taiwan, two in Korea, and one each in Bangladesh, Hong Kong, India, Malaysia, and the Philippines. In Europe, two studies were done in more than one European country, two in Belgium, and one for each in the Czech Republic, Luxembourg, Spain, Romania, and the United Kingdom. In

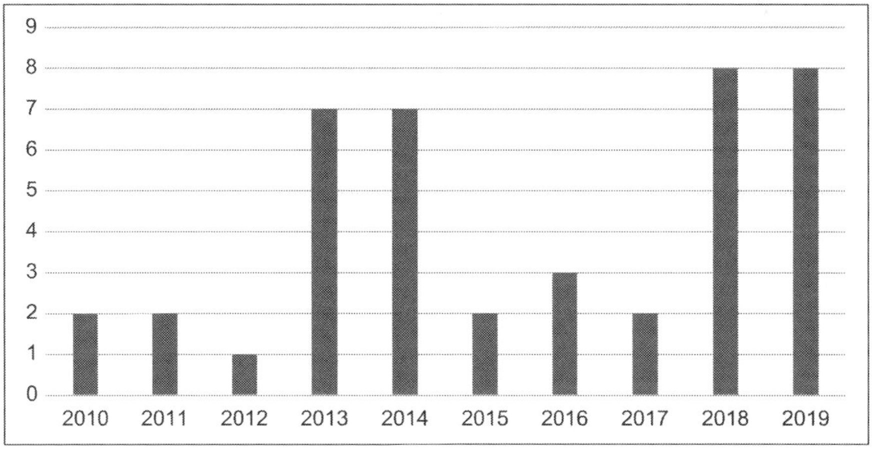

Figure 1.1 Numbers of selected studies in years 2010–2020.

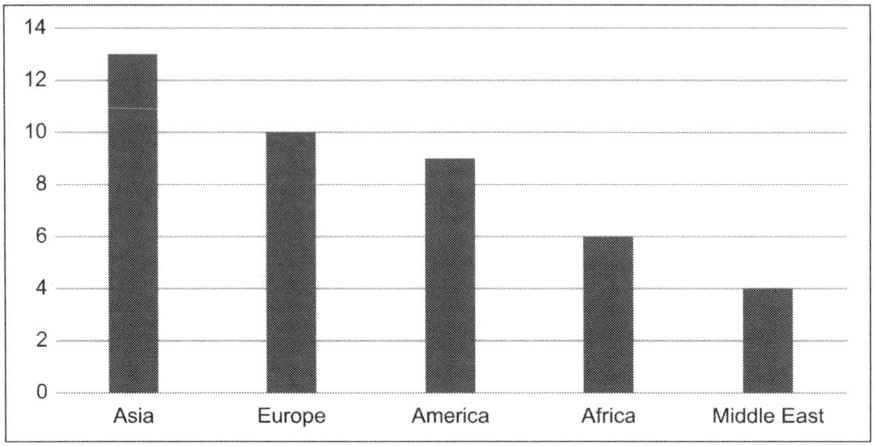

Figure 1.2 Numbers of selected studies in different areas.

America, eight studies were done in the United States and one in Colombia. In Africa, one study each was done in Cameroon, Ethiopia, the Republic of Benin, Rwanda, and Zambia. In the Middle East, two studies were done in Turkey, one in Iran, and one in Yemen. This shows that researchers from different parts of the world have been interested in adopting a competency-based approach in teacher education.

Different studies researched different topics. One study (Bhavana & Kousalya, 2011) intended to develop student teachers' competency for framing questions by analyzing their errors. Another study (Yigzaw, 2013) examined the assessment used in their outcome-based education. Some studies (Johnstone & Soares, 2014; Vail, 2019) examined personalized (self-paced) learning for diverse learners while some (CCSSO, 2013; Johnstone & Soares, 2014) advocated collaborative support. Many other studies (e.g., Agudo, 2017; Al-Jaro & Asmawi, 2019) evaluated their EFL teacher education and suggested possible solutions which align with CBE. On reviewing the literature, several themes emerged, including (1) teacher education redesign; (2) interdisciplinary curriculum; (3) real teaching experience; (4) inquiry-based theory; (5) teaching standards; (6) teacher roles; (7) technology; (8) curriculum implementation; and (9) problems or challenges. The following paragraphs present the themes.

Teacher education redesign

In EFL teacher education, studies have been carried out to shed light on problems occurring in recent years, and many studies (e.g., Chang, 2018; Chen, 2018; Nkwetisama, 2012; Wu, 2018) suggested that EFL teacher education can be improved when bringing CBE on board. Several studies proposed to use CBE to redesign teacher education (e.g., Chang, 2018; Chen, 2018; Serdenciuc, 2013; Tabaro, 2018; Wu, 2018; Yook & Lee, 2016). These studies (e.g., Chang, 2018; Chen, 2018; Nkwetisama, 2012; Serdenciuc, 2013; Tabaro, 2018; Wu, 2018) analyzed the current curricula and interviewed teachers in its area to highlight some important competencies that teacher education needed to address.

Interdisciplinary curriculum

When calling for teacher education redesign, many studies (e.g., Chang, 2018; Chen, 2018; Wu, 2018) thought of curriculum design as one of the key factors for nurturing preservice teachers with competency-based instruction. Serdenciuc (2013), Chang (2018), and Chen (2018) all pointed out the importance of transdisciplinary or interdisciplinary curriculum and recommended preparing teachers with the ability to design interdisciplinary curriculum.

Real teaching experience

Another important issue in CBTE is real teaching experience. Some researchers (e.g., Karim et al., 2019) argued that the problem of lacking practical experience in conventional EFL teacher education could be solved via the internship and teacher residency. Some studies (e.g., Agbayahoun, 2018; Agudo, 2017; Yook & Lee, 2016) have drawn a similar conclusion through collecting opinions from student teachers or in-service teachers. Many scholars (e.g., Cator et al., 2014; Chang, 2018) iterated the importance of actual teaching experience for preparing future CBE teachers. Still, some studies (e.g., Ali et al., 2014; Cabaroglu, 2014) expressed concerns about the teaching practicum. Problems such as student management (Ali et al., 2014; Cabaroglu, 2014) and professional identity (Cabaroglu, 2014) have been reported.

Inquiry-based learning

Different theories in teacher education have been blooming in recent years and inquiry-based theory is one of them (Fwu, 2018). Many scholars (e.g., Agbayahoun, 2018; Hadiyanto et al., 2017) criticized how EFL teacher education falls short in problem-solving skills training. By adopting inquiry-based learning in CBE, the courses can be designed with high relevance to real-life and troubleshooting skills (MOE, 2014; Serafín et al., 2015). Some follow-up studies on inquiry-based CBE were made (Fwu, 2018; Ortlieb & Lu, 2011; Serafín et al., 2015). Fwu (2018) stressed the importance of student teachers developing the ability to derive research problems from the teaching field and develop the research abilities using a backward design. Ortlieb and Lu (2011) noted that student teachers should accept the training of inference. Also, Serafín et al. (2015) mentioned that problem-solving skills are essential for student teachers to learn how to apply learning materials in new situations.

Teaching standards

In addition to the above observational studies, some empirical studies (e.g., Johnstone & Soares, 2014) experimented with CBE and provided suggestions for designing teacher education programs or lessons in the classroom. Among them, Johnstone and Soares (2014) provided principles, and the Council of Chief State School Officers (CCSSO, 2013) proposed core teaching standards based on successful empirical models in the United States. Though with some differences, both studies (CCSSO, 2013; Johnstone & Soares, 2014) illustrated the following four themes: (1) personalized learning for diverse learners; (2) a strong focus on valid competencies; (3) reliable and improved assessment; and (4) collaborative support and learning resources.

Teacher roles

CBE teachers play different roles, including course design (Casey, 2018; Struyven & Meyst, 2010), learning media application (Rodriguez Buitrago, 2013), giving feedback (Zhao, 2010), and assisting interaction (Sert & Walsh, 2013). According to Richards and Rodgers (2014) and Casey (2018), CBE educators have at least four different roles: needs analyst or instructional designer, materials developer and resource assembler or manager, assessor and learner guide, and learner coach. In addition to the role of an academic expert, other roles are also implied, such as a mentor (Cator et al., 2014), a life counselor (Springer, 2020), and leadership roles (CCSSO, 2013).

Technology

The adaptability of foreign language teaching materials (Karim et al., 2019) is also a problem for EFL teacher education. In CBE, Information and Communications Technology (ICT) (Casey, 2018) and online learning resources (Cator et al., 2014; Ford, 2014) are utilized to help students to learn with rich and multiple aids. With the expectation of teachers to manage ICT in education, several studies (e.g., Hadiyanto et al., 2017; Rodriguez Buitrago, 2013; Twining & Henry, 2014) investigated teacher competencies in the digital age. Among them, Hadiyanto et al. (2017) explored soft skills; Rodriguez Buitrago (2013), online tutoring; and Twining and Henry (2014), ICT teaching. Two studies (Egbert & Shahrokni, 2019; Tseng & Yeh, 2019) researched computer-assisted language learning (CALL) competencies for CBE teachers. Online intercultural exchanges and telecollaboration (e.g., Müller-Hartmann, 2016) are important themes. Additionally, according to a report (Roll, 2017), the instruction in an innovative CBTE program involves online, in-person, and virtual reality.

Curriculum implementation

In countries where CBE has been promoted for some time, researchers would examine its implementation. Many studies (e.g., Agbayahoun, 2018; Alata, 2019; Glyanenko, 2016; Hobbs, 2013; Kabombwe & Mulenga, 2019; Koenen et al., 2015; O'Dowd, 2018; Struyven & Meyst, 2010; Yook & Lee, 2016) looked into how English teachers implement CBE in their respective contexts. Among them, several studies (e.g., Agbayahoun, 2018; Alata, 2019; Al-Jaro & Asmawi, 2019; Kabombwe & Mulenga, 2019; Struyven & Meyst, 2010) noted the gap between the stated CBE curriculum and the implemented curriculum. Hobbs (2013) and Glyanenko (2016) described the respective features of CBTE in the United States and the United Kingdom. On the other hand, both Koenen et al. (2015) and O'Dowd (2018) observed eclectic approaches in teacher training, a mix of traditional and competency-based teaching.

Problems or challenges

There are certainly concerns about CBE. According to Gallagher (2014), research has been conducted to indicate the disadvantages or obstacles of CBE in the late 20th century, including hyper-individualization, high drop-out rates, poor student self-monitoring, and higher-than-expected costs. For contexts where individualized learning is not the focus of its CBE, researchers indicated problems about CBE, including vague concepts about CBE (Chen, 2018; Wu, 2018), teacher educators without CBE backgrounds, difficulties for developing competency-based assessments, and the lack of supporting system (Wu, 2018) have also been mentioned. In response to the current needs for CBTE, teacher education institutions have been urged to equip preservice teachers with competency-based teaching ability (Wu, 2018) and build a sound evaluation system (Chang, 2018).

The above review regarding CBE and EFL teacher education in the past decade shows that researchers in different countries have been interested in adopting a competency-based approach in EFL teacher education. Based on a majority of the studies that urged EFL teacher education to be redesigned with the principles of CBE, more studies are necessary. Possible directions are revealed through research topics such as interdisciplinary curriculum, real teaching experience, inquiry-based learning (with backward design), the consideration of teaching standards and teacher roles, and the use of technology (such as telecollaboration). In addition, based on the studies on curriculum implementation, there should be still a long way to go for EFL teachers or teacher educators to be able to implement competency-based teaching thoroughly, and there are certainly challenges left for researchers and educators to conquer when adopting a competency-based approach in teacher education.

Conclusion

The purpose of this chapter was to provide a clear vision for the current status of CBE research for educators and researchers to consider the EFL teacher education in their teaching contexts. The chapter presents the historical and theoretical backgrounds of CBE, defines "competency" and CBE in the 21st century, summarizes the core competencies for lifelong learning, describes features of CBE, and reviews studies on CBE and EFL teacher education during the period from 2010 to 2020. CBE in the 21st century is different from that in the 1970s. With the same spirit of bridging education and life, CBE nowadays emphasizes not only academic abilities but also lifelong learning skills that transfer knowledge to different contexts. In this complex world of the 21st century, CBE aims to prepare core competencies for learners to function independently and interdependently.

In EFL teacher education, the emphasis of CBE on performances in real-life scenarios appears to be the solution to the problems that EFL teacher education has encountered. CBE provides new ways for learning and teaching and changes the current state of EFL teacher education, causing an impact on teacher training theories, teaching standards, assessments, and teacher roles. Issues that draw research attention in EFL teacher education may include interdisciplinary curriculum, real teaching experience, inquiry-based learning blended in a learning environment with rich and multiple technological aids.

Many major educational organizations (e.g., EU, 2019; MOE, 2014; OECD, 2018; UNESCO, 2015; US Department of Education, 2015) accentuate the importance of core competencies and competency-based learning. Many studies (e.g., CCSSO, 2013; Chen, 2018; Johnstone & Soares, 2014) suggested that more research on instructional practices of CBE is necessary. Compared to CBE research, studies on CBE in EFL settings are still scarce. After reflecting on the results, this chapter concludes that future work on better understanding CBE, be it language education or teacher education, in EFL settings can benefit from the following: (1) research on how EFL education can be redesigned, including the aspects of interdisciplinary curriculum, real teaching experience, inquiry-based learning, backward design, integration of teaching standards, teacher roles, and the use of new technology; (2) research evaluating the implementation and challenges of CBE in different EFL settings; and (3) research on what CBE objectives are and how they are related to learner effectiveness. The following chapters of this book provide examples of the research and practices.

References

Agbayahoun, J. P. (2018). Teaching materials and the knowledge base of EFL teachers. *Studies in English Language Teaching*, *6*(1), 47–64.

Agudo, J. (2017). What EFL student teachers think about their professional preparation: Evaluation of an English language teacher education programme in Spain. *Australian Journal of Teacher Education*, *42*(8), 62–76.

Akane, (2019). 無私珍愛-教師調查： 108 課綱正式啟動八成教師還沒準備好 [A survey on teachers: Curriculum Guidelines of 12-Year Basic Education is officially launched, 80% of the teachers are not ready]. https://kingcar.org.tw/survey/500882

Akos, P., Wasik, S. Z., McDonald, A., Soler, M., & Lys, D. (2019). The challenge and opportunity of competency-based counselor education. *Counselor Education and Supervision*, *58*(2), 98–111.

Alata, E. J. P. (2019). Evaluation of outcomes-based private junior high school English curricula. *International Journal of Curriculum and Instruction*, *11*(1), 43–64.

Ali, M., Othman, A., & Karim, A. (2014). Issues and concerns faced by undergraduate language student teachers during teaching practicum experiences. *The Malaysian Online Journal of Educational Sciences, 2*(3), 22–30.

Al-Jaro, M. S., & Asmawi, A. (2019). An EFL teacher education program: Issues and concerns from a Yemeni university. *Arab World English Journal, 10*(1), 139–154.

Anderson, L. (2018). Competency-based education: Recent policy trends. *Competency-based Education, 3*(1). https://doi.org/10.1002/cbe2.1057

Ashworth, P. D., & Saxton, J. (1990). On competence. *Further and Higher Education, 14*(2), 3–25.

Bhavana, A. R., & Kousalya, L. (2011). A study on the problems and perspectives of student teachers in the construction of 'wh' questions. *Journal on English Language Teaching, 1*, 51–57.

British Columbia. (n.d.). Core competencies. https://curriculum.gov.bc.ca/competencies

Burke, J. (1989). *Competency-based education and training*. Falmer Press, Taylor & Francis Inc.

Butova, Y. (2015). The history of development of competency-based education. *European Scientific Journal, 1*, 250–255.

Cabaroglu, N. (2014). Re-visiting the theory and practice gap through the lens of student teacher dilemmas. *Australian Journal of Teacher Education, 39*(2), 89–109.

Cangelosi, J. S. (1975). Competency-based teacher education: A cautionary note. *Contemporary Education, 46*(2), 124–126.

Casey, K. (2018). *Moving toward mastery: Growing, developing and sustaining educators for competency-based education*. iNACOL.

Cator, K., Schneider, C., & Ark, T. V. (2014). *Preparing teachers for deeper learning: Competency-based teacher preparation and development*. https://digitalpromise.org/wp-content/uploads/2014/05/FINAL-Preparing-Teachers-for-Deeper-Learning-Paper-1.pdf

Chang, C. H. (2018). 素養導向的未來師資培育 [Cultivating teachers for core competence orientation]. *School Administrators, 113*, 11–18.

Cheetham, G., & Chivers, G. (1996). Towards a holistic model of professional competence. *Journal of European Industrial Training, 20*(5), 20–30.

Chen,Y.H.(2018).以素養導向觀點探討中等學校藝術師資培育教材教法課程現況與實踐 [Discussion from a competence-oriented perspective on the status quo and practice of the secondary school teacher training "Arts teaching material and methods" curriculum]. *Journal of research in education sciences, 63*(4), 89–117.

CCSSO (Council of Chief State School Officers). (2013). Interstate Teacher Assessment and Support Consortium (InTASC) standards: Model Core Teaching Standards and Learning Progressions for Teachers 1.0. https://ccsso.org/sites/default/files/2017-12/2013_INTASC_Learning_Progressions_for_Teachers.pdf

Curran, C. M., & Petersen, A. J. (2017). *Handbook of research on classroom diversity and inclusive education practice*. IGI Global.

DU (Deakin University). (1994). *A collection of readings related to competency-based training* (ED 384 695). Deakin University.

Edwards, C. H. (1973). Competency-based teacher education: A critique. *Contemporary Education, 44*(3), 188–193.

Egbert, J. L., & Shahrokni, S. A. (2019). Balancing old and new: Integrating competency-based learning into CALL teacher education. *JALT CALL Journal, 15*(1), 3–18.

Eldridge, D. (2020). Editorial. *Competency-based Education*, *5*(3). https://doi.org/10.1002/cbe2.1222

EU (European Union). (2010). *New skills for new jobs: Action now, A report by the Expert Group on New Skills for New Jobs prepared for the European Commission*. http://ec.europa.eu/social/main.jsp?catId=568&langId=en

EU (European Union). (2018). *Council recommendation on key competences for lifelong learning*. https://eur-lex.europa.eu/legal-content/EN/TXT/PDF/?uri=CELEX:32018H0604(01)&from=EN

EU (European Union). (2019). *Key competences for lifelong learning*. https://op.europa.eu/en/publication-detail/-/publication/297a33c8-a1f3-11e9-9d01-01aa75ed71a1/language-en

Ford, K. (2014). *Competency-based education: History, opportunities, and challenges*. Center for Innovation in Learning and Student Success. University of Maryland University College. http://files.eric.ed.gov/fulltext/ED114384.pdf

Fwu, B. J. (2018). 素養導向國教新課綱的師資培育：國立臺灣大學「探究式–素養導向的師資培育」理想芻議 [Teacher preparation in response to competence-based curriculum reform for k-12 education: National Taiwan university's proposal of inquiry-based and competency-based Teacher education]. *Journal of research in education sciences*, *63*(4), 59–87.

Gallagher, C. W. (2014). Disrupting the game-changer: Remembering the history of competency-based education. *Change: The magazine of higher learning*, *46*(6), 16–23.

Garrison, M. J. (2018). Resurgent behaviorism and the rise of neoliberal schooling. In K. Saltman, & A. Means (Eds.), *Handbook of global education reform* (pp. 323–349). Wiley-Blackwell.

Gervais, J. (2016). The operational definition of competency-based education. *The Journal of Competency-Based Education*, *1*(2), 98–106.

Glyanenko, K. (2016). Professional training of language teachers in the context of British experience. *Comparative Professional Pedagogy*, *6*(3), 74–78.

Hadiyanto, M. A., Failasofah, A. N., Fajaryani, N., & Habibi, A. (2017). In search of quality student teachers in a digital era: Reframing the practices of soft skills in teacher education. *Turkish Online Journal of Educational Technology – TOJET*, *16*(3), 71–78.

Henri, M., Johnson, M., & Nepal, B. (2017). A review of competency-based learning: Tools, assessments, and recommendations. *Journal of Engineering Education*, *106*, 607–638.

Hobbs, V. (2013). "A basic starter pack": The TESOL certificate as a course in survival. *ELT Journal*, *67*(2), 163–174.

Hodge, S. (2007). The origins of competency-based training. *Australian Journal of Adult Learning*, *47*(2), 179–209.

Hohn, R. L., & Meinke, D. L. (1978). Competency-based education and educational psychology. *Contemporary Education*, *49*(4), 211.

Hoogveld, A. W. M. (2003). *The teacher as designer of competency-based education*. (Doctoral dissertation, Open University of the Netherlands, Netherlands). https://core.ac.uk/download/pdf/55534027.pdf

Johnstone, S. M., & Soares, L. (2014). Principles for developing competency-based education programs. *Change: The Magazine of Higher Learning*, *46*, 12–19.

Karim, A., Shahed, F. H., Mohamed, A. R., Rahman, M. M., & Ismail, S. A. M. M. (2019). Evaluation of the teacher education programs in EFL context: A testimony of student teachers' perspective. *International Journal of Instruction*, *12*(1), 127–146.

Kabombwe, Y. M., & Mulenga, I. M. (2019). Implementation of the competency-based curriculum by teachers of history in selected secondary schools in Lusaka district, Zambia. *Yesterday & Today*, *22*, 19–41.

Koenen, A. K., Dochy, F., & Berghmans, I. (2015). A phenomenographic analysis of the implementation of competency-based education in higher education. *Teaching and Teacher Education*, *50*, 1–12.

Lai, Z. Y. (2019). 淺談國語文課綱對國中國文教師的影響 [Discussion on the impact of the new Chinese curriculum on junior high school Chinese teachers]. *Taiwan Educational Review Monthly*, *8*(5), 164–170.

Levine, E., & Patrick, S. (2019). *What is competency-based education? An updated definition*. Aurora Institute.

Louiza, B., & Sarnou, H. (2018). Measuring the effectiveness of competency-based e-learning in EFL classes. *International Journal of Social Sciences & Educational Studies*, *5*(2), 54–63.

Lunce, L. M. (2006). Simulations: Bringing the benefits of situated learning to the traditional classroom. *Journal of Applied Educational Technology*, *3*(1), 37–45.

Makulova, A. T., Alimzhanova, G. M., Bekturganova, Z. M., Umirzakova, Z. A., Makulova, L. T., & Karymbayeva, K. M. (2015). Theory and practice of the competency-based approach in education. *International Education Studies*, *8*(8), 183–192.

Malan, S. (2000). The 'new paradigm' of outcomes-based education in perspective. *Journal of Family Ecology and Consumer Sciences*, *28*, 22–28.

Merriam-Webster Dictionary. (2020). *Online dictionary*. https://www.merriam-webster.com/dictionary/competency.

MOE (Ministry of Education). (2014). *Curriculum guidelines of 12-Year basic education*. https://cirn.moe.edu.tw/WebContent/index.aspx?sid=11&mid=9900

Moon, Y. L. (2007). Education reform and competency-based education. *Asia Pacific Education Review*, *8*(2), 337–341.

Mulder, M. (Ed.), 2017). *Competence-based vocational and professional education: Bridging the worlds of work and education*. Springer International Publishing.

Müller-Hartmann, A. (2016). A task is a task is a task is a task... Or is it? Researching telecollaborative teacher competence development—The need for more qualitative research. https://files.eric.ed.gov/fulltext/ED571355.pdf

Nkwetisama, C. M. (2012). The competency-based approach to English language education and the walls between the classroom and the society in Cameroon: Pulling down the walls. *Theory and Practice in Language Studies*, *2*(3), 516–523.

Nodine, T. R. (2016). How did we get here? A brief history of competency-based higher education in the United States. *Competency-based Education*, *1*, 5–11.

O'Dowd, R. (2018). The training and accreditation of teachers for English medium instruction: An overview of practice in European universities. *International Journal of Bilingual Education & Bilingualism*, *21*(1), 1–11.

OECD (Organization for Economic Cooperation and Development). (2014). *Competency framework*. https://www.oecd.org/careers/competency_framework_en.pdf

OECD. (2018). *The future of education and skills. Education 2030*. https://www.oecd.org/education/2030/E2030%20Position%20Paper%20(05.04.2018).pdf

Ortlieb, E. T., & Lu, L. (2011). Improving teacher education through inquiry-based learning. *International Education Studies*, *4*(3), 41–46.

Pérez-Llantada, C. (2011). Integrated language and competency-based learning. A proposed pedagogical framework for stepping into academia. *Considerations on Educational issues*, *7*(2), 117–129.

Richards, J. C., & Rodgers, T. S. (2014). *Approaches and methods in language teaching* (3rd ed.). Cambridge University Press.

Roll, N. (2017). *Green light for competency-based teacher ed.* https://www.insidehighered.com/news/2017/11/01/competency-based-teacher-education-program-receives-state-approval

Rodriguez Buitrago, C. (2013). Identifying training needs of novice online English language tutors. *Gist Education and Learning Research Journal, 7*, 134–153.

Senge, P. M. (2000). The academy as a learning community: Contradiction in terms or realizable future? In A. F. Lucas (Ed.), *Leading academic change: Essential roles for department chairs* (pp. 275–300). Jossey-Bass Inc.

Serafín, Č, Dostál, J., & Havelka, M. (2015). Inquiry-based instruction in the context of constructivism. *Procedia-Social and Behavioral Sciences, 186*, 592–599.

Serdenciuc, N. L. (2013). Competency-based education—Implications on teachers' training. *Procedia-Social and Behavioral Sciences, 76*, 754–758.

Sert, O., & Walsh, S. (2013). The interactional management of claims of insufficient knowledge in English language classrooms. *Language and Education, 27*(6), 543–565.

Springer, S. B. (2020). Forty years: Where is competency-based education? *Adult Learning, 31*(2), 54–56.

Struyven, K., & Meyst, M. D. (2010). Competence-based teacher education: Illusion or reality? An assessment of the implementation status in Flanders from teachers' and students' points of view. *Teaching and Teacher Education, 26*(8), 1495–1510.

Sturgis, C., & Casey, K. (2018). *Designing for equity: Leveraging competency-based education to ensure all students succeed.* iNACOL.

Sturgis, C., Patrick, S., & Pittenger, L. (2011). *It's not a matter of time: Highlights from the 2011 competency-based learning summit.* International Association for K–12 Online Learning and the Council of Chief State School Officers.

Tabaro, C. (2018). The Rwandan secondary school competence-based curriculum: Knowledge, skills and attitudes to incorporate in the university of Rwanda-College of education programs to align them with the current curriculum. *International Journal of Education and Practice, 6*(2), 64–75.

Timothy, J. J. (2018). *Competency-based education implementation and leadership case study.* (Doctoral dissertation, Creighton University, Omaha). http://pqdd.sinica.edu.tw.nthulib-oc.nthu.edu.tw/doc/10827598

Tseng, S.-S., & Yeh, H.-C. (2019). Fostering EFL teachers' CALL competencies through project-based learning. *Educational Technology & Society, 22*(1), 94–105.

Tuxworth, E. (2005). Competence-based education and training: Background and origins. In J. Burke (Ed.), *Competency-based education and training* (pp. 9–22). Falmer Press.

Twining, P., & Henry, F. (2014). Enhancing "ICT teaching" in English schools: Vital lessons. *World Journal of Education, 4*(2), 12–36.

UNIDO (United Nations Industrial Development Organization). (2002). UNIDO Competencies. http://www.unido.org.

UNESCO (United Nations Educational, Scientific and Cultural Organization). (2015). *UNESCO Competency Framework.* https://en.unesco.org/sites/default/files/Competency%20Framework_E.pdf

Urofsky, R. I., & Bobby, C. L. (2012). The evolution of a student learning outcomes focus in the CACREP standards in relation to accountability in higher education. *Counseling Outcome Research and Evaluation, 3*, 63–72.

US Department of Education. (2015). *Every student succeeds act.* https://www.congress.gov/114/plaws/publ95/PLAW-114publ95.pdf

Vail, T. (2019). Self-paced English as a foreign language in a competency-based education program for Korean learners. *The Journal of Competency-Based Education*, *4*(3), 1–10.

Westera, W. (2001). Competences in education: A confusion of tongues. *Journal of Curriculum Studies*, *33*(1), 75–88.

Wu, C.-S. (2018). 素養導向教師教育內涵建構及實踐之研究 [Construction and practice of competency-based teacher education]. *Journal of Research in Education Sciences*, *63*(4), 261–293.

Wu, P. C., & Chan, J. C. (2018). 從能力本位到素養導向教育的演進、發展及反思 [Reflecting on the perspective transformation of competency-based education]. *Journal of Educational Research and Development*, *14*(2), 35–64.

Yigzaw, A. (2013). High school English teachers' and students' perceptions, attitudes and actual practices of continuous assessment. *Educational Research and Reviews*, *8*(16), 1489–1498.

Yook, C., & Lee, Y. (2016). Korean EFL teachers' perceptions of the impact of EFL teacher education upon their classroom teaching practices. *Asia-Pacific Journal of Teacher Education*, *44*(5), 522–536.

Zhao, H. (2010). Investigating learners' use and understanding of peer and teacher feedback on writing: A comparative study in a Chinese English writing classroom. *Assessing Writing*, *15*(1), 3–17.

Zeichner, K. M. (1983). Alternative paradigms of teacher education. *Journal of Teacher Education*, *34*(3), 3–9.

2 Competency-based teacher education and sociocultural theory

Exploring connections

Ana Cristina Biondo Salomão and Patrícia Fabiana Bedran

Introduction

The knowledge base of language teacher education has been reexamined contemporarily by questioning the traditional position of language-based disciplines as the major source of the knowledge needed by the profession. The knowledge base is a professional self-definition, which is neither static nor neutral, and has its foundations in values, assumptions, and interpretations grounded in a specific epistemological perspective that informs what knowledge is, who the knower is, and how knowledge is produced (Johnson, 2009).

The way educational research has conceptualized teacher learning and, consequently, informed teacher education has changed greatly in the past 40 years, influenced by epistemological shifts in relation to the conceptualization of human learning—behaviorist (i.e., by habit formation), cognitivist (driven by the mind), or socially situated (arising from interpersonal relationships in a given context). Learning to teach today is understood as a long and complex process of development, resulting from participation in social practices and contexts associated with teaching and learning.

This chapter aims at presenting an overview of language teacher education, discussing concepts such as teacher training and teacher development, and implications of how contemporary perspectives on practice situations are driving forces toward the reconceptualization of the knowledge base of teacher education. We intend to explore the possible connections between competency-based language education and sociocultural theory.

Our main focus of discussion is how a sociocultural perspective meets an interpretative view of reality and provides elements for the (re)construction and transformation of teaching practices, placing knowledge as intimately and dynamically linked to experience and highlighting the role of human agency in professional development. As more attention has been paid to teacher learning and its complexity from an epistemological practice, the new challenges in teacher education include seeking to plan, implement, and sustain programs that focus on learning in, from, and for foreign language teaching practice.

DOI: 10.4324/9781003212805-3

Language teacher education: An overview

Johnson (2009) states that language teacher education has been much more something that teacher educators have done than something that has been studied. What the author means is that, in fact, the education of language teachers as an independent field has been built in a way that is often more pragmatic than theoretical in terms of the way teachers learn to teach. Freeman (2009) resonates this statement by stating that the scope of teacher education had widely been understood implicitly before it became an activity recognized as an area of study.

Clarke (2008) presents the different educational models adopted for teacher education in Western societies in the middle of the last century. During the 1950s, according to the author, the dominant model would be the "craft approach." The English word "craft" is generally used to describe the work of the artisan, which underlies the view of this approach in teacher education as favoring practice over theory. Because of criticism on the lack of academic rigor of such a perspective, the following decades placed teachers as implementers of theories—the traditional model of application of science (Wallace, 1991).

In the 1980s, according to Freeman (2002, 2009), the scope was refined as more attention was increasingly given to the teacher. According to the author, this was a period of change and reconceptualization, placing classroom processes and decision-making as the focus of many studies, and focusing on how teachers' learning was defined and understood. The concept of a blank slate gave way to that of teachers' implicit theories, which led, in the 1990s, to the end of the process-product paradigm, bringing teachers emic concerns about their professional development (Freeman, 2002). It was in the late 1980s that American researchers coined the term teacher-learner, which placed teachers in two fields of activity: with students in the classroom, where they taught, and in formal and informal training or development courses, where they learned (Freeman, 2009).

Richards and Farrell (2005) distinguish between teacher training and development. According to the authors, training refers to activities directly focused on the responsibilities of the teacher and is typically aimed at immediate and short-term objectives, involving the understanding of basic concepts and principles as a prerequisite for applying them to teaching, in addition to the ability to demonstrate principles and practices in the classroom. Among the objectives of the training perspective are: learning to use effective strategies to start a lesson, adapting the textbook to meet the needs of the class, learning to use group activities, using effective questioning techniques, and using classroom resources (e.g., video) and techniques to give feedback to learners about their performance.

On the other hand, development refers to growth in general, not focusing on a specific job. It serves a long-term goal and seeks to facilitate the growth of the teacher's understanding of teaching and of himself or herself as a teacher, involving the examination of different dimensions of teaching practice as the basis for a reflective review. Among the objectives of the development perspective are: to understand how the second language learning process occurs, to understand how our roles change according to the type of learners we are teaching, to understand the types of decision-making that occur during a class, to review our own theories and principles of language teaching, to develop an understanding of different teaching styles, and to determine learners' perceptions of classroom activities.

Vieira-Abrahão (2006) summarizes the change that occurred in relation to a paradigm shift in this area pointing to the change in training practice, common in the 1970s and 1980s, for the practice of development, called "teacher training or education." The author differentiates the training perspective from the education perspective by stating that training means the preparation of the teacher for activities to be performed in the short term, such as, for example, the beginning of teaching work in a language course, which involves concepts and principles seen as "static knowledge" and "a one-way relationship between theory and practice." However, a development perspective seeks to develop the ability to learn and develop throughout the career, and seeks to promote in the teacher the understanding about teaching and about himself or herself as a professional.

Since learning to teach today is understood as a long and complex process of development resulting from participation in social practices and contexts associated with teaching-learning, we intend to discuss how a sociocultural perspective meets an interpretative view of reality and provides elements for the (re)construction and transformation of teaching practices. This places knowledge as intimately and dynamically linked to experience and highlights the role of human agency in professional development.

Perspectives on sociocultural theory in language teacher education

Theoretical assumptions about biological and social factors in the psychological development of the individual have been used to understand the process of teaching and learning and teacher education from a more contemporary perspective, based on the sociocultural approach to mind (Dellagnelo & Vieira-Abrahão, 2020; Johnson, 2009; Johnson & Golombek, 2016). Sociocultural theory highlights the social aspect as a fundamental factor for the social and cognitive development of human beings (Vygotsky, 1987, 1999, 2010). A sociocultural approach to the mind, according to Werstch (1993, p. 18), is fundamentally based on the conception that action is mediated and that "it cannot be separated from the milieu in which it is carried out."

For Vygotsky, human beings are constituted as such in their relationship with others, and culture is part of human nature in a historical process, which shapes their psychological functioning (Oliveira, 1992). According to the conceptions of sociocultural theory, contrary to the precepts of a universalistic approach,[1] as presupposed by Piaget's ideas, human development can only occur within a social context. As stated by Johnson and Golombek (2016), it emerges out of participation in external forms of social interaction that become internalized psychological tools for thinking (internalization). Psychological processes are at the same time both socially derived—embedded within the historical practices of a culture—and individually unique. Transformation from external (interpsychological) to internal (intrapsychological) operations is always a mediated process (Johnson & Golombek, 2016).

One of the criticisms made by Werstch (1993) about research in psychology is the tendency, especially in the United States, to analyze human mental functioning disconnected from social issues, in a kind of vacuum, under the justification of simplifying problems in order to start with a more concrete research, which can later proceed with cultural, institutional, and historical "variables." Such criticisms are not recent. In 1901, as the author points out, Dewey had already signaled that psychology would have to come to terms with how individuals are culturally, historically, and institutionally situated in order to understand their mental functioning. The social role in development seems to gain, therefore, a prominent position in Dewey's reflections, influenced by the theories of G. H. Mead (1932), as pointed out by Ajello (2005). According to Mead (1932), intelligence of the mind arises through the internalization of the social processes of experience and behavior, which allows one to state that there is no mind or thought without language.

As pointed out by Ajello (2005), Dewey (1916), as a philosopher of education, adds another element to the development of the individual in society: the role of schooling in the development of cooperative and socially oriented behavior. The concept of reflective practice had a significant focus with Dewey's book, *How We Think*, published in 1933, followed by Schön's published work in 1993, *The Reflective Practitioner*, which, according to Zeichner (2008), influenced researchers on teacher education to turn to the discussion on reflective teaching. In Dewey's perspective, the function of the social dimension is linked to the fact that the individual develops in society through shared activities, the first of them being language, and through the role of education in a "special environment" such as the school institution. In this sense, schooling is assigned a social role in the development of learners, leading to a review of the role of teachers and students toward an appreciation of social interaction through practical activities that allow the active participation of those involved.

The sociocultural perspective of teacher education is based on the epistemology of practice, giving value to (re)construction through reflection, analysis, and problematization (Pimenta & Ghedin, 2002). As Bedran (2020) points out, based on Wallace (1991), Richards and Lockhart (1996), Pimenta and Ghedin (2002) and Vieira-Abrahão (2006, 2007), the conception of teacher learning is based on the idea that teachers learn through practice and through reflection on the nature and meaning of teaching. In this vein, Johnson and Golombek (2016), grounded in a sociocultural perspective of teacher education, turn to the need for teacher educators to direct their attention not to practice itself but to how and what they are trying to accomplish through practice and, most importantly, what teachers are learning as they engage in these practices, which can be moment-to-moment interactions, oral and written, as well as tasks and activities to be developed face to face or remotely. It is precisely in teacher training practices of L2 that professional development can always be enhanced and developed in a planned and intentional way.

We start from the sociocultural assumption that the knowledge taught in school cannot be transmitted as such to the students; it must be given with the aim of inciting a "know-how" constituted by students themselves (Friedrich, 2012). The achievement of such an endeavor in practical terms stems from Wittgensteinian tradition, which conceptually distinguished "knowing that" and "knowing how." Friedrich (2012) argues that knowledge necessarily requires the function of a psychological instrument, and as soon as the student becomes capable of interweaving it between him/herself and the world, it means that he/she is capable of a "know-how." This is different from the "know that," in the forms of manuals and definitions since they are only "known" and "redictated" knowledge. Such definitions allow us to understand and utilize Vygotsky's reflections on learning and development.

Learning and development are two processes that, for Vygotsky (2010), are in complex interrelationships without coinciding immediately. For the author, learning is only good when it is ahead of development, since it triggers functions that were in a maturing situation and in the zone of immediate development. Learning influences development in a formal school situation, and the formal discipline of each school subject is the field in which this substantial influence on development takes place. It is important to clarify that this is what distinguishes the education of the child from the training of animals, for example. In this sense, he also argues that the education of the child, whose goal is multilateral development, is different from specialized education or technical skills such as typing, riding a bicycle, etc., which have no substantial influence on development.

The distinction between everyday and scientific concepts, according to Friedrich (2012), enables the understanding of the role that Vygotsky attributes to the school, because the development of scientific concepts at school age is a key issue in the face of schools' responsibilities. According to Vygotsky (1987, 2010), scientific concepts are not assimilated or memorized by the child, but emerge and constitute themselves through an immense tension of all the activity of their own thought, which makes it impossible and sterile to teach them directly. These concepts, unlike everyday concepts, are second-order generalizations, since they are related to objects in the world and to other concepts, which implies that they are always based on everyday concepts and always exist within a system of concepts. They are more systematized knowledge that is based on general principles and, therefore, more easily applicable to new situations, unlike everyday concepts that do not need this institutional framework for learning and are, therefore, formed and learned in informal practical experiences (Friedrich, 2012; Vygotsky, 1987, 2010).

In this sense, there would be no need for teaching if it used only what is already mature in development, that is, if it were not a source of development and emergence (Vygotsky, 2010). Such considerations lead us to the conceptualization and function of formal teaching contexts and the school contexts at different levels, as well as the revision and (re)formulation of how we understand teacher education should be. Teacher education programs are the ideal place for systematic learning to teach L2 in an intentional and organized way; schools are physical and sociocultural environments where learning to teach, teaching, and learning take place. Schooling refers to the sociocultural and historical processes that take place in schools over time (Johnson & Golombek, 2016).

As Johnson and Golombek (2016) state:

> We believe that it is inside the practices of L2 teacher education, both the 'moment-to-moment' interactions (oral and written) between teacher educators and teachers as well as the assignments and activities that teacher educators ask teachers to engage in, perhaps face-to-face but many times 'at-a-distance,' where teacher education can best see, support, and enhance the professional development of L2 teachers. By exploring these interactions as they unfold and within the sociocultural contexts in which they occur, we, as teacher educators, not only open ourselves up for closer scrutiny, but we hold ourselves accountable to the teachers with whom we work and, of course, the L2 students they teach. (…) We firmly believe that learning to teach should not be a process of 'discovery learning' or 'learning by doing,' but rather learning that is intentional, deliberate, goal-directed by expert teacher educators who are skilled at moving teachers toward more theoretically and pedagogically sound instructional practices and greater levels of professional expertise.
>
> (Johnson & Golombek, 2016, pp. 3–4)

Considering teacher education programs as a context for systematic learning to teach, as Johnson and Golombek (2016) rightly argue, brings teacher education a focus on the internalization of "true concepts."[2] This is significantly important as teacher educators assist teachers in their process of transforming tacit knowledge and beliefs throughout their education, enabling them to rethink what they thought they knew about teaching, and learning. Teacher education programs would therefore be responsible for teaching teachers to think about possibilities and paths that transcend their everyday experiences. It is important to say that, based on the Vygotskian perspective, this does not mean privileging scientific concepts to the detriment of everyday concepts, but uniting them and transforming them into "true concepts," in such a way that "an academic concept 'gradually comes down to concrete phenomena' and an everyday concept 'goes from the phenomenon upward toward generalizations'" (Johnson & Golombek, 2016, p. 5; Vygotsky, 1986, p. 148).

In this sense, training teachers goes far beyond curriculum delivery or skill acquisition. As Johnson and Golombek (2016, p. 91) describe, traditional microteaching simulations, where teachers plan and deliver "mini-lessons" (5–10 minutes) as a component of course methodology, originated in the 1960s grounded in a technicist view of teaching and learning. They consist of a "discrete set of behaviors that could be broken down into its smallest parts, studied, practiced, and mastered largely through imitation and repetition." Such activities, according to the authors, sought to "acclimatize new teachers to the 'real world' of teaching." With the reflective teaching movement, as opposed to technicism, these activities underwent considerable changes, which provided opportunities for systematic reflection that allowed teachers to move beyond practices based on intuition or routine. While recognizing that in many programs due to local circumstances microteaching is an opportunity for teacher education and is viewed very positively by theorists in the field, Johnson and Golombek criticize and ponder these simulations on the grounds that social, institutional, and historical factors, which are endemic to teaching, are not present in this activity. Thus, they defend that microteaching does not simulate reality and present a proposal for teacher education in a sociocultural perspective. Within the context of a TESOL methodology course, they address the "structured mediational spaces" created in the project for teachers "(...) to develop a sense of the instructional setting in which they will teach, to conceptualize and materialize the subject matter to be taught, to enact an initial lesson in, for and with their classmates and through critical reflection and dialogic interaction, to become consciously aware of the theoretical and pedagogical reasoning for their instructional practices" (Johnson & Golombek, 2016, p. 92).

In their analysis, Johnson and Golombek (2016) use SCDA (sociocultural discourse analysis), a methodology that is characterized by exploring the nature of classroom dialog and its educational significance. Turning less to mere description and more to intentional and well-organized intervention, the authors present an analysis of the moment-to-moment, asynchronous, and at-a-distance teacher educator/teacher dialogic interactions that take place in five different practices. The data for study were collected in the L2 teacher education programs where the authors work in the United States. The analysis of activities designed to prepare teachers to teach lessons shows dialogic interaction that can emerge and becomes fundamental to the process of learning to teach. For each practice, the authors focus on highlighting the linguistic, rhetorical, and pragmatic characteristics of the dialogic interaction between teacher educators and teachers. These include tracing the psychological processes that emerge in "interthinking" in interactions between teacher educators and teachers, identifying the emergence of potential "growth points" in cognitive/emotional dissonance, following the emergence and preservation of an Intermental Development Zone (IDZ) developed in practice, describing the quality and character of "responsive mediation," and exploring the ways in which teachers begin to enact their instructional practices (Johnson & Golombek, 2016, p. 54).

The practical activity, brought by Johnson and Golombek (2016), allows us to visualize the role of dialogic, negotiated interaction, which is based on a directed, organized, and planned teacher education practice, with the introduction of psychological instruments responsible for contributing to the reconceptualization of instructional action. For the authors, the comments throughout the negotiated interaction allow the focus to be on how the participants experienced the lesson and not on what the teachers could or should have done. It is, therefore, as the authors point out, a practice that is not only reduced to the staging of the class but also allows awareness of what happens. It thus lays it open for social mediation, in which it is possible to visualize the interdependence between content (what) and pedagogy (how), laying the basis for the development of conceptual thinking.

We resonate with Johnson and Golombek (2016, p. 8) that teacher education involves the construction of agency, which is related to knowledge about the ability to manipulate a repertoire of linguistic, cultural, pedagogical, and interactional resources, aiming at the development of student learning. Teacher education programs must create opportunities for teachers to engage in instructional practices in sociocultural contexts where they work or will work and mainly provide expert mediation. It would be a fundamental role of teacher educators to engage student-teachers in appropriate educational practices and expose them to psychological tools[3] for their development, which, as the authors clearly state, should not be discovered or invented by the teacher educator, but explicitly presented through theoretical learning and practical activities in moment-to-moment and at-a-distance dialogic interactions.

Competency-based teacher education: Exploring connections with sociocultural theory

Contemporary research and public policies emphasize the need for education to develop individuals with deep ethical commitment, who can reflect and act upon relevant social, economic, cultural, and political issues. Documents, such as the "Key competences for lifelong learning"[4] released by the European Union, as well as the "UNESCO Competency Framework,"[5] the "Competency Framework" (UNESCO, 2015),[6] and the "Position paper with the vision on the future of education and skills"[7] published by the OECD, attempt to provide spaces for the exchange of ideas, practice, and research to contribute to thinking about education in a globalized world. The words "competence" and "skills" are often used along with knowledge, attitudes, and value aiming to assist instructional systems to prepare students for the world in which they will live when they become adults.

The OECD defines competency as such:

> A competency is more than just knowledge and skills. It involves the ability to meet complex demands, by drawing on and mobilising psychosocial resources (including skills and attitudes) in a particular context. For example, the ability to communicate effectively is a competency that may draw on an individual's knowledge of language, practical IT skills and attitudes towards those with whom he or she is communicating.
>
> (OECD, 2005)

And, more recently, the definition of competency has been extended to include the idea of transforming society:

> Building on the "OECD Key Competencies" identified through the DeSeCol project, the OECD Learning Compass 2030 defines "transformative competencies" as the types of knowledge, skills, attitudes and values

> students need to transform society and shape the future for better lives. These have been identified as creating new value, reconciling tensions and dilemmas, and taking responsibility.
>
> (OECD, 2019)

The definition of competence is complex and has multiple dimensions, anchored in different theoretical and conceptual matrices. Competence has usually been linked to a recognized ability to act or express oneself. However, it should not only be defined in terms of readiness to the performance of an action, but also rather be built up in the daily sociocultural and relational situations of everyday life as they require the identification of relevant knowledge, the mobilization of resources, and an active posture toward challenges or problems (Marinho-Araujo & Almeida, 2016).

As Gallagher (2014) cautions, competency-based education poses the risk of promoting hyper-individualization. For teacher education, it is important to reflect on competencies in relation to the individual's ability to relate prior knowledge and "scientific" and "everyday concepts" with practical issues. This will enable the construction of "true concepts" and professional teacher identity in each singular situation of the pedagogical experience. It is in the ability to relate prior knowledge to issues experienced in concrete situations that a competence is recognized. Assuming this conception allows to underscore the epistemology of practice as a moment of fundamental importance for the construction and verification of professional competence. This means that aligning competency-teacher education with sociocultural theory should enable teacher-educators to educate teachers with a critical-reflective, intellectual, and transforming posture for questioning and promoting systematized reflection in all the broad and comprehensive dimensions of their professional experience as teachers.

Freeman and Johnson (1998) strongly believe that the dialogic interactions that emerge in L2 teacher education practices cannot be considered detached from the sociocultural environments and social values of which the participants are part. This means that "teacher education cannot be understood apart from the sociocultural environments in which they take place and the processes of establishing and navigating the social values in which these practices are embedded (see also Edwards, 2010)." (Johnson & Golombek, 2016, pp. 6–7). In relation to competence, it states that:

> Given its dynamic nature, 'pedagogical content knowledge develops' as teachers engage in the actual activities of teaching. And this creates a conundrum for teacher education programs because it requires that learners of teaching perform as self-regulated teachers before they have the necessary competence to do so, or before they have the appropriate pedagogical content knowledge to do so. Yet, we see the developmental value of performance preceding competence (Cazden, 1981; Miller, 2011), in a sense, placing teachers ahead of themselves, as it is precisely through engaging in the activities of teaching and the dialogic interactions (spoken and written)

> related to those activities that teachers will develop deeper understanding of their actions and become consciously aware of the subject matter content and pedagogical resources that form the basis of their instructional decisions and activities.
>
> (Johnson & Golombek, 2016, p. 9)

In this sense, it is communicative interaction that drives cognitive development. It is in our interaction with others that our competence develops, as we receive support to perform beyond our own competence. As stated by Van Compernolle (2015), what we typically do in schools is teaching for competence before we support students' performances, but we in fact should be doing the opposite. When assuming a more technicist conception of competence and restricting it to the development of skills, schools do not create conditions for learning to actually happen, as the interactions are focused on carrying out tasks and not on "being able to perform." By doing so, schools do not consider the individual as the one who, in the relationship between the world and the school routine, constitutes and realizes a "know-how," as Friedrich (2012) points out when discussing the subject in Vygotsky's theory.

According to Marinho-Araujo and Almeida (2016), learning to identify, mobilize, and use resources such as knowledge, skills, mental schemes, affections, beliefs, principles, attitudes, and behaviors in relationships and in action, is what leads to building the materiality of a competence, understanding it as a dimension of the human development process. The different resources to be mobilized constitute differentiated symbolic contents that will be transformed reflexively and intentionally into more complex activities.

In this vein, it is worth establishing a relationship between the Wittgensteinian tradition (Friedrich, 2012) regarding performance in practical terms, that is, to "know what" and "know-how." As Perrenoud (1999) points out, to be competent, it is necessary to know how to mobilize knowledge and skills in a pertinent and timely manner in work situations, which, in our area, is seen as practical learning situations of teaching—teacher education—and in teaching situations in different and unique contexts. If the resources to mobilize are missing, there is no competence; if the resources are present, but not mobilized in a timely and conscious manner, then, in practice, it is as if they did not exist (Perrenoud, 1999). This reveals the importance of the systematized, intentional, organized learning process for teachers led by communicative interaction as a form of interpsychological functioning in which cognitive processes are externalized through speech.

Conclusion

A sociocultural perspective in competency-based teacher education can underpin teachers to act with intentionality by making choices and decisions in complex contexts within a cultural and historical reality. It should not be defined merely as a set of skills or abilities that are trainable and used for a certain purpose by an individual, but imply a collective character through a formative process mediated in teacher education.

Sociocultural theory brings about resources of recursive mediation for the competence approach by relating the construction of knowledge and everyday social action. In this way, resources should be mobilized in an interdependent way to help professors articulate the critical points identified in the situation, enabling them to make decisions in appropriate and useful ways in their social and work contexts.

By adopting a perspective that recognizes the intersection between cognitive and social elements, teacher education must lay the foundation for teaching to be understood as a dynamic process of (re)construction and transformation of practices, so that it responds to local needs. This enables teachers to become innovative in the unpredictable nature of the classroom, and highlights the role of human agency in (trans)forming the world.

Notes

1 For Werstch (1993, p. 19), universalistic approaches do not overtly preclude an analysis of sociocultural situatedness, but they tend to be formulated in a way that makes such situatedness seem trivial.
2 True concepts are reframed scientific concepts, which result from the dialectical interaction between "everyday concepts" and "scientific concepts" (Vygotsky, 2010).
3 On psychological instrument functioning, Vygotsky posits that "all higher psychic functions, for example voluntary attention or logical memory, arise with the aid of psychological instruments and consequently constitute themselves as mediated psychic phenomena." (Friedrich, 2012, pp. 53–54). As Friedrich (2012) points out, the psychological instrument functions as an intermediary element between man's activity and his object. It is found in the psychic activity of the subject, functioning as a form of influence of the subject over himself, as a form of self-regulation and self-control.
4 https://op.europa.eu/en/publication-detail/-/publication/297a33c8-a1f3-11e9-9d01-01aa75ed71a1/language-en
5 https://en.unesco.org/sites/default/files/competency_framework_e.pdf
6 https://www.oecd.org/careers/competency_framework_en.pdf
7 https://www.oecd.org/education/2030/E2030%20Position%20Paper%20(05.04.2018).pdf

References

Ajello, A. M. (2005). A perspectiva pedagógica no estudo dos processos sociais na escola. In C. Pontecorvo, A. M. Ajello, & C. Zucchermaglio (Eds.), *Discutindo se aprende: interação social, conhecimento e escola* (Tradução de Cláudia Bressan e Susana Termignoni). Artmed.

Bedran, P. F. (2020). Recursos tecnológicos e metodológicos no desenvolvimento de prática(s) reflexivas(s) em um contexto de formação de professores de língua com foco na (co)construção de conhecimento. In A. C. K. Dellagnelo, & M. H. Vieira-Abrahão (Eds.), *Estudos sobre ensino-aprendizagem e formação do professor de línguas sob uma perspectiva sociocultural.* Pontes Editores.

Cazden, C. (1981). Performance before competence: Assistance to child discourse in the zone of proximal development. *Quarterly Newsletter of the Laboratory of Comparative Human Cognition*, *3*, 5–8.

Clarke, M. (2008). *Language teacher identities: Co-constructing discourse and community*. Multilingual Matters.

Dellagnelo, A. C. K., & Vieira-Abrahão, M. H. (2020). *Estudos sobre ensino-aprendizagem e formação do professor de línguas sob uma perspectiva sociocultural*. Pontes Editores.

Dewey, J. (1916). *Democracy and education*. The Macmillan Company (trad. It. *Democrazia edededucazione*, La Nuova Italia, Firenze, 1949).

Edwards, A. (2010). How can Vygotsky and his legacy help us to understand and develop teacher education? In V. Ellis, A. Edwards, & P. Smagorinsky (Eds.), *Cultural-historical perspectives in teacher education and development* (pp. 61–77). Routledge.

Freeman, D. (2002). The hidden side of the work: Teacher knowledge and learning to teach. *Language Teaching*, *35*, 1–13.

Freeman, D. (2009). The scope of second language teacher education. In A. Burns, & J. C. Richards (Eds.), *Second language teacher education* (pp. 11–19). Cambridge University Press.

Freeman, D., & Johnson, K. E. (1998). Reconceptualizing the knowledge-base of language teacher education. *TESOL Quarterly*, *32*, 397–417.

Friedrich, J. (2012). *Lev Vigotski: mediação, aprendizagem e desenvolvimento: uma leitura filosófica e epistemológica* (Tradução de Anna Rachel Machado e Eliane Gouvêa Lousada). Mercado de Letras.

Gallagher, C. W. (2014). Disrupting the game-changer: Remembering the history of competency-based education. *Change: The Magazine of Higher Learning*, *46*(6), 16–23. https://doi.org/10.1080/00091383.2014.969177

Johnson, K. E. (2009). *Second language teacher education: A sociocultural perspective*. Routledge.

Johnson, K. E., & Golombek, P. R. (2016). *Mindful L2 teacher education: A sociocultural perspective on cultivating teachers' professional development*. Routledge.

Marinho-Araujo, C. M., & Almeida, L. S. (2016). Abordagem de competências, desenvolvimento humano e educação superior. *Psicologia: Teoria e Pesquisa*, *32*(spe), e32ne212. Epub 23 de março de 2017. https://doi.org/10.1590/0102-3772e32ne212

Mead, G. H. (1932). *Mind, self and society*. The University of Chicago Press (trad. It. Mente, sé e società, Giuint Barbera, Firenze 1966).

Miller, R. (2011). *Vygotsky in perspective*. Cambridge University Press.

OECD. (2005). The definition and selection of key competencies. Executive Summary. http://www.oecd.org/pisa/35070367.pdf (Accessed 03/31/2021).

OECD. (2019). OECD Future of education and skills 2030. Concept Note. https://www.oecd.org/education/2030-project/teaching-and-learning/learning/transformative-competencies/Transformative_Competencies_for_2030_concept_note.pdf (Accessed 03/31/2021).

Oliveira, M. K. (1992). Vygotsky e o processo de formação de conceitos. In Y. Taille, M. K. Oliveira, & H. Dantas (Eds.), *Piaget, Vygotsky, Wallon: teorias psicogenéticas em discussão*. Summus.

Perrenoud, P. (1999). Construir competências é virar as costas aos saberes? *Pátio Revista Pedagógica*, *11*, 15–19. http://www.unige.ch/fapse/SSE/teachers/perrenoud/php_main/Perrenoud_livros_e_artigos.html (Acesso: 31 mar 2020).

Pimenta, S. G., & Ghedin, E. (2002). *Professor Reflexivo no Brasil: gênese e crítica de um conceito*. Cortez Editora.

Richards, J. C., & Farrell, T. S. C. (2005). *Professional development for language teachers: Strategies for teacher learning*. Cambridge University Press.

Richards, J. C., & Lockhart, C. (1996). *Reflective teaching in second language classrooms*. Cambridge University Press.

UNESCO (United Nations Educational, Scientific and Cultural Organization). (2015). *UNESCO Competency Framework*. https://en.unesco.org/sites/default/files/competency_framework_e.pdf

Van Compernolle, R. A. (2015). *Interaction and second language development: A Vygotskian perspective*. John Benjamins Publishing Company.

Vieira-Abrahão, M. H. (2006). A formação inicial e o desenvolvimento profissional do professor de línguas estrangeiras: Práticas e pesquisas. *Horizontes de Linguística Aplicada*, *5*(2), 3–23.

Vieira-Abrahão, M. H. (2007). A formação inicial do professor de língua estrangeira: Parceria universidade e escola. In M. L. Ortiz, & K. A. Silva (Eds.), *Linguística Aplicada: Múltiplos Olhares* (pp. 155–166). Pontes.

Vygotsky, L. S. (1986). *Thought and language* (A. Kozulin, Trans.). MIT Press.

Vygotsky, L. S. (1987). *Pensamento e Linguagem* (Tradução de Jefferson Luiz Camargo). Martins Fontes.

Vygotsky, L. S. (1999). *A formação social da mente* (Tradução de José Cippola Neto et al. 6. ed.). Martins Fontes.

Vygotsky, L. S. (2010). *A construção do pensamento e da linguagem* (Tradução de Paulo Bezerra. 2. ed.). WMF Martins Fontes.

Wallace, M. J. (1991). Teacher education: Some current models. In M. J. Wallace (Eds.), *Training foreign language teachers*. Cambridge University Press.

Werstch, J. V. (1993). *Voices of the mind: A sociocultural approach to mediated action*. Harvard University Press.

Zeichner, K. M. (2008). Uma análise crítica sobre a "reflexão" como conceito estruturante na formação docente. *Educação & Sociedade*, *29*(103), 535–554.

3 Integrating language teacher identity into competency-based language teacher education

Eric K. Ku and Yeu-Ting Liu

Introduction

Language teacher identity (LTI) has been recognized as an important aspect of language teacher education (Barkhuizen, 2017b; De Costa & Norton, 2017; Rudolph et al., 2020; Varghese et al., 2016; Yazan & Rudolph, 2018; Yazan & Lindahl, 2020). Scholars have also called for more holistic and transdisciplinary approaches toward language teacher education (De Costa & Norton, 2016; Douglas Fir Group, 2016; Johnson, 2019), which can be seen as part of a broader "humanistic-based" approach to teacher education that focuses on the development of "the teacher as a person" (Korthagen, 2016, p. 315). And yet, at the same time, competency-based education, which, unlike humanistic-based teacher education (HBTE), focuses on the mastery of concrete skills (Korthagen, 2016), has become increasingly prevalent in higher education worldwide due to an emphasis by institutions and policy-makers on accountability, relevance, effectiveness, efficiency (Burnette, 2016; Hopcraft, 2010; Pantić & Wubbels, 2010; Selingo, 2015; Struyven & De Meyst, 2010), and international competitiveness (Cheng, 2017).

In this chapter, we present a review of current understandings of LTI and competency-based language teacher education (CBLTE), exploring the perceived incompatibility between competency-based approaches (focus on the teacher's skillset) and humanistic approaches (focus on who a teacher is). We argue that the focus of teacher education should not be a matter of choosing one approach over the other because both competencies and identities are core concepts in teacher development. Rather, the focus should be on understanding what role LTI plays in CBLTE. We present a review of current approaches that have been proposed and/or implemented in integrating identities into competency-based frameworks. Finally, we argue that recognizing the role of LTI in CBLTE is not an inherently paradoxical endeavor, nor does it take away from the integrity of a competency-based approach. In fact, acknowledging that the development of competencies is inseparable from the development of identities strengthens competency-based frameworks.

DOI: 10.4324/9781003212805-4

Competency-based language teacher education

What is CBLTE?

CBLTE refers to the application of competency-based teacher education (CBTE) toward language teachers. CBTE became popular in the 1960s and 1970s (Forzani, 2014) and can be described as structuring teacher education based on a set of skills (or competencies) that teachers-in-training must show mastery of to be a competent teacher (Robinson & Mogliacci, 2019). CBTE was introduced as a way of moving teacher education away from a more traditional emphasis on a teacher's "ability to demonstrate knowledge" and toward an "ability to do" (Houston & Howsan, 1972). The specific competencies that are necessary for teachers to acquire vary depending on the teachers, institutions, and policy-makers within each educational context (Day, 2017). Despite the inconsistencies, the overall assumption underlying CBTE is that a "good teacher" can be determined from a set of professional competencies acquired through teacher education.

In recent decades, CBLTE, or the application of CBTE toward language teacher education, has become more common. For example, in Australia, language teacher competencies play a major role in Teaching English to Speakers of Other Languages (TESOL) teacher education, particularly in acquiring TESOL accreditation from short courses offered outside university settings (Murray, 2009). Likewise, the ways language teacher competence as a construct has been theorized and/or implemented has expanded greatly. Early conceptualizations of language teacher competence focused on language proficiency and pedagogical content knowledge (Shulman, 1987; Thomas, 1987). Similarly, language teacher competence has also been described in terms of the interrelationship between language, linguistics, and teaching, an approach that still influences the structure of language teacher education programs today (Cots & Arnó, 2005). However, Freeman (2020) argues that what language teachers need to know (i.e., their knowledge-base) has shifted in the past 20 years from being defined by "the actual work of classroom teaching" to "English in the world – who is using it and how" (p. 6). One example of how CBLTE is actually implemented is the *European Portfolio for Student Teachers of Languages*, a document developed by the European Centre for Modern Languages of the Council of Europe to guide students in teacher education programs in self-assessing their language teacher competencies (Newby et al., 2007). The document describes seven categories of "core competences which language teachers should strive to attain," which in accordance with Freeman's argument, includes not only pedagogical and content knowledge (e.g., methodology, lesson planning) but also knowledge of the educational and social context (Newby et al., 2007, p. 5).

Criticisms of CBTE

One of the main criticisms of CBTE is the lack of a coherent, universal definition of competency (Day, 2017; Gervais, 2016; Le et al., 2014; Whitty & Willmott,

1991). One reason why there has been a lack of uniformity is that conceptualizations and implementations of competencies have been changing over time. Many scholars point to two definitions of competency, with early definitions limited to competency as the ability to perform tasks and later definitions expanding competency to include not only skills but also knowledge, attitudes, values, and motives (Chappell et al., 1995; Whitty & Willmott, 1991). Most contemporary implementations of CBTE use the latter definition (Day, 2017; European Commission, 2013; Fernández & Hughes, 2013; Pantić & Wubbels, 2010). In fact, current research emphasizes competency as complex, operating on a continuum as a dynamic process of learning, rather than the possession of a fixed trait (Toom, 2017).

Definitions of competency also vary because they are implemented in wide-ranging global contexts. CBTE has been implemented globally, including the European Union (Fernández & Hughes, 2013; Struyven & De Meyst, 2010), East Asia (Cheng, 2017), the United States (Gervais, 2016), and Australia and New Zealand (Murray, 2009). In global contexts, translating the term *competency* to retain the original concept while also maintaining local linguistic and cultural relevance has been challenging. For example, in Taiwan, the national public education curriculum originally translated the term competency as *néng lì* (能力), which translates to ability, but later revised the translation to *sù yǎng* (素養), which more broadly "involves the cultivation of character, dispositions, and morality" (Chen & Huang, 2017, p. 5). Other terms that have been used include "basic abilities" (France), "basic skills" (the United States), "core skills" (the United Kingdom), "key competencies" (Australia), and "basic competences" or *competencias básicas* (Spain) (Fernández & Hughes, 2013).

In addition to the lack of a consistent definition, competencies have also been criticized for being reductionist and oversimplified (Day, 2017; Fernández & Hughes, 2013; Korthagen, 2016), ignoring the complex interpersonal, situational, emotional, and intellectual factors that impact teacher education. This is due to the behaviorist origins of competency approaches and the need for CBTE to interpret teacher development into technical, measurable units (Murray, 2009). The reductionist nature of competencies can lead to major problems in the pedagogical validity or predictive value (Lucas, 1999) of teacher competencies. In other words, scholars question whether the teacher competencies used in CBTE accurately represent or measure the qualities of good teachers (Day, 2017; Hyland, 1994; Willbergh, 2015).

Some scholars argue that competencies may be more appropriate for describing straightforward technical skills common in vocational training but less suitable for teaching practices that involve complex sets of knowledge, skills, and abilities (Chappell et al., 1995). Brundrett and Silcock (2002) frame this as the difference between *training* and *education*, with the former focused on imparting knowledge and skills to improve job performance while the latter not necessarily focusing on job performance. Thus, Brundrett and Silcock (2002) argue that teachers need a form of *education* that prepares them to tackle the wide range of problems they face and that competency-based frameworks are unable to provide that form of education.

Competency-based vs. humanistic-based approaches in teacher education

While CBTE has been valued and criticized for its focus on the development of a teacher as a purveyor of a set of skills, HBTE focuses on the development of the teacher as a person (Korthagen, 2016). Robinson and Mogliacci (2019) describe HBTE as a "teacher identity approach" to teacher education, in which teacher education creates opportunities for teachers to explore the connections between their personal experiences and their practices and beliefs in teaching.

While HBTE has never been implemented as a mainstream approach to teacher education, scholars have discussed the significance of the teacher identity approach to teacher education. In a comprehensive review of historical and current teacher education programs that focus on teaching awareness of identity, Rodgers and Scott (2008) found several common approaches in contemporary HBTE programs, including making time and space for reflection, building communities of trust, and using stories to think through experiences. Danielewicz (2001) also discussed ways of enacting HBTE by proposing a "pedagogy for identity development" consisting of ten principles that guide teacher educators in transferring theories of identity development into practice in the classroom.

The contrast between CBTE and HBTE presents an ongoing debate that pits one approach against the other. However, in actuality, CBTE and HBTE have a closer relationship than one would expect. Ironically, it is because HBTE provides such a different perspective that it has been able to challenge and influence CBTE to evolve (Korthagen, 2016). Namely, as CBTE has become increasingly prevalent worldwide, it has had to address common criticisms of being too reductionist and narrowly focused on competencies. Thus, proponents of CBTE have attempted to rebalance competency-based frameworks by incorporating other aspects of teacher development emphasized in HBTE (e.g., knowledge, attitudes) into contemporary definitions of competency (Korthagen, 2016; Struyven & De Meyst, 2010). In this way, we argue that CBTE and HBTE should not be mutually exclusive approaches to teacher education, but rather complementary and interconnected. With this is mind, teacher identity is one of the important aspects of teacher development emphasized in HBTE that has also been discussed as contributing to CBTE. The following section will provide an overview of the current literature on LTI and how it pertains to CBLTE.

Language teacher identity

What is language teacher identity?

Research in applied linguistics has adopted various theoretical perspectives when it comes to studying LTI, namely identities-in-discourse, identities-in-practice, and identities-in-activity.

A poststructuralist view of identity argues that identity is relational and discursively constructed through language, or identities-in-discourse, in contrast to the individual as having a core, essential self (De Costa & Norton, 2017; Lindahl & Yazan, 2019; Varghese et al., 2005; Varghese et al., 2016). An individual's identity changes over time and space, often in diverse and contradictory ways, and is constructed by and through language. Thus, language is used not only for communication but also for creating a sense of who one is and how one relates to others.

On the other hand, Lave and Wenger's theory of situated learning introduced identities-in-practice (Lave, 1996; Wenger, 1998), in which identity develops from learning the ways of being in a certain community. As individuals' identities develop through participating in the community, so do their practices. This means that for language teachers, LTI and teaching practices mutually impact each other (Kanno & Stuart, 2011). Moreover, language teachers do not enter the classroom with well-formed LTIs. Rather, LTIs are developed over time through working with communities of teachers and students and participating in being a language teacher. Both notions of identities-in-discourse and identities-in-practice appear in current definitions of LTI (Barkhuizen, 2017a; Block 2017). For example, Block (2017) defines LTIs as "... an ongoing, narrated process which brings together experiences in the past, present, as well as those anticipated in the future. LTIs are constructed via (or emerge from) interactions (both face-to-face and electronically mediated) with others..." (p. 34). While the first half of the above definition reflects the "identities-in-discourse," the second half is reminiscent of "identities-in-practice." In fact, Cross (2020) argues that "identities-in-activity," which is grounded in activity theory, combines both discourse and practice perspectives by approaching identity as "a personal (discursive, meaning making) construction of one's self grounded in, and emergent from, the (practical) activity within which that individual is situated as subject" (p. 39) (see also Dang, 2013). In sum, conceptualizations of LTI incorporate the construction and negotiation of identities through both language and social interactions.

Developments in language teacher identity research

Early research in the 1990s on identity in language learning focused on *learner* identities, such as Norton Peirce's (1995) seminal work on the identities of five immigrant women learning English in Canada. In the late 1990s and early 2000s, identity research in language teaching and learning began transitioning from studying learners to teachers (Kayi-Aydar, 2015), with many studies focusing on linguistic identities, such as how being a non-native speaker impacted teachers' careers (Amin, 1997; Pavlenko, 2003; Tang, 1997). In the 2000s, LTI research also investigated the sociocultural identities of language teachers using sociocultural theory (Johnson, 2006), Lave and Wenger's (1991) communities of practice framework, and Anderson's (1991) concept of imagined communities (Kanno & Norton, 2003; Pavlenko, 2003). These studies (e.g., Tsui, 2007; Varghese et al., 2005) examined how LTIs are not passively acquired, but are constructed and negotiated through social interaction. In addition, other LTI studies during this period (e.g., Lin et al., 2004; Menard-Warwick, 2008; Motha, 2006) explored the role of intersectional identities (e.g., race, gender, class) in the development of LTI.

While new studies examining LTI as identities-in-practice are still being conducted, LTI research in recent years has more often adopted a poststructuralist approach to LTI (i.e., identities-in-discourse; Norton & De Costa, 2018), which focuses on LTIs as complex and multiple and in relation to conflicting discourse and ideologies (Kayi-Aydar, 2019). Furthermore, these studies continue to explore the relationship between LTI and intersectional identities (e.g., race, gender, class) while also exploring new issues, such as the role of emotions in LTI (Song, 2016; Wolff & De Costa, 2017; Yazan & Lindahl, 2020) and translingual teacher identity (Ishihara & Menard-Warwick, 2018; Zheng, 2017).

Role of LTI in language teacher education

Arguably, the most significant claim LTI research has made is that LTIs shape classroom teaching practices (Kanno & Stuart, 2011; Reis; 2012; Simon-Maeda, 2004). For language teacher education, this means that designing a curriculum that fosters the development of LTIs may affect teachers' performance as new teachers. For example, Kanno and Stuart (2011) documented two novice TESOL teachers and found that changes in their teaching practices were impacted by how their LTIs changed over time. Thus, scholars have argued that LTIs need to be at the forefront of teacher education because the foundation of teacher education is less about learning new knowledge and more about developing LTIs (Fairley, 2020; Kanno & Stuart, 2011; Varghese et al., 2016).

In the next section, we will extend this line of thinking (i.e., the role of LTI) to CBLTE and present our argument for the need to address LTI in CBLTE. We will explain the current state of LTI in CBLTE and perspectives on how to implement LTI as part of CBLTE.

Why does LTI matter in CBLTE?

Fairley (2020) presents one of the few studies that has explicitly attempted to bridge the gap between LTI and CBLTE. In this pioneering study, Fairley proposes an LTI-centered model of LTE that is transformative, agentive, and advocacy-oriented while also presenting four key competencies necessary for this model (i.e., critical reflexivity, emotional literacy, collaboration, and responsiveness). Though her theorization of identity is thorough, her theorization of competency is sparse. In this sense, Fairley proposes an LTI-centered model of LTE that is only lightly framed from a competencies-based approach.

Besides Fairley's study, most of LTI research has avoided specifically addressing CBLTE. One reason might be that CBLTE is still relatively new to the field of language teacher education, so LTI scholars have not yet covered this specific area of research. Another reason might be a tendency to avoid considering LTI's role in CBLTE because of how different identity-based and competency-based approaches are. However, what does exist in the current literature are teacher education studies that point out the shortcomings of CBTE and suggest identity as one of the ways of addressing those shortcomings. In other words, the main rationale for considering the role of LTI in CBLTE is *to provide a more holistic, comprehensive approach to teacher education by incorporating and addressing identities into competency-based frameworks.*

One of the major limitations of CBLTE is the overemphasis on competencies because skills are most easily observed and measured as data for accountability or performance judgment purposes (Day, 2017). Day (2017) sums up this perspective well by noting that "teaching is more than the sum of competences" (p. 179). An overemphasis on competencies oversimplifies the qualities that are needed to be a competent teacher by ignoring the softer, less apparent, but equally important aspects of language teaching, such as values, attitudes, and identities. This leads scholars to question the relevancy and pedagogical validity of teacher competencies (Hyland, 1994; Lucas, 1999); in other words, do teacher competencies accurately measure and reflect the actual teaching practices required of a competent teacher?

This does not mean that competencies are never useful in teacher education (Murray, 2009). Quite the contrary, scholars not only recognize the value of competencies but also point out the need for CBTE to go beyond "narrowly defined competences" by providing opportunities to address the development of teachers' identities (Day, 2017). For example, adapted from Varghese et al. (2016), a language teacher competency based on identity work could guide teachers "to disrupt or at least question the identity categories that teacher candidates come with as well as in what ways such categories are privileged and/or marginalized." Furthermore, this is also an example of how competencies and identities are, in fact, interconnected (Jarvis-Selinger et al., 2012; Korthagen, 2016, 2017), and language teacher education presents a good arena for the integration of both (Fernández & Hughes, 2013). In this sense, addressing the development of LTIs can make a CBLTE program more well-rounded and relevant to the complexity of classroom teaching.

Current approaches for integrating competencies and identities

In the following section, we present two categories representing the current approaches toward integrating identities in a CBTE framework. We created the two categories based on a review of current CBTE studies featuring frameworks that integrate identities in competency-based frameworks. Examples are provided to illustrate the two approaches, with some examples documenting frameworks that have actually been implemented while others proposing new frameworks.

Approach 1: Identity as a competence

The "identity as a competence" (IAC) approach involves incorporating identity into CBTE by listing it as one of the teacher competencies in a framework among other competencies. This is arguably the least obstructive way of incorporating identity into CBTE because it maintains the original competency-based structure while adding identity by revising existing competencies or adding new ones. Because the degree of change and actual presence of identity is minor in the IAC approach, the impact is likely also minor. For example, the IAC approach does not incorporate identity as a way of rebalancing or reconceptualizing the core elements of a CBTE program. In addition, identity is not conceived as conceptually equal to competence; rather, identity is treated as one of the many issues that competencies can be designed to address.

The IAC approach has been implemented in several national CBTE frameworks, due to the ease with which adding an extra identity-oriented competency into existing teacher competency frameworks. The IAC approach in three national CBTE frameworks will be discussed from Taiwan, Flanders, and Finland. It should be noted that in all three cases, the specific term "identity" was not used; rather, alternative terms close in meaning to identity (i.e., "self," "teacher as…") were used.

Taiwan

Taiwan presents an example of real-world implementation of IAC at the national educational level. It's important to note that the following competency frameworks from Taiwan were not specifically designed for language teacher education. Rather, they were created as national curriculum standards for primary and secondary public education.

Taiwan created two versions of the national competency framework called the 9-year curriculum and the 12-year curriculum, implemented in 1998 and 2014, respectively. Both of these curriculum guidelines were designed to follow the global trend of competency-based frameworks (Chen & Huang, 2017). Chen and Huang (2017, pp. 3–4) present a comparison of the two frameworks. Both competency frameworks are composed of three categories with three to four competencies in each category. In both frameworks, the parts that are most characteristic of the IAC approach are the first three competencies in the first category. In the 9-year curriculum, the first category is "relation to the self" with the first competency as "self-understanding and development of potentials." In the 12-year curriculum, the first category is "self-directed action" with the first competency as "a sound body and mind and self-improvement." Though the two frameworks are similar, the 12-year curriculum describes the categories and competencies in more concrete and actionable terms than that of the 9-year curriculum. For instance, in terms of the competency categories, the framework transitioned from an *internally* oriented perspective (i.e., *relations* to self, society, and nature) to an *externally* oriented perspective (i.e., self-directed *action*, communicative *interaction*, social *participation*).

In addition, the following are more specific descriptions of the identity-oriented competencies from the 9-year and 12-year curriculum, respectively:

> Self-understanding and exploration of potentials, which involves thorough understanding of one's physical conditions, capabilities, emotions, needs, and personalities, loving and caring for oneself, self-reflection on a regular basis, self-discipline, an optimistic attitude, and morality, showing one's individuality, exploring one's potentials, and establishing suitable values.
>
> (Ministry of Education, n.d.)

> [Students should] Possess the ability to conduct sound physical and mental developments, and maintain an appropriate view of humans and self. Through decision-making, analyses, and knowledge acquisition, students can effectively plan their career paths, search for meaning in life, and continually strive for personal growth.
>
> (Ministry of Education, 2014)

Both descriptions of the identity-oriented competencies incorporate themes around understanding and reflecting on one's identity. The main difference between these two descriptions lies in the latter descriptions' emphasis on *the desired result* of reflecting on identity, namely career planning and personal growth.

Flanders (Belgium)

The example of the IAC approach from Flanders, Belgium comes from the competence framework designed in 1998 for teacher education (Struyven & De Meyst, 2010). This competence framework was created as a way of transforming teacher education consistent with changes in the United Kingdom in 1996 (Struyven & De Meyst, 2010). Struyven and De Meyst (2010, p. 1497) present an overview of the Flanders' framework detailing the "basic competences for teacher education," which are composed of *functional components* and *attitudes*. In other words, basic competences consist of what roles teachers should play (i.e., functional components) and what types of thoughts and behavior teachers need to have (i.e., attitudes). These basic competences outline the goals for preparing beginning teachers to fully function as a faculty member of an institution (Struyven & De Meyst, 2010).

The part of Flanders' framework that is most pertinent to the IAC approach are the functional components, which highlight the roles a teacher plays (e.g., "teacher as a guide," "teacher as innovator"). Though the framework never uses the term "identity," the functional components focus on *who* teachers can be. In sum, while the Taiwanese competency framework used identity as a competency (namely, adding identity as a new entry to existing competencies), the Flanders competency framework incorporated identity into the way competencies are written (namely, adding identity by revising existing competencies).

Finland

The Finnish teacher education also provides an example of the IAC approach. The Finnish education system has long been recognized internationally delivering high quality, equitable education, and putting more emphasis on the holistic development of students as whole individuals rather than simply cognitive skills (Tirri, 2014). This can be seen in the current Finnish teacher education system's aim to "educate pedagogically thinking teachers who can combine research findings about teaching with the profession's practical challenges" based on an awareness of their values, beliefs, and goals (Tirri, 2014, p. 603). In other words, a core component of producing pedagogically thinking teachers is for teachers to reflect on who they are and what they believe as a teacher. Since 2015, Finnish policy-makers have claimed that "the educational system was no longer promoting twenty-first-century competences nor adequately preparing students for the future" (Lavonen, 2020, p. 67). Thus, a national teacher education forum was developed to plan new teacher education reforms to face the challenges of the future. Specifically, the forum drafted teacher education goals in line with the competencies framework established by the Organisation for Economic Co-operation and Development's (OECD) Definition and Selection of competencies (DeSeCo) project, with competencies such as developing "awareness of the different dimensions of the teaching profession: the social, philosophical, psychological, sociological, and historical bases of education as well as the school's societal connections" (Lavonen, 2020, p. 74). These new directions in teacher education seek to address challenges in equality and diversity in urban schools due to increasing number of immigrant students as well as children with learning difficulties (Tirri, 2014). Similar to Taiwan's and Flanders' frameworks, Finland has also implemented an IAC approach by including holistic aspects of teacher development as competencies into the teacher education system.

Approach 2: Identity and competencies as complementary

While the IAC approach situates identity as a type of competency, the "identity and competencies as complementary" (ICC) approach positions identity and competencies as equally important factors in teacher education. The ICC approach is less common than the IAC approach, possibly because the former demands a greater revision of CBTE frameworks at the conceptual and structural level than the IAC approach does. Finally, because the ICC approach requires significant changes, there are few, if any, real-world applications of the ICC approach. In the following sub-section, we present two frameworks as examples of the ICC approach, both of which are theoretical in nature.

The onion model

The onion model is an example of a conceptual model in teacher education that treats competencies and identities as complementary constructs within a greater system of teacher development. The onion model was first introduced by Korthagen (2004) and as consisting of seven nested layers (like the layers of an onion) of teacher development: core qualities, mission, identity, beliefs, competencies, behavior, and environment (please see Figure 8.2 in Korthagen, 2016, p. 334). Korthagen (2016) argues that teacher development is influenced by all layers, including both competencies and identity, but teachers may not be aware of the inner layers of identity, mission, and core qualities because those layers may not be immediately observable and require deeper forms of self-reflection.

In conceptualizing competency and identity as distinct layers, the onion model treats competency and identity as complementary constructs, unlike the IAC approach which treats identity as a type of competency. In other words, the IAC approach treats identity as a type of competency, while the ICC approach treats identity not as a competency but as its own layer. Therefore, the onion model assumes that competencies and identity can coexist within the same model of teacher education. Moreover, the onion model recognizes the importance of competencies in teacher education while also not being limited to a solely competency-based model. The onion model takes a holistic approach to teacher education by including all elements of teacher development and showing that they are interconnected parts of a greater system.

KARDS: A modular model of language teacher education

Kumaravadivelu (2012) introduced KARDS, a modular model of language teacher education consisting of five modules: Knowing, Analyzing, Recognizing, Doing, and Seeing (KARDS). Visually, these five modules are positioned in a circle at the ends of a five-pointed star and each module is connected with double-headed arrows to the other four (please see Kumaravadivelu, 2012, p. 125). Here is a brief summary of each of the modules:

- Knowing: developing professional, procedural, and personal knowledge
- Analyzing: analyzing learner needs, motivation, and autonomy
- Recognizing: recognizing your own identities, beliefs, and values
- Doing: teaching, theorizing, and dialogizing
- Seeing: monitoring your own teaching

Each of the modules describes what conditions and capabilities language teacher education programs must foster for prospective teachers. Each module operates independently with specific aims and functions while also engaging interdependently as "a network of mutually reinforcing sub-systems" (Kumaravadivelu, 2012, p. 17).

While Kumaravadivelu (2012) does not use the term competency, the category of "doing" is a close descriptor. Like the onion model, KARDS conceptualizes competencies (i.e., doing) and identity (i.e., recognizing) as complementary parts of a greater whole. Furthermore, each of the modules reinforces each other, so a teacher's engagement with competencies will also be oriented by their identities.

The onion model and KARDS both provide an expansive approach to teacher education that addresses how competencies interact with other aspects of teacher development. However, they have different assumptions of how teacher development functions in teacher education. The onion model assumes that the various aspects of teacher education are hierarchical, that the outer layers are more apparent and easily accessible and the inner layers require deeper introspection to reach. Furthermore, it assumes a linear order such that competencies would come before beliefs and before identity. This might be problematic when implemented in an actual teacher education program; not all teachers experience development in this order. The structure of the onion model imposes an artificial rigidity that may result in difficulties if implemented in many different teacher education contexts.

On the other hand, KARDS presents five interrelated aspects of teacher education that are not structured in a hierarchy. In fact, because the model is designed to be modular, it allows for greater flexibility and adaptability (Kumaravadivelu, 2012). While the onion model may appear easier to implement because of its simplicity, KARDS provides a more practical model because of its ability to be customized for different teacher education contexts.

Implications for CBLTE

The examples of the IAC and ICC approach to integrating identities into CBLTE offer three implications.

A need to expand traditional teacher competency-based frameworks

First, scholars recognize the need for competency frameworks within teacher education around the globe, and that traditional competency frameworks are lacking. This is no exception within language teacher education. The problem the IAC and ICC aim to address is providing broader frameworks that retain the benefits of competency-based models (i.e., offer accountability, measure progress) while also including other important aspects of teacher development (e.g., identity, values). Though the IAC approach has already been implemented, some may argue that simply changing competency entries to include identity is not enough. Further innovation requires experimentation with the implementation of the ICC approach in actual teacher education programs.

Kumaravadivelu (2012) suggests that local practitioners could use KARDS as “a compass” to guide them in designing a curriculum that is relevant for local teacher education programs. This could be implemented in teaching practicums, where pre-service teachers enter a classroom and learn about teaching from an in-service teacher. KARDS can be used as a guideline for the different aspects of teaching that pre-service teachers should pay attention to. In addition, KARDS could also be used to make sure that language teacher education coursework addresses all aspects of this approach.

Variation in local implementation

The second implication is that the actual implementation of integrating identities into CBLTE will likely vary based on multiple factors. First, the level of specificity in designating or emphasizing the type of identities may vary. For instance, while Flanders' and Finland's frameworks specifically focus on "teacher" as the main identity, the other frameworks discussed in this chapter do not focus on a certain identity and simply use the generic term "identity." Since one can have multiple, interconnected identities, using the generic term "identity" may be beneficial in keeping the frameworks adaptable to different contexts. Second, integrating identities into CBLTE may be implemented at different timeframes. While Taiwan's framework targeted primary and secondary education, Flanders', Finland's, the onion model, and KARDS were designed to be implemented for teacher education. As the literature has shown that identities continuously evolve, integrating identities into CBLTE can be implemented at different and possibly multiple timeframes. Lastly, the method of implementation may also vary. For example, the IAC approach requires micro-level reforms (i.e., revising individual competencies) while the ICC approach requires macro-level reforms (i.e., restructuring an entire framework). Also, Taiwan's, Flanders', and Finland's frameworks were designed to be implemented as official government-based guidelines, while the onion model and KARDS seem more suitable for implementation at the classroom or institutional level.

A call for further theorizing, innovation, and implementation

Finally, the examples we have presented only represent early efforts to theorize or implement the integration of identities into CBTE. From the IAC and ICC examples, while some scholars have presented a vision for better approaches to CBTE, there is also room for further theorization and implementation. This means a call for more scholars to document and reflect on the outcomes and experiences of IAC approaches, experiment with implementing the ICC approaches, and introduce new approaches beyond IAC or ICC.

Conclusion

In this chapter, we have argued for the need to consider the role of LTI in CBLTE. This argument is based on literature from teacher education regarding the shortcomings of CBTE. Furthermore, we have also reviewed the literature on current conceptualizations of LTIs and the potential contributions LTIs can have for language teacher education. We also discussed the rationale for integrating LTI into CBLTE and current examples of frameworks that have done so. We hope that this chapter inspires new possibilities about how the role of LTI in CBLTE can be re-envisioned and implemented.

References

Amin, N. (1997). Race and the identity of the nonnative ESL teacher. *TESOL Quarterly, 31*(3), 580–583. https://doi.org/10.2307/3587841

Anderson, B. (1991). *Imagined communities. Reflections on the origin and spread of nationalism* (Rev. ed.). Verso.

Barkhuizen, G. (2017a). Language teacher identity research: An introduction. In G. Barkhuizen (Ed.), *Reflections on language teacher identity research* (pp. 1–11). Routledge.

Barkhuizen, G. (Ed.). (2017b). *Reflections on language teacher identity research*. Routledge.

Block, D. (2017). Journey to the center of language teacher identity. In G. Barkhuizen (Ed.), *Reflections on language teacher identity research* (pp. 31–36). Routledge.

Brundrett, M., & Silcock, P. (2002). *Achieving competence, success, and excellence in teaching*. New York, NY: Psychology Press/Taylor and Francis Group.

Burnette, D. M. (2016). The renewal of competency-based education: A review of the literature. *The Journal of Continuing Higher Education*, 64(2), 84–93. https://doi.org/10.1080/07377363.2016.1177704

Chappell, C., Gonczi, A., & Hager, P. (1995). Competency-based education. In G. Foley (Ed.), *Understanding adult education and training* (pp. 175–187). Sydney: Allen & Unwin.

Chen, H. L. S., & Huang, H. Y. (2017). *Advancing 21st century competencies in Taiwan*. Retrieved from Asia Society Center for Global Education. http://asiasociety.org/files/21st-century-competencies-taiwan.pdf

Cheng, K. (2017). *Advancing 21st century competencies in East Asian education systems*. Retrieved from Asia Society Center for Global Education. https://asiasociety.org/files/21st-century-competencies-east-asian-education-systems.pdf

Cots, J. M., & Arnó, E. (2005). Integrating language teachers' discipline knowledge in a language course. In N. Bartels (Ed.), *Applied linguistics and language teacher education* (pp. 59–78). Boston, MA: Springer.

Cross, R. (2020). The 'subject' of Freeman & Johnson's reconceived knowledge base of second language teacher education. *Language Teaching Research, 24*(1), 37–48.

Dang, T. K. A. (2013). Identity in activity: Examining teacher professional identity formation in the paired-placement of student teachers. *Teaching and Teacher Education, 30*, 47–59.

Danielewicz, J. (2001). *Teaching selves: Identity, pedagogy, and teacher education*. SUNY Press.

Day, C. (2017). Competence-based education and teacher professional development. In M. Mulder (Ed.), *Competence-based vocational and professional education* (pp. 165–182). Cham: Springer.

De Costa, P. I., & Norton, B. (2016). Identity in language learning and teaching: Research agendas for the future. In S. Preece (Ed.), *The Routledge handbook of language and identity* (pp. 586–601). Routledge.

De Costa, P. I., & Norton, B. (Eds.) (2017). Transdisciplinarity and language teacher identity. *The Modern Language Journal*, 101(S1), 1–105.

Douglas Fir Group. (2016). A transdisciplinary framework for SLA in a multilingual world. *The Modern Language Journal, 100*(S1), 19–47. https://doi.org/10.1111/modl.12301

European Commission. (2013, July). *Supporting the teaching professions for better learning outcomes*. https://ec.europa.eu/assets/eac/education/policy/school/doc/teachercomp_en.pdf

Fairley, M. J. (2020). Conceptualizing language teacher education centered on language teacher identity development: A competencies-based approach and practical applications. *TESOL Quarterly*, *54*(4), 1037–1064. https://doi.org/10.1002/tesq.568

Fernández, D. M., & Hughes, S. (2013). Competences and foreign language teacher education in Spain. In M. L. P. Cañado (Ed.), *Competency-based language teaching in higher education* (pp. 63–75). Springer.

Forzani, F. M. (2014). Understanding "core practices" and "practice-based" teacher education: Learning from the past. *Journal of Teacher Education*, *65*(4), 357–368.

Freeman, D. (2020). Arguing for a knowledge-base in language teacher education, then (1998) and now (2018). *Language Teaching Research*, *24*(1), 5–16. https://doi.org/10.1177/1362168818777534

Gervais, J. (2016). The operational definition of competency-based education. *The Journal of Competency-Based Education*, *1*(2), 98–106.

Hopcraft, G. B. (2010). Competency-based education. In T. C. Hunt, J. C. Carter, T. J. Lasley, & C. D. Raisch (Eds.), *Encyclopedia of educational reform and dissent*. Thousand Oaks, CA: Sage.

Houston, W. R., & Howsan, R. B. (1972). *Competency-based teacher education: Progress, problems and prospects*. Chicago, IL: Science Research Associates.

Hyland, T. (1994). *Competence, education and NVQs: Dissenting perspectives*. London: Cassell.

Ishihara, N., & Menard-Warwick, J. (2018). In "sociocultural in-betweenness": Exploring teachers' translingual identity development through narratives. *Multilingua*, *37*(3), 255–274. https://doi.org/10.1515/multi-2016-0086

Jarvis-Selinger, S., Pratt, D. D., & Regehr, G. (2012). Competency is not enough: Integrating identity formation into the medical education discourse. *Academic Medicine*, *87*(9), 1185–1190.

Johnson, K. E. (2006). The sociocultural turn and its challenges for second language teacher education. *TESOL Quarterly*, *40*(1), 235–257. https://doi.org/10.2307/40264518

Johnson, K. E. (2019). The relevance of a transdisciplinary framework for SLA in language teacher education. *The Modern Language Journal*, *103*, 167–174. https://doi.org/10.1111/modl.12524

Kanno, Y., & Norton, B. (2003). Imagined communities and educational possibilities: Introduction. *Journal of Language, Identity, and Education*, *2*(4), 241–249.

Kanno, Y., & Stuart, C. (2011). Learning to become a second language teacher: Identities-in-practice. *The Modern Language Journal*, *95*(2), 236–252. https://doi.org/10.1111/j.1540-4781.2011.01178.x

Kayi-Aydar, H. (2015). Multiple identities, negotiations, and agency across time and space: A narrative inquiry of a foreign language teacher candidate. *Critical Inquiry in Language Studies*, *12*(2), 137–160. https://doi.org/10.1080/15427587.2015.1032076

Kayi-Aydar, H. (2019). Language teacher identity. *Language Teaching*, *52*(3), 281–295. https://doi.org/10.1017/S0261444819000223

Korthagen, F. A. J. (2004). In search of the essence of a good teacher: Towards a more holistic approach in teacher education. *Teaching and Teacher Education*, *20*(1), 77–97.

Korthagen, F. A. J. (2016). Pedagogy of teacher education. In J. Loughran & M. L. Hamilton (Eds.), *International handbook of teacher education* (Vol. 1, pp. 311–346). Springer.

Korthagen, F. A. J. (2017). Inconvenient truths about teacher learning: towards professional development 3.0. *Teachers and Teaching: Theory and Practice, 23*(4), 387–405. https://doi.org/10.1080/13540602.2016.1211523

Kumaravadivelu, B. (2012). *Language teacher education for a global society: A modular model for knowing, analyzing, recognizing, doing, and seeing*. Routledge.

Lave, J. (1996). Teaching, as learning, in practice. *Mind, Culture, and Activity, 3*(3), 149–164. https://doi.org/10.1207/s15327884mca0303_2

Lave, J., & Wenger, E. (1991). *Situated learning: Legitimate peripheral participation*. Cambridge University Press.

Lavonen, J. (2020). Curriculum and teacher education reforms in Finland that support the development of competences for the twenty-first century. In F. M. Reimers (Ed.), *Audacious education purposes* (pp. 65–80). Cham: Springer. https://doi.org/10.1007/978-3-030-41882-3_3

Le, C., Wolfe, R., & Steinberg, A. (2014). *The past and the promise: Today's competency education movement. Students at the center: Competency education research series*. Boston, MA: Jobs for the Future.

Lin, A., Grant, R., Kubota, R., Motha, S., Sachs, G. T., Vandrick, S., & Wong, S. (2004). Women faculty of color in TESOL: Theorizing our lived experiences. *TESOL Quarterly*, 38(3), 487–504. https://doi.org/10.2307/3588350

Lindahl, K., & Yazan, B. (2019). An identity-oriented lens to TESOL teachers' lives: Introducing the special issue. *TESOL Journal, 10*(4), e506.

Lucas, C. (1999). *Teacher education in America*. New York, NY: St. Martin's Press.

Menard-Warwick, J. (2008). The cultural and intercultural identities of transnational English teachers: Two case studies from the Americas. *TESOL Quarterly, 42*(4), 617–640. https://doi.org/10.2307/40264491

Ministry of Education (MOE). (November 2014). *shí èr nián guó mín jī běn jiāo yù kè chéng gāng yào zǒng gāng* [General guidelines of the twelve-year curriculum]. Retrieved from http://www.naer.edu.tw/files/15-1000-7944,c1174-1.php?Lang=zh-tw.

Ministry of Education (MOE). (n.d.). General Guidelines of Grades 1–9 Curriculum for Elementary and Junior High School Education https://www.k12ea.gov.tw/files/92_sid17/%E6%96%B0%E7%B8%BD%E7%B6%B1%E8%8B%B1%E6%96%87%E7%89%88.pdf

Motha, S. (2006). Racializing ESOL teacher identities in U.S. K-12 public schools. *TESOL Quarterly, 40*(3), 495–518. https://doi.org/10.2307/40264541

Murray, J. (2009). Teacher competencies in the post-method landscape: The limits of competency-based training in TESOL teacher education. *Prospect: An Australian Journal of TESOL, 24*(1), 17–29.

Newby, D., Allan, R., Fenner, A. B., Jones, B., Komorowska, H., & Soghikyan, K. (2007). *European portfolio for student teachers of languages: A reflection tool for language teacher education*. Graz, Austria: Council of Europe Publishing.

Norton, B., & De Costa, P. I. (2018). Research tasks on identity in language learning and teaching. *Language Teaching, 51*(1), 90–112. https://doi.org/10.1017/S0261444817000325

Norton Peirce, B. (1995). Social identity, investment, and language learning. *TESOL Quarterly, 29*(1), 9–31.

Pantić, N., & Wubbels, T. (2010). Teacher competencies as a basis for teacher education—Views of Serbian teachers and teacher educators. *Teaching and Teacher Education, 26*(3), 694–703.

Pavlenko, A. (2003). "I never knew I was a bilingual": Reimagining teacher identities in TESOL. *Journal of Language, Identity, and Education*, *2*(4), 251–268. https://doi.org/10.1207/S15327701JLIE0204_2

Reis, D. S. (2012). "Being underdog": Supporting nonnative English-speaking teachers (NNESTs) in claiming and asserting professional legitimacy. *Journal on Excellence in College Teaching*, *23*(3), 33–58.

Robinson, M., & Mogliacci, R. (2019). Conceptions and models of teacher education. In G. W. Noblit (Ed.), *Oxford research encyclopedia of education*. Oxford University Press. http://doi.org/10.1093/acrefore/9780190264093.013.571

Rodgers, C. R., & Scott, K. H. (2008). The development of the personal self and professional identity in learning to teach. In M. Cochran-Smith, S. Feiman-Nemser, D. J. McIntyre, & K. E. Demers (Eds.), *Handbook of research on teacher education: Enduring questions in changing contexts* (3rd ed.). New York, NY: Routledge/Association of Teacher Educators.

Rudolph, N., Selvi, A. F., & Yazan, B. (2020). *The complexity of identity and interaction in language education*. Multilingual Matters.

Selingo, J. J. (2015). A new measure for collegiate learning: What presidents think about the promises and pitfalls of competency-based education. Retrieved from https://www.pearsoned.com/wp-content/uploads/CBE_Survey_v6_Pearson.pdf

Shulman, L. S. (1987). Knowledge and teaching: Foundations of the new reform. *Harvard Education Review*, *57*(1), 1–22. http://doi.org/10.17763/haer.57.1.j463w79r56455411

Simon-Maeda, A. (2004). The complex construction of professional identities: Female EFL educators in Japan speak out. *TESOL Quarterly*, 38(3), 405–436. https://doi.org/10.2307/3588347

Song, J. (2016). Emotions and language teacher identity: Conflicts, vulnerability, and transformation. *TESOL Quarterly*, *50*(3), 631–654. https://doi.org/10.1002/tesq.312

Struyven, K., & De Meyst, M. (2010). Competence-based teacher education: Illusion or reality? An assessment of the implementation status in Flanders from teachers' and students' points of view. *Teaching and Teacher Education*, *26*(8), 1495–1510.

Tang, C. (1997). The identity of the nonnative ESL teacher on the power and status of nonnative ESL teachers. *TESOL Quarterly*, *31*(3), 577–580. https://doi.org/10.2307/3587840

Thomas, A. (1987). Language teacher competence and language teacher education. In R. Bowers (Ed.), *Language teacher education: An integrated programme for ELT teacher training*. British Council, Modern English Publications.

Tirri, K. (2014). The last 40 years in Finnish teacher education. *Journal of Education for Teaching*, *40*(5), 600–609.

Toom, A. (2017). Teachers' professional and pedagogical competencies: A complex divide between teacher work, teacher knowledge and teacher education. In D. J. Clandinin & J. Husu (Eds.), *The SAGE handbook of research on teacher education* (Vol. 2, pp. 803–819). SAGE Publications Ltd. https://www.doi.org/10.4135/9781529716627

Tsui, A. B. M. (2007). Complexities of identity formation: A narrative inquiry of an EFL teacher. *TESOL Quarterly*, *41*(4), 657–680. https://doi.org/10.1002/j.1545-7249.2007.tb00098.x

Varghese, M., Morgan, B., Johnston, B., & Johnson, K. (2005). Theorizing language teacher identity: Three perspectives and beyond. *Journal of Language, Identity and Education*, *4*, 21–44.

Varghese, M., Motha, S., Park, G., Reeves, J., & Trent, J. (2016). Language teacher identity in (multi)lingual educational contexts [special issue]. *TESOL Quarterly, 50*(3), 541–783 https://doi.org/10.1002/tesq.333.

Wenger, E. (1998). *Communities of practice: Learning, meaning, and identity.* Cambridge University Press.

Whitty, G., & Willmott, E. (1991). Competence-based teacher education: Approaches and issues. *Cambridge Journal of Education, 21*(3), 309–318.

Willbergh, I. (2015). The problems of "competence" and alternatives from the Scandinavian perspective of *Bildung. Journal of Curriculum Studies, 47*(3), 334–354.

Wolff, D., & De Costa, P. I. (2017). Expanding the language teacher identity landscape: An investigation of the emotions and strategies of a NNEST. *The Modern Language Journal, 101*(S1), 76–90. https://doi.org/10.1111/modl.12370

Yazan, B., & Lindahl, K. (2020). *Language teacher identity in TESOL: Teacher education and practice as identity work.* Routledge.

Yazan, B., & Rudolph, N. (2018). *Criticality, teacher identity, and (in)equity in English language teaching.* Springer.

Zheng, X. (2017). Translingual identity as pedagogy: International teaching assistants of English in college composition classrooms. *The Modern Language Journal, 101*(S1), 29–44. https://doi.org/10.1111/modl.12373

Section II

Research

4 Undergraduate EFL majors' agency in ELT lesson designs

Chin-Wen Chien

Introduction

The 12-Year Basic Education Plan has been implemented since September 2019. Competency-based assessment, interdisciplinary studies, and integration of major social issues into curricula (e.g., gender, environment) are new trends included in the English curriculum reforms (Ministry of Education, 2014). These new teaching initiatives should be introduced in the language teacher education programs (Tang et al., 2012).

Teacher agency refers to "teachers' curriculum work and their understanding of educational purposes" (Root, 2014, p. 76). Understanding teacher agency is vital in teacher education research (Goodson & Numan, 2002). Teacher agency is critical to the process of implementing curriculum reform (Nguyen & Bui, 2016; Yuan & Lee, 2014). Developing a lesson aligned with the aims, procedural steps, and assessment standards of an educational program is challenging for teachers, regardless of whether they are experienced or a novice (Boyd, 2012; Liyanage & Bartlett, 2010).

The purpose of the current investigation was to train 26 Taiwanese undergraduate English as a foreign language (EFL) majors to be curriculum makers, as a means of activating their agency in curriculum work. The setting was a Teaching English to Speakers of Other Languages (TESOL) method class in a language teacher education program in a northwest Taiwanese city. These undergraduates were language learners majoring in English instruction. This study explored their agency in English lesson design and implementation of the 12-Year Basic Education Plan and in addition, answered the following research questions. First, what features mainly characterize English majors' teacher agency, as revealed in their lesson planning and implementation? Second, what is the attitude of English majors toward their teacher agency in lesson planning and implementation? Third, what factors facilitated increases in EFL majors' teacher agency? Suggestions on effective curriculum design for integration of teacher agency into EFL teacher education courses were provided.

DOI: 10.4324/9781003212805-5

Literature review

The literature considered herein addresses issues relating to definitions and features of teacher agency, factors contributing to teacher agency, influences on teacher agency with respect to curriculum reforms, empirical studies, literature gap, and the conceptual framework. Biesta et al. (2015) argued that agency denotes "the quality of the engagement of actors with temporal-relational contexts-for-action, not a quality of the actors themselves" (p. 626).

Teacher agency in curriculum design is defined by Paris (1993) as "involving initiating the creation or critique of curriculum, an awareness of alternatives to established curriculum practices, the autonomy to make informed choices, an investment of self, and on-going interaction with others" (p. 16). Teachers might exert their agency in terms of curriculum development, implementation, and evaluation, since deriving curricula is multifaceted (Fleming, 1998).

Tang et al.'s (2012) longitudinal study explored the influence of training on four Hong Kong ESL pre-service teachers' beliefs and agency; they were involved in implementing a new English teaching method. The analysis of descriptive accounts, belief inventories, tasks, and interviews indicated that inconsistencies between their beliefs and practice resulted from their personal agency. A lack of sufficient teaching experience affected their classroom practice.

Teacher agency is generally explored along three dimensions (Priestley et al., 2012, 2015). First, teacher agency is iterational between a teacher's personal and professional histories and experience. Second, their curriculum agency is projective and consists of expectations for the short term and the long run. Third, the practical evaluative dimension concerns cultural (ideas, values, and discourses), structural (social relations, trust, and power), and material (environment and resources) aspects.

Various factors might affect teachers' achievement of agency during curriculum planning and innovation. Agency can vary from context to context, because beliefs, values, and attributes can be held by teachers in relation to a given situation or relative to conflicting demands—otherwise put, "input regulation" (e.g., prescription of content, methods, and/or teaching materials) or "output regulation" (e.g., steering through outcomes; Priestley et al., 2012, 2015). Macaro (2001) analyzed six French as a second language student teachers' videos and interviews to explore the relationship among teachers' agency, training programs, and governmental policy. One student teacher's agency was influenced by the government policy of "using the target language only for instruction"; that attitude (and consequent agency) further affected his classroom practice.

Limited studies (e.g., Fleming, 1998; Kayi-Aydar, 2015; Molina, 2016; Nguyen & Bui, 2016; Rasti & Sahragard, 2017; Yang, 2012) have focused on language teacher agency in ESL or EFL contexts. Nguyen and Bui (2016) analyzed 15 Vietnamese EFL teachers' interviews and classroom observations to explore their change agency in responding to English education policies. These teachers were aware of the importance of meeting minority students' needs. They activated their agency by democratizing teaching practices, providing high-quality, practical teaching and fostering their students' awareness of both educational and social concerns. In the ESL setting, Fleming (1998) explored ESL instructor's agency relative to the curriculum. Fleming used interview protocols along with observations and documents to explore five Canadian ESL program instructors' response to curriculum development. The analysis revealed that these instructors desired to exert their agency over curriculum development; however, they failed to do so due to their lack of time to prepare materials and activities for classroom learning and, as well, assessing their students.

Empirical studies use Priestley et al.'s (2012, 2015) teacher agency theories to explore its influence on curriculum development, innovations, or reforms (e.g., Alvunger, 2018; Biesta et al., 2015; Fleming, 1998; Molina, 2016; Rasti & Sahragard, 2017). Biesta et al. (2015) used observations and interviews (both individual and group) to explore six classroom teachers' agency. Biesta et al. (2015) concluded that teacher agency is highly dependent upon their personal qualities and, further, that it was iterational between their professional knowledge and skills. Limited empirical studies use Priestley et al.'s (2012, 2015) approach to explore the preparation of preservice or undergraduate students for application of teacher agency in response to curriculum reforms and innovations in language teacher education. The present study employed triangulated data to explore English majors' teacher agency in planning lessons for English instruction. The conceptual framework was based on the work of Priestley's group and other similar studies (e.g., Alvunger, 2018; Molina, 2016; Yang, 2012), as revealed in Figure 4.1.

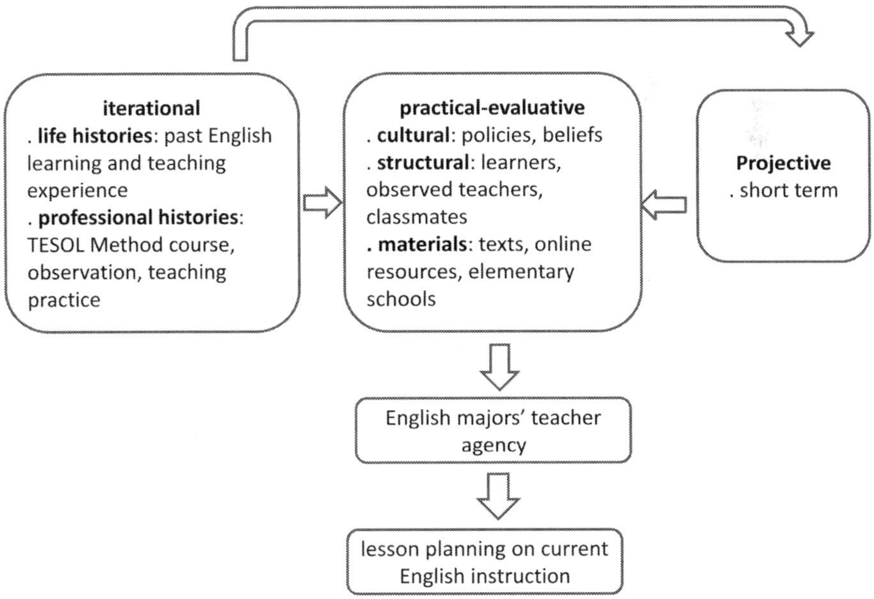

Figure 4.1 Conceptual framework.

The investigation involved two levels. For the iterational level, participants' life histories were considered. This included their past English learning and teaching experience as well as their professional histories (e.g., courses, their observations, and teaching practice) and all affected the teachers' agency. As for the practical-evaluative level, the government's English educational policies and the instructors' own beliefs affected and activated their own teacher agency. The interaction with their learners, observed teachers, and classmates also influenced their agency. Resource materials were used to activate teacher agency; they made professional decisions about how to adapt the materials to their teaching context (Gopinathan & Deng, 2006).

Lesson plans reflected the intended curriculum; this was an area where participants could discover and extend their teacher agency. These provided a valuable framework for articulating teachers' lesson objectives as well as delineating resources they could use. In this manner, lesson plans fostered the contingent decision-making and agency that teachers develop in the classroom (Boyd, 2012). Such agency was projective and consisted of expectations for the short term.

Methodology

A case study approach was employed in this investigation. The methodology was chosen because it provided the best basis for exploring the subject matter. No previous research was found that could serve as an appropriate basis for designing research in this specific context, so the case study approach was exploratory and descriptive. A single-case design with 26 multiple participants was employed. The participants shared many common characteristics and conditions; this enabled the researcher to "strengthen the precision, validity, stability, and trustworthiness of the findings" (Miles et al., 2014, p. 33). The case was a TESOL Method course; the unit of analysis was the participants' teacher agency in design and delivery of the lesson plan.

Participants and setting

Participants in this study were 26 English majors enrolled in "TESOL Methods," a 3-credit undergraduate course offered in a language teacher education program at a northwest Taiwan university. The course aimed to introduce students to second-language acquisition research, its educational implications, and instructional strategies that support English learners' development.

Of the 26 participants, 20 were female and 6 were male. With regard to their English proficiency levels, only one participant reached C1, "effective operational proficiency" of the Common European Framework of Reference for Languages (CEFR). Fourteen students reached B2 "vantage" and 11 reached only B1 "threshold" of the CEFR. Prior to this class, participants had taken one required course related to English instruction, "Introduction to English Methodology." Four of the participants had taken two elective courses ("Reading and Writing Instruction" and "Storytelling"), and two had taken "Children's English." A total of 20 participants had English teaching experience in language schools or being English tutors.

Data collection

Data collected for analysis included 22 final projects, semi-structured interviews, and self- and peer-evaluations on videos. The final course project included the following elements. First, the participants were asked to observe an English teacher's instruction using the student's chosen educational approach (e.g., competency-based, cross-disciplinary, theme or topic-based, issue-based, or school-based). Second, they were asked to describe the teaching procedure, strengths and weakness of that teacher's instruction based on the English language teaching methods and theories. Next, they designed a 40-minute lesson plan including goals, learners' age, English proficiency levels, teaching procedure, assessments, worksheets, and supplementary teaching materials. Fourth, they were asked to share their lesson plan in class; feedback was provided by their classmates and the instructor. Fifth, based on the feedback, they revised their lesson plan. Sixth, they taught this revised lesson to their target learners and videotaped it. Seventh, after the instruction, they asked the target learners for feedback regarding the lesson. They used the readings and concepts covered in class to critique their own teaching practice. Finally, they made a 5-minute video clip of their final project and uploaded it to YouTube. On the last day of class, each participant showed his/her video and completed their self- and peer-evaluation. Participants worked individually on their own final projects, but four pairs worked together on the final group projects. The 7-point Likert scale self- and peer-evaluations were developed based on empirical studies (e.g., Borich, 2013).

Each participant was interviewed once for approximately 30 minutes at a time. The interview protocol was developed based on the studies by Abednia (2012), Fleming (1998), and Yang (2012), among others. The interview protocol was comprised of three sections. The first section was designed to elicit participants' beliefs and self-agency on curriculum innovations, such as "What was your ideal lesson in the teaching style you chose to focus on?" The second section was designed to explore participants' designs and implementation of curriculum innovations, such as "What curriculum documents/resources were your lesson plan based on?" The third section aimed to analyze the factors that affected participants' activation of agency, such as "What helped you design and teach this lesson?"

Data analysis

During analysis, participants were identified with pseudonyms, thus making reviewers "blind" to their identity. The videos were transcribed, coded, and analyzed based on the conceptual framework and the research questions. All the data were coded in two steps. First, the researcher read through all the data and tentative codes were marked. Then, patterns or themes were gleaned from the data. Themes that were aligned were categorized.

The researcher applied a number of measures to ensure trustworthiness of the data. Data triangulation, including documentation, interview, and videos, increased its confirmability.

Results

Based on the data analysis of final projects, self-evaluations, peer evaluations, and interviews, issues were discussed in terms of agency. This was revealed in participants' lesson planning and implementations, participants' attitude toward agency exerted in their lesson planning and implementation, and factors facilitating their agency in lesson planning and implementation.

Agency revealed in lesson planning

Participants' agency was revealed in the topic selection and lesson planning. It was also affected by governmental policy and the training received in the "TESOL Method" course and other courses, and their past English learning experience. Of all the 22 final projects, the most popular topic designed by the participants was reading literacy (*n*=7), followed by character education (*n*=5), multi-culture education (*n*=4), and human rights education (*n*=3). Other issues included family education (*n*=1), environmental education (*n*=1), and information education (*n*=1). Participants exercised their agency and developed their competence and knowledge through the influence of sociocultural factors, such as policies, curriculum guidelines, and/or trainings on innovative teaching methods.

First, participants thought that the content of the instruction should go beyond textbooks. Instead, picture books, videos, or recent news reports were chosen as the content for instruction. Ada suggested, for instance, "Both textbooks and other teaching materials are good for students. There are a lot of aids and issues in these materials as suggested by the government K-12 curriculum guidelines." Leo said, "Learning English may be a little boring and torturing for the EFL learners. I learned from the Storytelling course that integrating story books into the lesson may attract students' attention and increase their willingness to engage in the activities related to the lesson." Leo's teaching procedure was shown in Final Project 1. He showed the cover of the picture book, *Handa's Surprise,* and asked his student questions for the warm-up and began to tell the story as the presentation.

Final Project #1: Leo's Storytelling Activities

WARM-UP: Greet the student and tell him/her we are going to read a story. Introduce the story and ask him/her questions about the cover.
QUESTIONS: What can you see? What is the girl doing? Where is the girl?
PRESENTATION: Read the story book, "Handa's Surprise." During the storytelling, throw some questions to the student in order to let him focus on the story.

Teachers can play the agentive role in responding to and implementing the policies (Nguyen & Bui, 2016). Prospective teachers, such as Leo in this study, can exercise their agency as policy implementers. Teachers do so by refraining from using textbooks alone, instead working toward meaningful curriculum and pedagogical transformation using authentic materials, emphasizing reading literacy, or issue-based lesson.

Secondly, participants thought that topics chosen for the instruction should be relevant to learners' lives. Amy said, "In the TESOL Method course, I learned that the authentic context was crucial for learners to practice vocabulary and sentence patterns. Food is what we eat every day, so food would be a good topic. So students can learn vocabulary and sentence patterns related to food." Ada said, "In the TESOL Method course, I learned that picture books can be used not only to teach vocabulary and sentence patterns but also reading strategies and core values. I think animals are related to students' life. Students can learn the vocabulary and realize the importance of friendship." Lesson plan designs revealed teachers' agency, expertise, experience of and beliefs in English teaching and learning. The lesson plan designs are cognitively processed for requiring teachers to effect synergies of factors involved in their knowledge of content, pedagogy, learners, and the contexts that optimize the best practice for learners (Liyanage & Bartlett, 2010).

As revealed in Final Project 2, Ada identified "friendship" as the theme of the picture book, so she asked her students a question, "What animals come to help?" during the practice and asked them to write down their good friends as the production.

Final Project #2: Ada's Instruction on Animal's Picture Book

PRACTICE: *The teacher will review the story and ask students what the animal is.*
THE TEACHER WILL ASK ONE QUESTION ABOUT THE STORY: *What animals come to help? Students will name these animals.*
PRODUCTION: *Write down your good friend and draw some pictures.*

Prospective teachers actively respond to and enact policies on topic selections relevant to learners' needs. Teachers exercise their agency for lesson planning and demonstrate the competence in alignment between purpose, content, results, and assessments (Alvunger, 2018).

Third, participants valued cultural differences and racial issues and such beliefs and agency were affected by the society that participants live. Their agency was exerted in their lesson designs and interviews. As Ann said:

> Recently, with globalization, there have been more and more people from different countries living in Taiwan. It seems that Taiwan is much more diverse and multicultural than before. However, there are a lot of problems derived from the differences and gaps between people, such as social inequality, harassment, or even attack. The main solution is to understand others' backgrounds. The competency-based teaching method can

> make students aware of the injustice and what lies in ethic gaps and also equip them with the attitude of respect for people from different social groups.

Such finding is in accord with previous studies suggesting that sociocultural forces might impact teachers' agency activation and construction. Teachers themselves develop reflective abilities and form a comprehensive understanding of the educational contexts and society (Yuan, 2016).

Pam also emphasized the importance of multicultural education, saying, "When I was in elementary school, I enjoyed different cultural activities my English teacher designed, particularly Christmas. I can integrate multicultural education and introduce how people in different countries celebrate Christmas." As revealed in Final Project 3, Pam introduced customs in different countries such as Japan and Sweden.

Final Project #3: Pam's Culture Differences

PRESENTATION: *Different culture & different activities*

TEACHER: *The first one is the special tradition in Japan. The Japanese see Christmas as KFC day. They will wait in long lines to buy KFC Christmas meals. For Japanese, KFC is a symbol of family reunion.*

STUDENT: *Wow! It's so cool!*

TEACHER: *The second one is the special tradition in Sweden. They will eat rice pudding after the Christmas meal. It is said that people will marry this year if they find an almond in the pudding.*

Multicultural education was integrated into the English classroom as Final Project 3. Teachers like Pam can exercise their agency by consolidating their past English learning experience and theoretical knowledge on English instruction into classroom practice (Yuan & Lee, 2014).

Fourth, critical thinking, reflective thinking, and problem solving were emphasized in lesson plans; these skills were highly emphasized in the 12-Year Basic Education Plan. Participants revealed such beliefs and activated their agency influenced by the policies and their past learning experience, as observed by Deb and Ava below.

> I want my students to be aware of the environmental issues, because environmental education is highly emphasized in the 12-Year Basic Education Plan. Learners can make connections between what they have learned and their daily life through reflection and paragraph writing. Learners can reflect how to conserve the environment by their own contribution. (Deb 01)
>
> When I learned English, my teachers focused on grammar and vocabulary memorization. English instruction should go beyond understanding reading texts, vocabulary, and sentence patterns. Students are exposed to racial issues in their daily lives. I plan to use the reading text to guide students

to think about the problems discrimination will cause. I want to develop learners' critical thinking. (Ava 01)

Such findings were affirmed by the empirical studies that teachers' agency and identity can be influenced by their previous learning and coursework in language teacher education programs. Their agency can be strengthened in the course of guiding their lesson planning and teaching practice (e.g., Yuan, 2016).

Project 4 revealed Ida's activity design on reflective thinking; she raised questions that guided students to think and discuss environmental issues.

Final Project #4: Ida's Reflective Thinking

Teacher will ask students questions and discuss the paragraph with him/her.
T: *What kind of pollution did you read about in the paragraph?*
T: *What does the paragraph want to tell us?*
T: *What can we do to protect our environment?*

The lesson plan reveals the iterational dimension of the teachers' learning experience in personal and professional histories. Teachers exercise their agency in activity designs by taking into account the interaction between their pedagogical competence, policies, and learners in the educational setting (Alvunger, 2018).

Agency in lesson implementations

Participants activated their agency through lesson implementations. Their agency was influenced by governmental policies, the teachers they observed, the training they received, and their past teaching and learning experiences. First, participants intentionally taught the lessons in English and tried to avoid using Chinese. Their choice of instructional language was affected by the language policy that classes should be taught completely in English. Ina said, "I used Chinese to explain the worksheet when students did not understand how to write it. I should have explained it in another way or used gestures. I should not speak Chinese immediately. It's an English class, so I should use more English as required by the government." Teacher agency is affected by the sociocultural factors, such as language policy, the educational context, and learners' needs.

Excerpt 1 revealed Ina's explanations of the friendship worksheet. She explained how learners should do the worksheets. After Ina finished her explanations, a student responded that he did not understand. Another student asked Ina what she had to do. Ina used Chinese to explain how to complete the friendship worksheet.

Excerpt 1: Ina's Explanations of the Friendship Worksheet

INA: *Here is the worksheet. Write your name here. My good friend is__. Write your good friend's name here. We ___ together. Write what you two do together. My friend means a lot to me. Write your friend's name here. Draw a picture here.*

S1: wo ting bu dong (I don't understand.)
S2: xian zaiyaozuo shenmo (What do we have to do now?)
INA: (shrug and smile). zhe shi xi dan (This is the worksheet.) zhe li xie ni de ming zi (Write your name here).

Teachers attempt to demonstrate their capacity to become a change agent in curriculum innovation and implementation (Nguyen & Bui, 2016), such as Ina's desire and visions about using English for instruction in Excerpt 1. Hence, English teachers need to be equipped with sufficient capacity and competence to become such change agents in the context of English educational reforms.

With regard to English as the medium for learning that language, participants thought that they were English majors, so they should speak fluently and accurately. Liz said, "Since my teaching practice was by using CLIL (content language-integrated learning), it was necessary that I speak English fluently. It's still hard for me to speak English since I still make some grammar mistakes sometimes and it was hard to avoid those mistakes, especially when I was concentrating on what I was going to say."

While English teachers have the "ideal self" (Higgins, 1987), the attributes participants ideally like to possess, such as competency in accurate grammar as native speakers, they have the "ought self" (Higgins, 1987), the attributes individuals are supposed to possess as a result of certain responsibilities (e.g., using English as medium for CLIL instruction. English teachers or majors might struggle when they activate their agency and their different selves can contradict each other during lesson implementation such as Liz in this study; Nguyen & Bui, 2016; Yuan, 2016).

Second, participants aimed to have interactions with their students. Their agency and intentions were affected by English teachers they observed and the TESOL Method course. Eve said, "I originally looked forward to having a heated interaction; however, things turned out to be different from what I expected. It was necessary to have some ice-breaker games and group games as we experienced in the TESOL Method course." Sue said, "The discussion was supposed to be interactive between the teacher and students as the class I observed before. Unfortunately, it turned out to be a very silent period with my students who just wrote down answers on the worksheets."

English teacher agency can be strongly influenced by social engagement when they are in the process of learning to teach (Charteris & Smardon, 2015; Kayi-Aydar, 2015; Yuan, 2016). The instructor of the TESOL Method courses or the teachers who participants observed in this study played crucial roles in shaping participants' agency, so they insisted on having interaction with their learners.

Excerpt 2 revealed the interaction between Sue and her students. She expected her students to work on the worksheet, read through the paragraphs, and think out loud, so she could have discussions with them about the racism they were studying. However, her students did not pay attention to her guiding question but worked hard on their worksheets.

Excerpt 2: Sue's interaction with her student

SUE: *You use the hints to search for the words below. Fill in the blanks. Read through the paragraphs. Tell me how you feel. How do you feel when people mistreat new immigrants?*
S1: *(She is working on her worksheet.)*
S2: *(She is looking up an unknown word in the online dictionary).*

Prospective or novice teachers, such as Sue in this study, activated their agency and beliefs on engagement with their students during the instruction. However, their lack of experience and inadequate competencies prevented them from meeting the needs of their students and match expectations for interactive instruction (Yuan, 2016).

Participants' attitude toward agency in their lesson planning and implementation

As revealed in Table 4.1, participants held a positive attitude toward and satisfaction in lesson planning and implementation, particularly in the logical flow of instruction (mean=5.42) and students' active engagement (mean=5.38), followed by adhering to English teaching approaches (mean=5.31).

Participants' English abilities influenced their attitude toward and satisfaction with their agency, as activated in lesson planning and implementation, particularly in students' knowledge bank (r=.41), the varieties of content and process (r=.40), and students on task (r=.40), followed by students' active engagement (r=.24) and logical flow of instruction (r=.23).

Overall, the final project by Leo was rated the highest (mean=6.8) by the participants, followed by Ada's (mean=6.6) and Ana's and Ben's (mean =6.55). In these three final projects, picture books were used to teach vocabulary words for animals, literacy, reading and comprehension as revealed in Final Project 1 and 2 "animals." Friendship was emphasized in Leo's and Ada's lesson plans, while personality was the main focus in Ana's and Ben's lesson plan as in

Table 4.1 Participants' self-evaluation

	Statements	*Mean*	*SD*
1	Adhering to English teaching approaches	5.31	0.88
2	Including required elements	5	1.23
3	Varieties on content and process	5.11	1.07
4	Logical flow	5.42	1.14
5	Students' active engagement	5.38	1.39
6	Students on tasks	4.92	1.20
7	Task orientation	4.58	1.30
8	Appropriate assessments	4.77	1.45
9	Fund of students' knowledge	5	1.50
10	Teacher's vigor and involvement	5.27	1.25

Skill Focus **Vocabulary**	*Sentence Pattern: - I always finish my works on time. I am as principled as an elephant. -Although I am sometimes as timid as a mouse, I am energetic as an otter. *Vocabulary: Positive personalities: bear(powerful), elephant(principled), otter(energetic), rabbit(nimble), dolphin(creative) Negative: mouse(timid), lion(self-centered), fox(cunning), sloth(slow), mule(stubborn)

Presentations (15 minutes)	Teaching aids
1. Teacher introduces the vocabulary of animals and characters with flashcards and PPTs. The class will repeat the word after teacher's reading. 2. Teacher teaches the conversation pattern "What is your personality?" "I am as personality as a(n) animal." Examples: a) I am a person who has many ideas. I am as creative as a dolphin. b) I am afraid of speaking to foreigners. I am as timid as a mouse.	flashcard PPT

Figure 4.2 Ana's and Ben's lesson plan.

Figure 4.2. Ana and Ben's used the sentence patterns to teach students to describe their personality.

As revealed in Table 4.2, peer evaluation was rated higher compared to self-evaluation. Participants held a positive attitude toward and satisfaction with peer evaluations in lesson planning and implementation, particularly in the logic flow of instruction (mean=6.2), followed by required elements in the lesson plans (mean=6.16).

Through different types of reflective practice (e.g., peer evaluation, self-evaluation, or discussions and feedback as employed in this study), participants in this study were engaged in reflective practice. Teachers can become agentive

Table 4.2 Participants' peer-evaluation

	Statements	*Mean*	*SD*
1	Adhering to English teaching approaches	6.08	0.99
2	Including required elements	6.16	0.89
3	Varieties on content and process	6.08	0.84
4	Logical flow	6.20	0.82
5	Students' active engagement	6.10	0.85
6	Students on tasks	5.94	0.85
7	Task orientation	5.94	0.89
8	Appropriate assessments	5.82	0.97
9	Fund of students' knowledge	5.63	0.82
10	Teacher's vigor and involvement	5.92	1.12

and reflective users of the pedagogical theories into their own classroom practice (Yuan & Lee, 2014).

Participants' English abilities influenced their attitude toward and satisfaction with peer evaluations in lesson planning and implementation, particularly in students' knowledge bank (r=.30). Participants' past trainings in different courses influenced their attitude toward and satisfaction with peer-evaluations in lesson planning and implementation, particularly in students' knowledge bank (r=.32), followed by their vigor and involvement (r=.29).

Discussion

The analysis of final projects, self-evaluation, peer-evaluations, and interviews based on the conceptual framework in Figure 4.1 reached the following major findings. Participants' life histories (past English learning and teaching experience), professional histories (TESOL Method course, observation, teaching practice, and relevant trainings), educational policies, and their potential students affected their agencies, particularly in topic selection and lesson planning. This study was in accord with empirical studies finding that teachers' agency is influenced by a wider array of personal, institutional, and sociocultural factors. Such teacher agency can be activated and shaped in the present and future professional practice (Charteris & Smardon, 2015; Nguyen & Bui, 2016; Yuan, 2016).

Next, the influence of different factors activated participants' agency to choose the issues in the lesson planning and activity designs on critical thinking, reflective thinking, and problem solving. Having a sense of agency can enable teachers to take up new roles or identity and to take actions in pursuit of curriculum reforms and innovations. Agency can also enable teachers to actively resist certain behaviors or classroom practices (Kayi-Aydar, 2015).

Moreover, the influence of different factors activated their agency to implement their lessons in English and follow through on intentions to have interactions with learners. The lesson plan implementation mirrors prospective teachers' professional expertise, competence, experience of, and beliefs in relation to English teaching and learning. It involves prospective teachers' synergies of content knowledge, pedagogy, learning, and conditions that optimize outcomes for their learners, so these prospective teachers, equipped with different knowledge bases, can function their agency in the instructional setting (Fleming, 1998; Liyanage & Bartlett, 2010).

In addition, "the logic flow of instruction" was rated the most satisfactory by participants in lesson planning and implementation in both self- and peer evaluations and their English abilities affected their satisfaction. This study was affirmed by the three processes designed by Liyanage and Bartlett (2010), including planning the content of the lesson, implementation of the content, and evaluation of the teaching and learning outcomes. The lesson plans were adjusted based on the instructor's and peers' feedback and later implemented. Self- and peer evaluation can be regarded as checking the effectiveness of the planning and implementation from the dynamic interactions of instructional context and the prospective teachers' knowledge base and agency (Liyanage & Bartlett, 2010).

In order to effectively integrate the value of teacher agency into EFL teacher education courses for pre-service teachers' curriculum designs, the three issues suggested are emphasis of key elements of the 12-Year Basic Education Plan, importance of field experience, and emphasis of reflective practice to activate teacher agency.

Emphasis of key elements of the 12-Year Basic Education Plan

Policies, TESOL Method courses, and other training courses affected participants' agency in lesson planning, particularly in choosing relevant themes or issues as well as activity designs. Learning to teach includes the knowledge of learners and their needs, aims for learning and instructional objectives, and teachers' perceptions of the language and learning (Liyanage & Bartlett, 2010). Elements of the 12-Year Basic Education Plan such as issues, authentic context, cultural awareness, critical thinking, etc., should be introduced and modeled in language teacher education. The quality and effectiveness of lessons and instructional decisions can be made wisely upon the prospective teachers' knowledge of the target language, teaching methods, experience, and styles (Liyanage & Bartlett, 2010).

Prospective teachers can have the potential to exercise their transformative roles and activate their agency to respond to the curriculum reforms. Hence, pre-service teachers need to be empowered with competencies to become proactive in designing their lessons and implementing their practice (Kayi-Aydar, 2015; Nguyen & Bui, 2016). Prospective teachers' agency should also be emphasized in terms of how their agency can be exercised productively in their own instructional settings. Their agency can function as the expected outcome (Liyanage & Bartlett, 2010).

Importance of field experience

Observing experienced English teachers' teaching practice affected participants' agency in decision-making on lesson plan implementation, particularly in using English as the medium for instruction and having interactions with their students. Potential or novice teachers can benefit from more opportunities to reflect upon authentic learning experiences in their classroom practice and construct their preferred teacher identities and agency (Liyanage & Bartlett, 2010). Field experience should be emphasized in language teacher education, so potential English teachers can be equipped with competence in effective lesson delivery (Farrell, 2008).

Emphasis of reflective practice to activate teacher agency

Participants received feedback on their lesson plans and implementations from their instructor, classmates, and students. Participants' agency was activated through constant feedback and led them to revise their lesson plans and implementations. Critical conversations and dialogue between English majors as learners and their instructor, among English majors, and English majors as prospective teachers with experienced teachers, can nurture their teacher agency as well as enable them to take a critical stance on educational policy and reforms (Nguyen & Bui, 2016). Hence, reflective practice and collaborative discussions should be emphasized to develop teacher agency in language teacher education (Biesta et al., 2015; Charteris & Smardon, 2015; Nguyen & Bui, 2016; Yuan & Lee, 2014). Prospective teachers can exercise their agency by engaging in reflective practice, so they can make connections between pedagogical theories and classroom practice and explore how they can apply beliefs of their learners, language, and English instruction to the contexts within which they might teach (Nguyen & Bui, 2016; Yuan & Lee, 2014).

Conclusions

The conceptual framework, based on Priestley et al.'s (2012) teacher agency, was used to explore 26 Taiwanese English majors' agency in developing lesson plans for current English instruction. In line with previous research, the analysis of final projects, self-evaluation, peer evaluations, and interviews identified Taiwanese EFL majors' contextualization of the curriculum in light of the knowledge requirements under the 12-Year Basic Education Plan implemented by the Ministry of Education. English major's agency was influenced personal, institutional, and sociocultural factors. Their agency was activated during the activity designs and implementation of their lessons. This study was situated within the concepts of teachers' agency and their knowledge stores of language education theory, so the major findings of this study can provide new perspectives from language teachers' agency. Three issues were provided in order to integrate the value of teacher agency into EFL teacher education courses for curriculum and lesson designs. Such insights gained through this study are useful for other language teacher education programs.

This study has three limitations. First, the research focused on the 26 participants in a language teacher education program and such findings may not be able to be generalized to other contexts. Next, participants were asked to observe the English teacher's instruction on their chosen educational trend. However, this study was limited by the lack of these teachers' voices in considering how they reacted to the 12-Year Basic Education Plan and the discussions they had with the participants. Another limitation was the short duration of this study. This study explored only the short-term influence of the agency on curriculum innovation.

The future research can continue to investigate the long-term impact of the agency on curriculum innovation in their practicum or educational service learning. Comparative studies are needed to explore the positive and negative influences of agency. This should yield a fuller understanding of how it can be effectively utilized to construct language teachers' agency and identity in curriculum innovation and reforms. Another exploration of these teachers' agency can be helpful in understanding the interactions between English majors as prospective teachers and in-service English teachers, which can be crucial for teacher agency.

References

Abednia, A. (2012). Teachers' professional identity: Contributions of a critical EFL teacher education course in Iran. *Teaching and Teacher Education, 28*(5), 706–717.

Alvunger, D. (2018). Teachers' curriculum agency in teaching a standards-based curriculum. *The Curriculum Journal, 29*(4), 479–498.

Biesta, G., Priestley, M., & Robinson, S. (2015). The role of beliefs in teacher agency. *Teachers and Teaching, 21*(6), 624–640.

Borich, G. D. (2013). *Effective teaching methods: Research-based practice.* Pearson Education.

Boyd, M. P. (2012). Planning and realigning a lesson in response to student contributions: Intentions and decision making. *The Elementary School Journal, 113*(1), 25–51.

Charteris, J., & Smardon, D. (2015). Teacher agency and dialogic feedback: Using classroom data for practitioner inquiry. *Teaching and Teacher Education, 50,* 114–123.

Farrell, T. S. (2008). Here's the book, go teach the class' ELT practicum support. *RELC Journal, 39*(2), 226–241.

Fleming, D. (1998). Autonomy and agency in curriculum decision-making: A study of instructors in a Canadian adult settlement ESL program. *TESL Canada Journal,* 19–35.

Goodson, I. F., & Numan, U. (2002). Teacher's life worlds, agency and policy contexts. *Teachers and Teaching, 8*(3), 269–277.

Gopinathan, S., & Deng, Z. (2006). Fostering school-based curriculum development in the context of new educational initiatives in Singapore. *Planning and Changing, 37,* 93–110.

Higgins, E. T. (1987). Self-discrepancy: A theory relating self and affect. *Psychological Review, 94*(3), 319–340.

Kayi-Aydar, H. (2015). Teacher agency, positioning, and English language learners: Voices of pre-service classroom teachers. *Teaching and Teacher Education, 45,* 94–103.

Liyanage, I., & Bartlett, B. J. (2010). From autopsy to biopsy: A metacognitive view of lesson planning and teacher trainees in ELT. *Teaching and Teacher Education, 26*(7), 1362–1371.

Macaro, E. (2001). Analysing student teachers' codeswitching in foreign language classrooms: Theories and decision making. *The Modern Language Journal, 85*(4), 531–548.

Miles, M. B., Huberman, A. M., & Saldana, J. (2014). *Qualitative data analysis: A methods sourcebook.* Sage Publications.

Ministry of Education. (2014). *Curriculum guidelines of 12-year basic education.* Ministry of Education.

Molina, S. C. (2016). English Language teaching in China: Teacher agency in response to curricular innovations. In P. C. L. Ng, & E. F. Boucher-Yip (Eds.), *Teacher agency and policy response in English language teaching* (pp. 19–37). Routledge.

Nguyen, H. T. M., & Bui, T. (2016). Teachers' agency and the enactment of educational reform in Vietnam. *Current Issues in Language Planning, 17*(1), 88–105.

Paris, C. (1993). *Teacher agency and curriculum making in classrooms.* Teachers College Press.

Priestley, M., Edwards, R., Priestley, A., & Miller, K. (2012). Teacher agency in curriculum making: Agents of change and spaces for manoeuvre. *Curriculum Inquiry, 42*(2), 191–214.

Priestley, M., Biesta, G. J. J., Philippou, S., & Robinson, S. (2015). The teacher and the curriculum: Exploring teacher agency. In D. Wyse, L. Hayward, & J. Pandya (Eds.), *The SAGE handbook of curriculum, pedagogy and assessment* (pp. 187–201). Sage.

Rasti, A., & Sahragard, R. (2017). Making sense of EFL teacher agency: Insights from an Iran case study. *Journal of English Language Teaching and Learning, 9*(19), 145–169.

Root, D. (2014). Debunking the myth of standardised education to promote equity and rigour. In A. T. Costigan, & L. Grey (Eds.), *Demythologizing educational reforms: responses to the political and corporate takeover of education* (pp. 68–86). Routledge.

Tang, E. L. Y., Lee, J. C. K., & Chun, C. K. W. (2012). Development of teaching beliefs and the focus of change in the process of pre-service ESL teacher education. *Australian Journal of Teacher Education, 37*(5), 90–117.

Yang, H. (2012). *Chinese teacher agency in implementing English as foreign language (EFL) curriculum reform: An activity theory perspective* (unpublished doctoral dissertation), University of New South Wales, Sydney, Australia.

Yuan, E. R. (2016). The dark side of mentoring on pre-service language teachers' identity formation. *Teaching and Teacher Education, 55*, 188–197.

Yuan, R., & Lee, I. (2014). Pre-service teachers' changing beliefs in the teaching practicum: Three cases in an EFL context. *System, 44*, 1–12.

5 Revamping pre-service English reading instruction

The reading specialist training at an education university in Taiwan

Ya-Chen Chien

Introduction

What is the beginning sound of the word "kite." "It is Kay. K - I -T - E." When asked what the word kite's initial sound is, a second-grade student spelled out the letter names instead of sounding out the /k/ sound. This has been a common problem for children learning English as a foreign language (EFL) in Taiwan. These children think that English is too challenging to learn because they memorize vocabulary by reciting the letters in words, learning English reading the hard way. They struggle with reading and writing. Moreover, with 30 students in a class, the teachers often cover what is in the textbook without having much time to tailor their instruction for struggling readers (Weng & Chien, 2015).

Most of the instruction in EFL setting draws inspiration from how English is taught to native speakers. Thus, looking at the United States, reading clinics have been developed since the 1920s, beginning at University of California Los Angeles (UCLA), and later at the University of Chicago, Iowa State University, and John Hopkins University. A medical model prevailed with a focus on diagnosing learners' reading difficulties and carrying out interventions. Students at these university-based reading clinics learned to complete diagnostic testing, make plans for instruction and teach, and monitored its success (Laster, 2013; Pletcher et al., 2019). These reading clinics offered an exemplary practicum for reading teachers and reading specialists while providing direct service to K-12 students (Morris, 2003). Although there were arguments that "clinic" sounds medically oriented, Laster (2013) explained that a "reading clinic" targets students' reading competency and helps enhance students' abilities, which is "much like a soccer clinic or basketball clinic [that] aims to advance skills (p. 5)." Reading specialists are teachers who have specialized training in students who find reading difficult (ILA, 2015). Reading specialists are responsible for collecting and analyzing data to plan, teach, and evaluate instruction for students who have difficulty with reading or writing.

Since Taiwan English education was only implemented for the last two decades, with elementary school students starting to learn English in third grade or first grade for large cities, university-based reading clinics have yet to be common locally. With the common practice of teaching pre-service teachers to

DOI: 10.4324/9781003212805-6

address reading competencies in the curricular framework, teaching in the past has had much emphasis on the teaching of phonics, vocabulary, sentence structure, and reading of picture books at the primary school level, with a focus on content coverage and mastery, not necessarily focusing on the learner. Most novice teachers were teaching a whole class of students as if teaching only one student (Weng & Chien, 2015).

Develop competency-based reading assessment and instruction

The new 12-year National Curriculum in Taiwan emphasizes promoting students' literacies, a drive for self-learning, and connecting what they learn to their real-life applications (Chen & Huang, 2017). For children and their parents to know how to enhance reading competence is much needed. However, pre-service elementary school English teacher training in the past has placed emphasis on training content knowledge and pedagogical knowledge for whole-class settings, and has yet to include teaching how to diagnose struggling reader's reading difficulties, address individual learning needs, and provide differentiated instruction (Chien, 2019). With the Taiwan government advocating transforming the country into a bilingual nation by 2030 (Financial Supervisory Commission, 2019), primary and secondary bilingual education has begun to take shape as one-third of the curriculum is being taught bilingually in both English and Chinese in the capital city. The focus on enhancing learners' English reading competence, reading skills, and attitudes toward reading in different content areas would be paramount. By providing clinical-based practice opportunities, prospective teachers may become more familiar with qualitative and quantitative reading assessments to monitor students' reading competencies. Thus, this calls for modifying our previous reading instructional training to move away from the focus of content coverage in reading skills to an emphasis on the learner and on diagnostic reading training to provide reading interventions based on assessment results. The author attempted to revamp the reading instruction course carrying out a reading clinic model implemented at the University of Central Florida (Kelley & Wenzel, 2013), based on the author's prior experience sending her son to the reading clinic in 2017 and auditing a reading course taught by Dr. Michelle Kelley, a professor of Reading Education and "Professor in Residence" at Evans Elementary where she teaches pre-service teachers.

Coaching for success in teaching reading

Replicating the reading clinic at the University of Central Florida, the author served as a reading coach to her pre-service teachers in assisting with assessing learners, helping with interpreting results, and co-planning for intervention to help children read. In Bean's (2004 as cited in Kelley & Wenzel, 2013) levels of coaching complexity applied to clinical settings adopted by Kelley and Wenzel (2013), three levels of coaching activities in which reading coaches engage were identified, and the protocols that are relevant to the present study are as follows.

1 Level one, Informal Coaching: a reading coach informally creates an environment that promotes conversations and encourages self-reflection; provides a setting for clinicians to apply knowledge of teaching and assessing reading and writing under supervision and scaffolding, and assists with assessment selection and implementation.
2 Level two, more Formal Coaching: hold data conferences with clinicians to analyze student work, interpret assessment data and determine instructional focus; provide suggestions for instruction and feedback on lessons; provide training for clinicians based on student needs.
3 Level three, Formal Coaching: observe clinicians working with students (both assessment and instruction). Have clinicians self-reflect on observation, meet with clinicians to debrief on observation, and provide feedback.

Therefore, the purpose of this study is to examine an implementation of reading specialist training for pre-service English language teachers and to address how pre-service teachers were trained, the assessment tools used to diagnose EFL learners, and the perceptions of pre-service teachers who took the training. The present study also described how the author adopted the "Coach for Success" practice from the University of Central Florida enrichment program in literacy for the undergraduate and graduate courses in training pre-service English teachers to implement assessment-informed reading interventions for young EFL learners. This study analyzes the implementation of reading specialist training for pre-service English language teachers to provide suggestions for pre-service teacher training institutes to set up university-based literacy centers for EFL learners. The study addresses the following research questions:

1 How do we educate our pre-service teachers and train them to become reading specialists for EFL learners?
2 What is needed to help these pre-service teachers recognize the reading struggles and diagnose young learners' reading difficulties accurately?
3 What are the perceptions of pre-service teachers toward reading specialist training?

Method

The study took a qualitative inquiry case study approach to examine reading clinician training implementation in an EFL university setting. The study was conducted over a three-semester period, with three iterations of the same course taught to graduate and undergraduate students. Students reading diagnostic reports and the reflections in classroom observations have been part of the tools to help the teacher-researcher reflect upon how best to adjust the coursework to help students develop the skills of becoming a reading clinician. Students' reflections and essential feedback were the focus of the implementation of the program. The end-of-course evaluation results, four items for the undergraduate students and six items for the graduate students, are reported as part of pre-service teachers' perceptions of the training.

Setting and participants

The study was undertaken in an education university in northern Taiwan in a two-year TESOL MA program and the undergraduate four-year program of children's English education. The reading clinician training was designed to be integrated into a three-credit elective course, "Word Recognition and Reading," that the author delivered in three consecutive semesters to graduate students and undergraduate students. The graduate students who took the courses differed in their teaching experiences, ranging from zero teaching experiences to 20 years of EFL teaching experiences. The undergraduate students had limited teaching experience, but some had English tutoring experiences.

The reading program

Before implementing the reading clinician training curriculum, the course consisted of only the knowledge base of word recognition, reading instruction, and microteaching scheduled at the end of the semester. To implement the reading clinic training model with different coaching complexity based on Bean (2004), the instructor modified the syllabus and implemented three components: knowledge base of reading, reading assessment measures, and reading clinical practices.

First: Knowledge of reading acquisition

The first part of the course is developing knowledge of reading acquisition, understanding the characteristics of language development, and stages of reading development for English language learners understanding of how English learning children learn to read. This includes identifying common difficulties in students' development of reading components: print awareness, the sounds of speech, phonemic awareness, phonics, vocabulary, fluency, and comprehension.

DeVries' (2015) *Literacy Assessment and Intervention for the Elementary School Classroom* (4th ed.) was the graduate-level course's assigned reading textbook. Students were asked to answer guiding questions for each chapter, and the class was conducted adopting a flipped learning approach. Class time was devoted to explaining and demonstrating teaching strategies covered in the textbook, which provided students with real-time teaching practices in class.

For the undergraduate course, Roe et al.'s (2018) *Teaching Reading in Today's Elementary Schools* (12th ed.) was a required textbook. Reading 101: A guide to teaching reading and writing (Carreker et al., n.d.) from the Reading Rockets program was adopted and assigned in Google classroom. The Reading Rockets is a national public media literacy initiative in the United States that offers information and resources on how young children learn to read. Although the program is for pre-K to grade 3 teachers in the United States, the program contents are suitable for elementary school level reading in an EFL setting. Students developed a solid foundation of reading by adopting this free professional development content in both text and video forms. Student teachers need to know the importance of auditory discrimination to reading and sound-letter correspondence. Oral language helps develop learners' reading; this is why kids in EFL settings without oral language development often struggle to read. After a solid understanding of how young learners learn to read, student teachers can then work on how to assess learners and base their instruction on the assessment results.

Second: Reading assessments

The second portion of the course was on formal, informal, and performance-based reading assessment measures, laying the foundation for students to assess children and diagnose reading difficulties. Students need to identify EFL children's strengths and needs in the following areas: motivation, emergent reading skills (such as letter identification, letter sounds, the concept of print), phonemic awareness, phonics, vocabulary, reading fluency, and comprehension. The students become competent in administering the assessment through direct instruction in class, experiential approaches with classmates, or pre-recorded videos.

There follows a list of assessments offered in DeVries (2015) in the course:

1. Personal Interest Survey and Reading Attitude Survey
2. Assessment for Phonemic Awareness (isolation of beginning sound, deletion of the initial sound, segmentation of phonemes, blending of phonemes, and phoneme manipulation)
3. Phonics Mastery Survey (Consonant sounds, CVC words, consonant blends, consonant digraphs, long vowel sounds, multisyllabic words)
4. Running Record with Miscue Analysis
5. Readability and text difficulty: Lexile

Third: Reading clinician practices

Arrangement of Clinician Practices: For an undergraduate class with 32 students enrolled, the author adopted informal coaching and asked students to seek individual student tutees, administer the assessments, and interpret the results without the supervisor's presence. The student tutees' grade level ranged from second grade to sixth grade. The author adopted level two and three coaching for two groups of graduate students, formal coaching being onsite where tutoring took place. Student teachers were paired up with children referred by elementary school English teachers. The children were mainly those who had difficulty with word recognition or reading comprehension. On average, children who attended the clinic performed below grade-level English word recognition accuracy and comprehension expectations. The first group of graduate students taught fifth graders, and the second group of graduate students taught second graders. Tutors met as a group before and after the clinician practices. Data conference meeting time was designated so that student teachers could demonstrate their comprehensive knowledge of the child's reading difficulty and share their perceived focus area for instruction.

The location for the tutorial sessions

The tutorial sessions for graduate student teachers took place in the affiliated Experimental Elementary School. Research showed that reading clinics housed on university campuses had tutee attendance problems; thus, many reading clinics' directors moved their reading clinics onto public school campuses (Coffey et al., 2013). Therefore, it was fortunate that the University has close ties with its affiliated elementary school for the clinician practices to be arranged.

How were students assessed upon entering the literacy clinic? Informal reading inventory was used to assess students. DIBELS 8th Edition was adopted, but only the alphabet one. Vocabulary was not assessed, but running records and retelling were: 50% reading connected text and 50% devoted to skill-driven work based on assessment data. The student teachers used leveled books for guided reading instruction, using the author's collection.

Timeframe for Clinician Practices: For the undergraduate students, the assessment was carried out at least three times on their own with feedback from the author. The first group of graduate students spent 12 weeks, once a week, with their tutees one-on-one; however, the second group of graduate students spent six weeks with their second-graders in the form of small group instruction with two to three students per group.

Results and discussions

Research question one: How do we educate our pre-service teachers and train them to become reading specialists for EFL learners?

First: Knowledge of reading acquisition

Part of the prerequisite of becoming a reading specialist lies in understanding the reading foundations, including reading theories, oral language development, phonemic awareness, phonics, vocabulary, reading fluency, and reading comprehension (Kern et al., 2018). The graduate students complimented the textbook selection on covering all aspects of the reading foundation, and the end-of-course feedback was very positive. The items on factual knowledge, important concepts, principles and rules of reading instruction, as well as application of professional knowledge for graduate students, ranged from a mean of 4.75 (SD=0.6) to 4.8 (SD=0.4) in a Likert scale of one being "strongly disagree" and five being "strongly agree."

> I am really thankful for the reading class and the professor. I got a valuable and helpful textbook and learned many theories and activities about teaching literacy and reading. Moreover, the professor also encouraged us to combine knowledge of textbooks with real teaching, and everyone tried their best to make the reading clinic interesting and effective.
>
> —graduate pre-service teacher reflection

> I learned strategies to read picture storybooks for my student, such as predicting a story by reading the cover of the book and retelling a story. I also tried to utilize these strategies in my teaching to enhance student's reading comprehension.
>
> —undergraduate pre-service teacher reflection

Despite the positive feedback on textbook adoption and the lively in-class activities to prepare them for assessment and intervention, the first group of graduate students expressed that they were overwhelmed by the course load. Having to answer guiding questions before class and assigning more than one chapter per week to fit the clinical reading practice in the semester, they were pressured to finish assigned reading and post the answers to the guiding questions online before class. Another challenging issue voiced by the first group of graduate students was the research aspect of coursework. Since this was a graduate-level course, reading research articles and methodologies were discussed and a concept paper was required at the end of the course. Students reported improvement in inquisitive ability in the teaching of reading with a mean of 4.7 (SD=0.6) from the end-of-course survey. However, for the statement on analyzing and commenting on ideas and opinions that have been learned, the mean was 4.67 (SD=0.62). Although the mean score indicated that students were positive about this aspect, the mean was slightly lower than other items. Students reflected that they did not know how to critique research papers and asked for more guidance.

Modifications for the graduate-level course

The task of answering the guiding questions online was eliminated in the second group of graduate students, and the questions were discussed in-class orally instead. The research article reading and concept paper written assignment for evidenced-based reading instruction was also eliminated entirely as a student-centered task. Research on evidence-based reading became a teacher-led discussion in class so that reading assessment and instruction are based on previous research studies results, in other words, providing discussions on research-informed teaching practices. As can be seen in Table 5.1, the mean scores for improved inquisitive ability and students being able to analyze and comment on ideas and opinions of reading research authors and findings were both 4.8 (SD=0.4) for the second group of graduate students, although a smaller class-size could also contribute to this positive feedback.

Undergraduate students were also quite positive on the end-of-course feedback with an average mean of 4.53 (SD=0.61).

Table 5.1 The end of course feedback on reading instruction

	Graduate (n=12)		Undergraduate (n=32)		Graduate (n=5)	
	M	*SD*	*M*	*SD*	*M*	*SD*
1 Obtain factual knowledge of reading instruction	4.75	0.60	4.53	0.61	4.8	0.4
2 Obtain important concept of reading foundations	4.75	0.60	4.53	0.61	4.8	0.4
3 Learn important principles and rules about reading instruction	4.75	0.60	4.53	0.61	4.8	0.4
4 Improve the application of professional knowledge	4.75	0.60	4.53	0.61	4.8	0.4
5 Improve inquisitive ability	4.75	0.60	n/a	n/a	4.8	0.4
6 Can analyze and comment on ideas and opinions that have been learned	4.67	0.62	n/a	n/a	4.8	0.4
7 Overall course evaluation	4.79	0.08	4.62	0.09	4.85	0.03

> I was amazed by the diverse activities we had in class, including debates, discussions, teaching demos, drawing to illustrate schemata in reading, etc.
>
> —undergraduate student teacher reflection

Suggestions for a reading curriculum

A fairly large amount of time was dedicated to teaching students the foundations of reading and how to assess and provide intervention accordingly. Evidenced-based research discussions and fostering the ability to conduct reading research could be separated from a teaching-oriented course. Thus, for pre-service teachers at the graduate level, there could be three separate reading courses: one on reading foundation, the second on reading diagnostics and assessment, and the last one for a more research-oriented course on reading. The study recommended the course developers consider providing at least one research article and ask students to look for others when assigning concept papers on topics such as "whether phonics is effective for EFL learners" or "whether one-minute reading fluency is a good indicator for reading comprehension." A preliminary reading specialist training should include at least a nine-credit hour course to start with for TEFL programs focusing on teaching Young EFL learners to read.

Research question two: What is needed to help diagnose students correctly?

The second step: Assessment

Dynamic Indicators of Basic Early Literacy Skills (DIBELS) for kindergarten was adopted with modification. The DIBELS Benchmark includes Letter Naming Fluency (LNF), a standardized, individually-administered test with a page of 100 uppercase and lowercase letters arranged in random order. Students were asked to name as many letters as they could. Phonemic Segmentation Fluency (PSF) assesses students' ability to fluently segment two to six phoneme words into their individual phonemes. For example, if the examiner said "sun," and the student said "/s/ /u/ /n/," the student would receive three points for the word. Word Reading Fluency (WRF) measures the accuracy and fluency in reading "sight" words, including words with irregular pronunciations such as the, was, and of, with common words with regular pronunciations such as in, we, and no. Nonsense word fluency was not adopted because it was not used to teach letter-sound relationships to students. Nonsense Word Reading Fluency (NRF) includes a measure of alphabetic principle and phonics. For kindergarten NRF, the phonics pattern assessed is CVC words with short vowel sounds. The Phonics Mastery Survey included in DeVries was more difficult for EFL learners; therefore, the Basic Phonics Skills Test-II was adopted. The test includes consonant names and sounds, consonant digraphs, short vowels, reading short vowel words, consonant blends in short vowel words, final e words, long vowel digraphs, r-controlled words, other vowel digraphs, inflectional endings, two-syllable words, polysyllabic words with affixes, and three and four-syllable words. See Table 5.2 for reading assessments administered.

For our first group of graduate students teaching fifth-grade students for 12 weeks, they were able to administer different reading diagnostic tests and running records three times. For the second group of graduate student teachers tutoring second-grade students for six weeks, due to learners' lack of English exposure, they only assessed students the first two parts of BPST-II (letter name, letter sound, and consonant digraphs) and ten items on the phonemic segmentation. For the performance of BPST-II, the fifteen second graders' mean score was 19.6 out of 30 letter sounds. In other words, at the end of the second grade, they were only able to identify 19 letter sounds, including 26 letter sounds and four consonant digraphs th, sh, ch, and wh. Only two students were assessed with running records with decodable books of short a sound. On the other hand, the undergraduate student teachers assessed their students mainly using

Table 5.2 Reading assessments administered

	Graduate— 5th grade students	*Undergraduate— 1–6 grade students*	*Graduate— 2nd grade students*
Personal Interest Survey	V	V	5 items
Reading Attitude Survey	V	V	V
Letter Name Fluency	V	V	V
Phonemic Segmentation Fluency	V	V	10 items
Nonsense Word Reading Fluency	V	V	
Word Reading Fluency	V	V	
Basic Phonics Skills Test-II	V		V
Running Record	V	V	

the DIBELS 8th Edition for Kindergarten and running records of books of their choice based on their students' interest surveys.

Different levels of coaching

For undergraduate students, the author has adopted a level one of Bean's coaching complexity model: Informal Coaching by providing an environment that promotes conversations and encourages self-reflection. Students conducted the reading assessments with their tutees at their own time because of the class size of 32 students. We had the data conferencing and discussion in-class to plan for instruction. Students were guided to write up the report as they applied knowledge of assessing reading learned in-class to assessing their tutees. For the graduate student groups, the author adopted level two of Bean's coaching complexity, more formal coaching for the first group, and level three formal coaching for the second group of graduate students, observing them work with students for both assessment and instruction. After tutoring, the group gathered to provide reflections, debrief on observations, and provide feedback.

> The 6 weeks after school literacy remedial program has been a big challenge for me. The biggest reward I learned during the program is to apply systematic assessment to diagnose students' learning problem in literacy. With directional and concreted data, I have more confidence and resources to adopt suitable teaching strategies for students. It's also a good chance for us to have more practical experience with real elementary school students.
>
> —graduate pre-service teacher reflection

One of the graduate students in the second group was an in-service English teacher. Despite having taught English for ten years, she expressed gratitude for the experience and explained that she had gained valuable experiences in providing differentiated instruction based on assessment. The following was her reflections:

> This was a special experience for me to make teaching plans for individual learning and what impressed me the most is to do the assessments in order to diagnosis students' learning and then give them appropriate instructions. It's important to provide differentiated instructions since students have different needs in learning.
>
> —graduate in-service teacher reflection

Understood the importance of assessment

All three groups of pre-service teachers were aware of the importance of assessment as it informed their instruction. They mentioned that they were not aware that children's reading difficulties need to be identified through assessments before giving instruction. By the end of the course, they were familiar with the different varieties of assessments for reading, allowing them to track students' improvement and design lessons accordingly.

> I was amazed by so many assessments that cat could be used to assess students' current reading level in order to provide appropriate instructions for enhancing their reading skills.
>
> I learn to assess my student's reading accuracy with Oral Running Record. Also, I learned the ways to assess reading fluency and reading comprehension.
>
> Step by step, I clearly know her problems of learning English and reading.
>
> After implementing the reading clinic, I have more understanding of Minnie's interests, reading attitude, personality, English reading ability, the way she learns English.

Running records: The most difficult part of assessment

One of the challenges of diagnosing learning difficulty was finding the right leveled text to test learners' oral reading fluency and comprehension through running records. For example, one of the learners was in 4th grade, but he started going to an English cram school from first grade. He scored 64 out of 84 on phonemic segmentation. For phonics, nonsense word fluency, he got 74 out of 85, needing more help with consonant digraphs and r-controlled words. However, he struggled with the first-grade DIBELS oral reading fluency because the passage was written in the past tense form, and there were a lot of multisyllabic words. He ended up taking 2.5 minutes to finish only half of the passage. The results of the reading accuracy were 18 words out of 90 words incorrect, which indicates that this reading passage was at this readers' frustration level. Both graduate and undergraduate student teachers shared similar frustrating experiences.

> For this story the oral reading accuracy is 81.4%, which means that it is way too difficult for him. So does it mean that the textbook the cram school is using is too difficult? To be honest, I'm a little upset about the results, because originally I was going to find the story by myself, but I'm not quite certain about his English level.
>
> I selected a text from his textbook he had read before to see if he would read it well. Due to a lack of basic phonics rules, his text level was assessed at frustration level with only 78% of reading accuracy.
>
> I chose a book that might be suitable for Chanel called "I used to be afraid." It's a book with lots of colorful pictures that I found quite suitable because the sentence patterns are fixed and easy for underachievers to follow. ...This time her accuracy rate had enhanced to 62%.

Only the ones who used decodable books or level one graded readers were successful in finding suitable text for fifth-grade learners. Readers such as "Sammy the Seal" by Syd Hoff or "The Mutt and the Bug" were the ones that were most often at the learner's independent reading level.

Suggestions on administering assessments for EFL learners

Most of the assessments available are somewhat difficult for beginners; therefore, some of these tools have been adapted to target our local Taiwanese EFL students, especially for our second-grade learners. The reading interest survey and reading attitude survey were informative in terms of the selection of books, the phonemic awareness and phonics diagnostic test for DIBELS had been modified to the sections suitable for second-grade students. Running record was more applicable for fifth graders than second graders because the second graders still needed to work on letter sounds and short vowel sounds. There should be more guidance on running record text selection because almost everyone had asked their learners to read at frustration level for running record at least once. Despite having explained about readability, the informal reading inventory and the use of Lexile measures in class, pre-service teachers needed more practice finding the right text. The use of Lexile measures for beginning readers is strongly suggested for lower grades. The picture book "Goodnight, Gorilla" was listed as recommended reading for lower grades because its Lexile measure is BR100L. Student teachers also need to familiarize themselves with book selections from BR100L to BR300L. Also, decodable books, phonics readers, and graded readers would be more helpful for struggling readers.

Research question three: What are the perceptions of pre-service teachers toward reading specialist training?

The third step: Instruction

After debriefing the reading data, student teachers made plans to teach the learners and they reflected that not only did they know what to teach, but they found a need to incorporate different instructional strategies. They reported benefiting from the coaching from the instructor, myself, and from their peers. Their learners were happy about the topics of books selected for them despite some learning difficulties. They were more confident about providing differentiated instruction, yet needed whole-class instruction experiences. In the end, they saw learners' progress and would like to devote more time for professional development in honing their reading specialist skills. The results of student teachers' perceptions are discussed in the following.

Knowing what to teach next: A variety of teaching strategies

Student Teachers were empowered by their ability to analyze the results of the assessments to make instructional plans and focus on particular skills. One student-teacher was aware of the difficulty in getting her students to focus if she used a teaching activity repeatedly. And another designed five different activities, "Parking Lot" phonics with short vowel "a" and "I" sound, "Race Car Blending Activity," "Digraphs Monopoly," "Christmas Tree" with /e/ (ai, ay, a_e) and Jake and Gail go to Spain, and "Dragon" activity for post-assessment. The following were reflections from graduate students:

> From this authentic teaching experience, I learned that I have to change my teaching instruments, materials, and approaches since my student got bored if she has played the activity several times. … Therefore, I have to research different ways every week for the next teaching.
>
> While I was administering the Basic Phonics Skills Test and Phonemic Awareness Skills, it became clear that Ray needed more practice with phonics, short vowels sounds, digraphs, and long vowel sounds. Therefore, according to the results of the personal interest survey, I designed five kinds of activities to engage him to read and learn the phonics rules.
>
> I instantly knew that more phonics activities should be added to my instruction plan, such as silent e vowels followed by /r/, etc. This can also be noted in Abby's running record, so she achieved over 90% in one running record, considering her potential to reach 95% of accuracy, some adjustments of my instruction plans are needed. For example, my students didn't understand why the ea sound should only pronounce the long e sound.

Got learners hooked with books

A challenging yet rewarding part of the reading specialist training was the pre-service teachers' struggles and breakthroughs in finding the books that sparked their learners' interest in reading. Although, as indicated earlier, they may have trouble finding the correctly leveled text, finding books that intrinsically motivate learners to read with the help of the instructor's support also resulted in a positive reading attitude on behalf of the learners.

> I had a lot of struggle to find a perfect book for him, because most of the picture book about basketball is autobiography. In the end, I chose the book "let's play basketball" because except the words beneath, most of the sentences are quite easy and heard frequently.
>
> —undergraduate pre-service teacher reflection

> Even though Abby always said that she doesn't like reading, she really engaged in reading when the book of this week is about animals, so selecting books that attract children's attention is important.
>
> —graduate pre-service teacher reflection

> I spent a lot of time choosing the appropriate books for Chanel. The inspiration of reading became a breakthrough for both of us.
>
> —graduate pre-service teacher reflection

> I enjoy seeing the glory of his face when he had fun about the book, like he enjoys reading scary books and he also loves the Santa book I brought him that he could actually have Santa go around the tracks on the book. I believe the books I brought him also increase the possibilities of reading for him.
>
> —graduate in-service teacher reflection

Coaching and modeling for student teachers

For both graduate-level courses, the coaching model ranged from adopted level two to level three formal coaching. This allowed more direct monitoring through the process and prompt feedback to the student teachers. Another benefit of having everyone practice together with a group of learners at the elementary school is that student teachers can form a community of practice and share what they have done for their students and learn from each other.

> I think it is good that the professor showed us the way she interacted with elementary school students and how she taught them. Professor....was quite a good teaching model for me. I didn't know I could teach that way.
>
> —graduate pre-service teacher reflection

> I really appreciate Professor Jane and my classmates at ... [the University]; we discussed the teaching plans together, showed different teaching styles and shared thoughts each time. It's really memorable!
>
> —graduate in-service teacher reflection

Expand students' interest in reading different genres

The way each reading specialist interprets the results of a reading attitudes survey may be very different. It was not uncommon for Taiwanese students to report not having been exposed to English poems. Without having read a poem, one cannot fill out their attitude toward poem reading. One of the student teachers was at first about to avoid teaching poems altogether, but after becoming aware of this insight, she decided to introduce learners to interesting poems after all.

> When I learned that Minnie does not like poetry, my first reaction was, in the future reading clinic, I could avoid teaching poetry. Not until the professor's suggestion did I realize that I can introduce Minnie to some interesting poetry and stimulate her reading interest.
>
> —graduate pre-service teacher reflection

Need whole-class reading instruction training

A couple of graduate students from the first group expressed their appreciation for the reading clinic practices set up for them to learn to diagnose and teach accordingly; however, some indicated that they were able to teach one-on-one, but did not have experience handling a whole class instruction. Therefore, in the following year, changes were made for student-teachers to have 20 minutes of one-on-one and 15 minutes of whole-class instruction for the second group of graduate students teaching second-grade students. Five picture books were taught with the content simplified for the students, and with emphasis on identifying word initial sounds. The books were "Should I share my ice cream?" "Z is for Moose," "Still a gorilla," "Pete the Cat and His Four Groovy Buttons," and "It's Christmas, David"!

> Although everyone chose a suitable English storybook to teach students, all of us had the same goal: to focus on the initial sounds, and strengthen learners' letter sounds.
>
> —graduate pre-service teacher reflection

Observed learners' progress

Most of the student teachers were very impressed with their own work as they spent time diagnosing their learners' reading difficulty and providing the intervention they needed. This was especially true for the first group of graduate students who had spent three months' time with their tutees, after noting that their progress in the three running records results and post-assessments was remarkable.

> I found that clinic meetings are so helpful for the slower learners. I was so surprised that Lucy and other classmates' students can make great progress.
>
> I think the main reason is that the teaching goal we set and lesson designed met students' level.
>
> —graduate pre-service teacher reflection

The desire to learn more

Despite all the coursework, reading, discussions, assessments and lesson planning, and experience teaching first-hand, several student teachers reflected the realization that they wanted to learn more. They felt the need to discover a greater variety of picture books, to learn how to use Lexile to choose readers for learners, and to use technology to assist learners in reading. They knew this was only the beginning of their journey to becoming a reading specialist.

> I have to explore more picture books.
>
> I have to learn how to use Lexile to choose the readers for my student more skillfully.
>
> I would like to find more apps, online games for my students to learn English with more interest and motivation.

Conclusion

Training student teachers to diagnose their English learners' needs and design individual reading instruction plans accordingly was very well perceived and deemed useful by all three groups of student teachers. This study examined the assessment tools used for reading clinics and student teachers' reflections after administering to clarify issues of assessment. Through three iterations of the same course, assessment adaptation based on learner level and finding the most appropriately leveled text for the learners for running records were the two biggest challenges during the assessment phase. For assessing EFL primary school learners, BPST-II and DIBELS Kindergarten or first grade are suggested, but BPST-II was more suitable for lower grade levels, as DIBELS could be used for up to grade six with struggling EFL readers. Introducing Lexile measures to assist students in selecting the right text is also suggested. Decodable books, phonics readers, and graded readers in the beginning reader Lexile range were suitable across all levels when working with readers who needed help. Finally, the study recommends that, from a reading specialist training standpoint, course developers consider having field experience with upper-level primary school students. Having pre-service teachers work with upper-grade level students would provide them more experience with different reading assessments and the opportunity to work with learners on reading comprehension, not just decoding.

References

Bean, R. M. (2004). Promoting effective literacy instruction: The challenge for literacy coaches. *The California Reader, 37*(3), 58–63.

Carreker, S., Goldberg, M., Liptak, E., Lubar, N., Seals, L., Spear-Swerling, L. (n.d.). *Reading 101: A guide to teaching reading and writing.* https://www.readingrockets.org/teaching/reading101-course/welcome-reading-101

Chen, H.-L. S., & Huang, H.-Y. (2017). *Advancing 21st century competencies in Taiwan.* Taipei, Taiwan: Center for Global Education. https://asiasociety.org/files/21st-century-competencies-taiwan.pdf.

Chien, Y. C. (2019). Differentiated English instruction: Diagnostic assessment. *Hello E.T., 111*, 3–5. https://www.cet-taiwan.com/drcet/detail.asp?serno=1225

Coffey, D., Hubbard, D., Holbein, M., & Delacruz, S. (2013). Creating a university-based literacy center. In E. Ortlieb & E. H. Cheek, Jr. (Eds.). *Advanced literacy practices: From the clinic to the classroom* (pp. 21–35). Emerald Group Publishing Limited.

DeVries, B. (2015). *Literacy assessment and intervention for the elementary school classroom* (4th ed.). Routledge. https://doi.org/10.4324/9781315109770.

Financial Supervisory Commission. (2019). *Taiwan's 2030 goal to become a bilingual nation.* https://www.fsc.gov.tw/en/home.jsp?id=253&parentpath=0,4,212,252.

International Literacy Association. (2015). Research brief: The multiple roles of school-based specialized literacy professionals. https://www.literacyworldwide.org/docs/default-source/where-we-stand/literacy-professionals-research-brief.pdf

Kelley, M. & Wenzel, T. (2013). Coaching for success: UCF enrichment program in literacy. In E. Ortlieb & E. H. Cheek, Jr. (Eds.). *Advanced literacy practices: From the clinic to the classroom* (pp. 63–86). Emerald Group Publishing Limited.

Kern, D., Bean, R. M., Dagen, A. S., DeVries, B., Dodge, A., Goatley, V., Ippolito, J., Perkins, J. H., & Walker-Dalhouse, D. (2018). Preparing reading/literacy specialists to meet changes and challenges: International Literacy Association's Standards 2017. *Literacy Research and Instruction*, *57*(3), 209–231. https://doi.org/10.1080/19388071.2018.1453899

Laster, B. P. (2013). A historical view of student learning and teacher development in reading clinics. In E. Ortlieb & E. H. Cheek, Jr. (Eds.). *Advanced literacy practices: From the clinic to the classroom* (pp. 3–20). Emerald Group Publishing Limited.

Morris, D. (2003). *Of Studebakers and reading clinicians.* http://www.americanreadingforum.org/03_yearbook/pdf/Morris.pdf

Pletcher, B., Robertson, P., & Sullivan, M. (2019). A current overview of ten university-based reading clinics. *Reading Horizons: A Journal of Literacy and Language Arts*, *58* (3). https://scholarworks.wmich.edu/reading_horizons/vol58/iss3/2

Roe, B., Smith, S.H., & Kolodziej, N.J. (2018). *Teaching reading in today's elementary schools* (12th ed.). Cengage Learning.

Weng, H. T. & Chien, Y. C. (2015). Differentiated instruction for 5th grade English learners. *Elementary Education*, 55(2), 60–81.

6 Developing competency-based teacher education with school-university partnerships

A case in Taiwan

Amber Yayin Wang

Introduction

Education reforms around the world (e.g., CCSS, 2014; MOE, 2014; National Curriculum, 2011; OECD, 2013, 2016, 2018) and trends in teacher education (e.g., Uusiautti & Määttä, 2013) have centered on developing core competencies among students. Efforts have been devoted to reform education at different levels, including teacher education (e.g., Cydis, 2014; Klebansky & Fraser, 2013; McLean & Rowsell, 2013). In Taiwan, the latest national curriculum guidelines made competency-based instruction its essential emphasis (Chen & Huang, 2017; MOE, 2014). Scholars in Taiwan such as Wu (2017, 2018) and Fwu (2018) have strongly advocated that teacher education in Taiwan needs to be redesigned to respond to the current needs.

In the field of teacher education, a large amount of research has been done on competency-based teacher education (CBTE). More than 3,200 entries about CBTE could be found in the Education Resources Information Center (ERIC). However, most studies were published in the 1970s or in European contexts or contexts where English is a native language; recent studies related to CBTE in the context of English as a foreign language (EFL) were few. Among the few studies, some investigated special education, while others compared perspectives. Even though some studies (e.g., Cydis, 2015; Egbert & Shahrokini, 2019; Egorov et al., 2007; Müller-Hartmann, 2016; Wong, 2008) evaluated the implementation of teacher education courses, their focuses were on the technology, cultural competencies, or attitudes. Thus, as Wu (2018) indicated after reviewing the related literature, there is a need for empirical studies about CBTE in EFL contexts.

In competency-based education, learning should encompass knowledge, skills, values, and attitudes that connect to real-life scenarios (MOE, 2014; OECD, 2013, 2016). Based on the concept, the Ministry of Education in Taiwan (MOE, 2018a) required teacher education courses to develop necessary professional knowledge, skills, attitudes, and values that help teachers function effectively in a real-life teaching context. As Adon and Leung (2014) suggested, student teachers are influenced by their own experience as learners in their teacher education courses. Learning theories about competency-based instruction would be

DOI: 10.4324/9781003212805-7

as important as providing student teachers real and direct learning experience in competency-based approaches.

Responding to such trends to situate learning in real-life teaching contexts, research on teacher education in recent decades (e.g., Gao, 2015; Grossman et al., 2009; Lampert, 2010; Rahimi et al., 2016) has emphasized practice-based teacher education. The idea of building a partnership and creating collaboration between universities and public schools has then been adopted in teacher education. A large amount of research (e.g., Gao, 2015; Jackson & Burch, 2019; Lieberman, 1992; Rahimi et al., 2016) advocated school-university partnerships (SUP) to bridge the theory-practice divide and provide clinical practices for student teachers. The National Council for Accreditation of Teacher Education in the United States openly supported clinically based preparation as a "promising practice" (NCATE, 2010, p. 13). Rahimi et al. (2016) emphasized that student teachers would develop more potent teacher competencies through clinical practices with the support of SUP. While a large amount of research (e.g., Gao, 2015; Jackson & Burch, 2019; Lieberman, 1992; Rahimi et al., 2016) recommended SUP as an effective and promising way for preparing future teachers, there seem to be few SUP studies for preparing teachers of EFL.

Even though competency-based approaches and SUP have been advocated for redesigning teacher education (Vitrella, 2015), usage in EFL teaching contexts has not been extensive. Among the few studies, Pope (1999) and Elamin et al. (2002) partnered with local schools and explored technology competencies for student teachers in the United States. Rahimi et al. (2016) and Sharma et al. (2021) examined the CBTE curriculum with SUP in Australia. Geldens and Popeijus (2014) investigated the characteristics of the learning environments in CBTE with SUP in the Netherlands. Ramsaroop and Gravett (2017) observed CBTE with SUP in South Africa;

All of the above studies proposed to establish CBTE with SUP for supporting pre-service and in-service teachers. However, there does not seem to be any study in Taiwan that integrates SUP to develop CBTE. Research related to CBTE with SUP in Taiwan can be beneficial for exploring and developing directions for EFL teacher education, especially for those in Asia.

Objectives

Therefore, this study incorporated a competency-based approach and SUP into the teacher education courses in Taiwan, later referring to as the CBTE courses, and investigated if the courses helped develop competencies among the student teachers. This chapter describes this empirical study regarding the development and evaluation of the CBTE courses. Three main aspects are explored: (1) the design of the CBTE courses; (2) the student teachers' competencies before and after the CBTE courses; and (3) feedback from the student teachers, schoolteachers, and elementary school students.

Defining competency

Before discussing CBTE, it is necessary to define the concept of competency in this study. The word "competency" has different definitions (Bunda & Sanders, 1979; Gervais, 2016). According to Whitty and Willmott (1991), two types of definitions could be identified: competency as (1) "an ability to perform a task" and (2) achievement "encompassing intellectual, cognitive, and attitudinal dimensions" (p. 310). The latter definition has generally been adopted because, as Hextall et al. (1991) stated, teaching should not be reduced to technical tasks. In recent years, the word "competency" has been recognized as the performance (output) that demonstrates a combination of knowledge, skills, attitudes, and values (input) (MOE, 2014; OECD, 2013, 2016, 2018a).

According to the Ministry of Education in Taiwan (MOE, 2018a), teacher competency is defined as the knowledge, skills, attitudes, and values for teachers to function effectively in a real classroom. Research on teacher knowledge and skills has identified the Technological Pedagogical Content Knowledge (TPACK) as most essential for effective teaching (Mishra & Koehler, 2006). As for attitudes and values, according to many EFL teacher education studies (e.g., Uusiautti & Määttä, 2013), research has identified teachers as decision-makers, active developers, reflective professionals, researchers, critical change-makers, and lifelong learners. When comparing those attitudes and values with the major aspects of core competencies in the national curriculum guidelines in Taiwan (MOE, 2014), three types of attitudes and values emerge as the necessary ones for teachers: (1) Spontaneity: decision-maker and active developer; (2) Communication: communicator and lifelong learner; and (3) Social Participation: reflective professionals and critical change-makers.

According to Chai et al. (2016), both quantitative measurement and qualitative observation help better understand teacher competencies. Therefore, in this study, teacher competencies refer to the knowledge, skills, and attitudes demonstrated by student teachers in their performances in real EFL classrooms. The knowledge and skills were measured by a teacher efficacy survey, namely EFL-TPACK (Technological Pedagogical and Content Knowledge in EFL settings) (Wang, 2019) and observed by pupils and teachers in real elementary school classrooms. The attitudes and values were analyzed through the comments of the English teachers and the learning journals written by the student teachers.

Theoretical foundations

The design of the CBTE courses followed findings in the literature about CBTE, curriculum design for inquiry, and SUP. The following paragraphs review the related literature.

Features of competency-based teacher education

Competency-based learning has been associated with different similar approaches, such as performance-based, problem-based, mastery-based, and outcome-based learning, and they all shared similar core concepts (Gervais, 2016; Tuxworth, 1989). Upon the review of related literature (Gervais, 2016; Malan, 2000; Norford & Mazano, 2016; OECD, 2016; Sturgies et al., 2011; Tuxworth, 1989), several common features emerged in competency-based instruction: (1) instruction is based on real-life needs; (2) assessment is meaningful and performance-based; (3) teaching materials serve as the means to achieve the objectives; (4) objectives are explicit, measurable, transferable, behavioral learning outcomes; (5) learner-centered instruction and individual learning needs are emphasized; and (6) students spontaneously engage in solving problems in real-life contexts.

In Taiwan, the Ministry of Education (MOE, 2018b) suggested four principles for designing competency instruction: (1) real-life contexts; (2) practical action; (3) affective education; and (4) process and strategies. Also, Wu (2017) reviewed research related to competency-based instruction in teacher education and proposed five core concepts for developing CBTE: (1) well-rounded whole-person education; (2) pragmatic approach; (3) integrative learning from different disciplines; (4) reflective and improvement; and (5) professional growth (p. 15). Based on the above common features in the related literature, five guiding principles can be summarized: (1) real-life needs; (2) performance-based assessment; (3) measurable and transferable learning objectives; (4) interdisciplinary inquiry process; and (5) reflective learning. The design of the CBTE courses in this study follows these five guiding principles.

Curriculum design for inquiry

For competency-based education, many scholars suggested different approaches for curriculum design. For example, Tucker (1982) proposed the interdisciplinary approach for well-rounded teacher education. Tassinari (2012) recommended a dynamic model of learner autonomy to develop competencies. Also, Ryan et al. (2014) considered elements such as transdisciplinary themes and inquiry learning crucial for designing teacher preparation. As for the competency-based curriculum design, Whitty and Willmott (1991) noted that the design needs to provide clear objectives of achievement and explicit evidence of progress.

Suggestions from the related literature lead to what Ritchhart et al. (2011) and Blythe and Associates (1998) have stressed in curriculum planning—teaching thinking and teaching for understanding. With the same concepts, Wiggins and McTighe (2005) advocated Understanding by Design (UbD). The UbD framework (Wiggins & McTighe, 2005) integrates backward design and essential questions. Aligned with the outcome-based feature of competency-based education, backward design starts with "a clear description of learning outcomes as the basis for curriculum planning" (Richards, 2017, p. 15). Essential questions (McTighe & Wiggins, 2013) engage learners in the inquiry.

According to Wiggins and McTighe (2005), backward design includes three stages: (1) identify desired results; (2) determine acceptable evidence; and (3) create the learning plans. Their (2005) teaching for understanding uses essential questions to provoke thinking and help students transfer the skills they learn in the classroom to unfamiliar real-life situations. That is to say, the instructional design starts from figuring out what evidence is needed to prove that the learning performance has been achieved and then developing provocative questions that "foster inquiry, understanding, and transfer of learning" (Wiggins & McTighe, 2005, p. 22). The course design in the CBTE used the UbD framework, and the development of the CBTE courses will be described later in the results section.

School-university partnerships

Recent reforms on teacher education have centered on providing clinical practices or field-based experiences (NCATE, 2010; Zeichner, 2010). Real-classroom practices are necessary for student teachers to use their knowledge and skills in an authentic context, especially in competency-based education where learning needs to build upon a real-life scenario. SUP provides such possibilities.

As early as the 1990s, Goodlad (1994) proposed the idea of partnerships in education for reforming teacher preparation curriculum. Later, researchers and educators in different countries (e.g., Chang & Yen, 2009; Green et al., 2020; Kleinsasser & Paradis, 1997; Lieberman, 1992; McLaughlin & Black-Hawkins, 2007; Rahimi et al., 2016) have suggested that SUP in teacher education could benefit participants from the university and partner schools in many different ways, including field-based experience, professional development, and curriculum development. As defined by Zeichner (2010), SUP in this study refers to the collaboration between school and university to support student teacher learning.

According to Chang and Yen (2009), SUP has been practiced in Taiwan for more than a decade, but most of the SUP cases include only teacher educators and schoolteachers. When the latest national curriculum guidelines were issued, the Ministry of Education in Taiwan (MOE, 2018b) encouraged SUP for teacher educators and teachers at elementary or secondary schools to work collaboratively on developing interdisciplinary teaching methods and materials. Still, student teachers usually did not have opportunities for real teaching until they started their practicum after completing all their teacher education courses. Many schoolteachers suggested the need for exposing pre-service teachers to a real teaching environment, and many researchers (e.g., Chang, 2017; Chang & Yen, 2009; Darling-Hammond, 2006) urged the involvement of student teachers to acquire clinical experience in real teaching fields. The SUP in this study, involving student teachers, referred to the collaboration groups established among schoolteachers, teacher educators, and student teachers.

Studies on competency-based teacher education and school-university partnerships

CBTE- and SUP-based preparation appear to share similar values. NCATE (2010) identified 10 principles for developing an effective curriculum with SUP, and several were the same as those of CBTE. For example, both value student learning, clinical experience, a balance of the three learning domains (cognitive, psychomotor, and affective), and the importance of continuous improvement. A large amount of SUP research has been done, and there have been some SUP studies that focus on the development of competencies among student teachers. Among the studies related CBTE with SUP, most studies (e.g., Elamin et al., 2002; Ramsaroop & Gravett, 2017; Sharma et al., 2021) confirmed that the collaborations enabled student teachers to learn the competencies necessary for the teaching profession. The related studies included cases in the United States, Australia, Finland, the Netherlands, and Israel, offering examples for design in this study. Many of the studies (e.g., Ramsaroop & Gravett, 2017) suggested the possibilities for SUP to align coursework and real teaching experiences in CBTE, such as observation of exemplary practices, participation in microteaching exercises, and mentoring student teachers.

Method

The study described in this chapter comes from a two-year observation involving both quantitative and qualitative data. In the first semester, two SUP groups were formed, a model for planning CBTE courses was designed, and suggestions were solicited from experts. In the following three semesters, two additional SUP groups were established, and four CBTE courses were implemented and evaluated.

Research sites

The research sites included a university and four elementary schools in central Taiwan. The university has had a long history of preparing teachers of English at elementary school, and the four elementary schools were selected based on the accessibility. The SUP groups were established initially for collaboratively developing the school-based curriculum designs and/or developments for the elementary schools, and they agreed to support the practice teaching for student teachers. Two elementary schools were located in the city, and the other two in suburban areas.

Participants

Different groups of participants were solicited in different periods of the study. During the process of designing the CBTE courses, nine participants were invited to review and provide suggestions for the CBTE design. The nine reviewers were eight teacher educators in the field of English teaching and one researcher in a national research center. The SUP groups consisted of the researcher/teacher educator, student teachers at the university, subject teachers, English teachers, principals, and directors of academic affairs at elementary schools. Among them, 19 schoolteachers, 3 males (15.8%) and 16 females (84.2%), were invited to provide feedback.

During the implementation of the CBTE courses, the student teachers would observe and learn from an English teacher and practice teaching at the elementary schools. Among the schoolteachers in the SUP groups, five English teachers, all female, were invited to advise student teachers when they planned the lessons and practiced teaching on-site. More than 500 pupils participated in the practice-teaching lessons with the consent of their parents, though only 334 valid surveys were collected from the pupils. Of the valid responses, around half the sample (51.8%) was female, and the other half (48.2%) male. Table 6.1 summarizes all the participants in this study.

To evaluate the effectiveness of the CBTE courses, the learning performances of the student teachers in the courses were observed. Student teachers who took different education courses were solicited, including courses such as Children's English, English Teaching Materials and Methods, and English Listening and Speaking Instruction. In total, 150 student teachers returned the consent forms and voluntarily participated in the study. Among them, 121 were female (80.7%), and only 29 were male (19.3%). Most of them were from the department of education (*N*=54, 36.49%), and the next largest number was from the department of English (*N*=45, 30.41%). The rest were from other different departments, such as Chinese education, Taiwanese language and literature, science education, social studies, music, counseling, digital technology, early childhood education, special education, cultural studies, and creative industry (Table 6.2). Most of the student teachers (*N*=99, 66%) did not have any experience of teaching English. A few of them (*N*=29, 19.3%) had experiences teaching English for less than a year. Ten percent of them (*N*=15, 10%) had taught English for one to five years, and only very few of them (*N*=7, 4.7%) had taught for more than five years. Table 6.2 indicates the background information of the 150 student teachers.

Table 6.1 Summary of participants

Stage	*Description*	*Total N*	*Gender*	*N*	*%*
Reviewer	Teacher educators and researchers	9	M	1	11.1
			F	8	88.9
SUP group	Elementary school teachers	19	M	3	15.8
			F	16	84.2
Practice teaching	English teachers	5	M	0	0
			F	5	100
	Student teachers	150	M	29	19.3
			F	121	80.7
	Elementary school pupils	334	M	161	48.2
			F	173	51.8

Table 6.2 Background of student teachers

Category	*N=150*	*No*	*Percent*
Gender	M	29	19.3
	F	121	80.7
Major	Education	54	36.0
	English	45	30.0
	Chinese	12	8.0
	Taiwanese	4	2.7
	Science	9	6.0
	Social Studies	8	5.3
	Other	18	12.0
English teaching experience	None	99	66.0
	Less than a year	29	19.3
	1–5 years	15	10.0
	More than 5 years	7	4.7

Procedure

To meet the needs of the new national curriculum guidelines, all elementary schools are expected to create or reevaluate their school-based curriculum. The researcher proposed SUP with three elementary schools, and one elementary school approached the researcher/teacher educator for collaborations. The collaborations of the SUP include two stages: (1) school-based curriculum design and (2) student-teacher teaching practice. In the first stage, a SUP group worked together to create a school-based curriculum framework along with a sample unit plan. In the second stage, new groups of student teachers created new lesson units based on the curriculum frameworks and practiced teaching at the elementary schools. The second stage is the basis for this study.

Figure 6.1 provides an overview of the procedure. The first step was to design a CBTE model based on the literature, review the design model, and discuss it with the SUP groups. The completed CBTE design model was used to plan teacher education courses, referring to as the CBTE courses. Prior to each CBTE course, the SUP group scheduled possible dates for the student

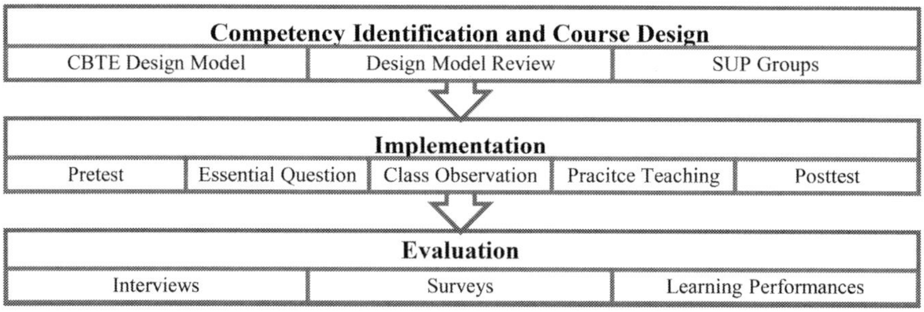

Figure 6.1 Overview of procedure.

teachers to observe real classes, discuss with schoolteachers, and practice their teaching; meanwhile, an interview was conducted with the schoolteacher by the researcher. The second step was to implement the CBTE courses. In the first week of the course, a pretest was administered to estimate the competencies of the student teachers. During the semester, learning journals written by the student teachers were collected each week. In the week of practice teaching, the student teachers collected feedback from the pupils after their lessons. In the final week of the course, the student teachers completed a posttest. After the course was completed, the schoolteachers were interviewed again. Finally, data were collected from different participants, including schoolteachers, elementary school pupils, and student teachers.

Data collection and analysis

To understand the effectiveness of the CBTE courses in helping student teachers achieve the established competencies, data were collected with four different tools, including a TPACK teacher efficacy survey, a pupil feedback survey, interviews, and learning journals. TPACK assessments have been extensively used to assess teacher efficacies (Chai et al., 2016; Koehler et al., 2012). The EFL-TPACK survey developed by Wang (2019) was adopted to measure the knowledge and skills of the student teachers. According to Wang (2019), the five-point Likert survey has high validity and reliability (Cronbach's $\alpha = 0.88–0.98$). The EFL-TPACK survey includes 49 statements investigating the knowledge bases of Pedagogical Content Knowledge (PCK) and Technological Pedagogical Content Knowledge (TPCK) and the ability to teach cognitive skills of different levels: remembering, understanding, applying, analyzing, evaluating, and creating. The survey results include a total score (TPACK scores=49–245) and eight sub-scores (scores=1–5). Higher scores indicate higher teacher efficacy on the different sub-domains. The pupil feedback survey was a five-point Likert scale with ten questions written in Chinese, inquiring if the children understood or liked the lessons taught by the student teachers. The semi-structured interviews with English teachers included questions related to the design of the CBTE courses and their evaluation of student teachers in the elementary school classrooms. The student teachers were required to submit their learning journals every week for 16 weeks. With the guide of a topical question of the week, the student teachers reflected and commented on what they had learned during the week.

The quantitative data were analyzed with SPSS and the qualitative data with MAXQDA. Descriptive statistics were examined to understand the overall thoughts and performances of the participants, and a *t*-test was performed to evaluate their performances before and after the courses. Interview scripts and learning journals were coded and categorized. All data in different CBTE courses were triangulated to analyze for similarities and differences, and themes were developed. Table 6.3 shows the outline of data collection and analysis.

Table 6.3 Summary of data collection and analysis

Competency	*Data collection*	*Data analysis*
Knowledge and skills Attitudes and values	1 EFL-TPACK survey 2 Pupil feedback survey 3 Interviews with schoolteachers 4 Reflective learning journal	1 Descriptive statistics & *t*-test 2 Descriptive statistics 3 Coding to look for themes 4 Coding to look for themes
Curriculum	*Data collection*	*Data analysis*
Course feedback	1 Pupil feedback survey 2 Interviews with schoolteachers 3 Reflective learning journal	1 Descriptive statistics 2 Coding to look for themes 3 Coding to look for themes

Results

The purposes of this study were to incorporate a competency-based approach and SUP in the teacher education courses in Taiwan and to examine if the CBTE courses helped develop the established competencies. The results are presented in the following three aspects: (1) the design of the CBTE courses; (2) the student teachers' competencies before and after the CBTE courses; and (3) the feedback about the CBTE courses.

Design of the CBTE courses

The integration of a competency-based approach and SUP in teacher education was based on the five principles summarized in the literature. During the discussions with the experts (M190422/M190905/M191204/M200213), all the design reviewers (*N*=9) agreed on the necessity of real teaching experiences and the idea that clinical experiences need to be integrated throughout every facet of teacher education, including theory courses. The finalized design model of the CBTE courses includes five essential elements: (1) it should be based on teaching English in a real classroom with SUP; (2) its comprehensive assessment system should require student teachers to act and perform like a real EFL teacher; (3) its activities should involve student teachers in observing and planning lessons to transfer learning; (4) its process should include inquiry-based learning through questions or tasks; and (5) its assignment should include something (e.g., reflective learning journal) that builds habits of a reflective teacher. According to the experts, the CBTE design model could be used in theory courses to help bridge theories and practices (TEA090422) as it provides student teachers opportunities to explore, observe, plan, reflect, teach, and perform like a real EFL teacher (STC191204).

Table 6.4 Example objectives of the CBTE courses

Aspect	*Children's English*	*Teaching listening & speaking*	*Materials and methods*
Knowledge	Language for instruction	Instructional design for the skills	Lesson planning
Skills	Use of language to guide	Strategies for teaching the skills	Use of materials/ methods
Attitudes	Communicator, decision-maker	Active developer, lifelong learner	Reflective professionals, critical change-makers
Action	Storytelling to children	Teaching EFL listening/speaking	Teaching EFL children

Course planning starts with setting the objectives. Under the overall aim, "developing competencies for teachers to function effectively in a real classroom" (MOE, 2018a), the learning objectives of each teacher education course were planned with different focuses, such as language use for children, teaching materials and methods, or instructional designs for specific language skills. The established competencies for each course covered knowledge, skills, and attitudes, and an action plan for each course was planned to observe the established competencies. Table 6.4 provides the example objectives of the CBTE courses implemented in this study.

Based on the objectives and the UbD framework, the desired results were decided. For example, in the course "English Teaching Materials and Methods," one objective is to learn how to plan lessons (see the last column in Table 6.4), the expected result would be for the teacher educator to observe the rationale presented in the lesson (See Stage 1 in Table 6.5). Table 6.5 shows an example of the CBTE course development in the UbD framework.

In the CBTE design model, the learning cycle is divided into three phases: (1) focused lesson; (2) guided instruction; and (3) independent learning. In the first phase, essential questions were the key, leading student teachers to explore and construct the core knowledge for the course. In the second phase, English practitioners played the major roles, providing a model for student teachers to create their lesson plans. In the final phase, authentic experiences were pivotal, putting their designed lesson plans into real practices. Table 6.6 summarizes the learning cycle in the CBTE design.

Table 6.5 A sample CBTE course in the stages of the UbD

Aspects of competency	*Stage 1*	*Stage 2*	*Stage 3*
	Desired results	*Acceptable evidence*	*Learning experience*
Knowledge	Rationale in lesson plans	Unit lesson plan	Essential question
Skills	Strategies in teaching	Lesson plan and materials	Teaching demonstration
Attitudes	Reflective researcher	Learning journal	Reflective discussion
Action	Teaching a planned unit	Real teaching video	Final teaching report

Table 6.6 The learning cycle in the CBTE design

Phase	*Key element*	*Example*
Focused lesson	Essential questions	Explore the questions with readings or discussions to construct knowledge
Guided instruction	Practitioner demonstrations	Observations in videos and/or a real class for ideas to plan lessons
Independent learning	Authentic experiences	Plan a real lesson to practice and reflect in real teaching experience

Demonstrated competencies

To claim the teacher education courses competency-based, it is imperative that the student teachers understand, can apply, and can perform the knowledge, skills, and attitudes that are expected to function effectively in a real classroom. Thus, this study assessed the teacher competencies before and after the CBTE courses. The following paragraphs present the results through the quantitative EFL-TPACK survey and the pupil feedback survey and the qualitative interview observations and learning journals.

The teacher knowledge self-reported by the student teachers in the EFL-TPACK survey indicated significant differences between the pretest and the posttest. As shown in Table 6.7, among the valid paired data (N=142), student teachers scored significantly higher in the posttest (M=185.96, SD=25.57) than in the pretest (M=151.88, SD=32.09) in their overall TPACK score (t-test p<0.001), as well as in every component dimension. It appeared that the student teachers were most confident in their PCK (Pretest M=3.32, SD=0.73; Posttest M=3.99, SD=0.54) and considered themselves weakest in teaching analyzing skills (Analyzing: pretest M=2.95, SD=0.70; posttest M=3.65, SD=0.57).

The teaching skills evaluated by the children (N=350) in the pupil feedback survey also showed positive results (all scored above average=3.50). The children

Table 6.7 A comparison on teacher knowledge before and after the CBTE courses

	Pretest		*Posttest*		*t-test*	
N=142	*M*	*SD*	*M*	*SD*	*t(df)*	*sig.(2-tailed)*
1 PCK	3.32	0.73	3.99	0.54	−8.55(259)	<0.001[a]
2 TPCK	3.16	0.70	3.83	0.64	−8.07(266)	<0.001[a]
3 Remembering	3.23	0.67	3.85	0.53	−8.36(263)	<0.001[a]
4 Understanding	3.11	0.69	3.86	0.53	−9.97(260)	<0.001[a]
5 Applying	3.10	0.67	3.79	0.56	−9.08(266)	<0.001[a]
6 Analyzing	2.95	0.70	3.65	0.57	−9.04(266)	<0.001[a]
7 Evaluating	3.02	0.71	3.75	0.57	−9.07(266)	<0.001[a]
8 Creating	3.01	0.76	3.73	0.64	−8.22(266)	<0.001[a]
TPACK	151.88	32.09	185.96	25.57	−9.53(266)	<0.001[a]

[a] Scaled scores for each dimension (1–8) =1–5; TPACK scores=49–245.

Table 6.8 Pupil feedback on the practice teaching lessons

Item		*M*	*SD*	Item		*M*	*SD*
1	I like their English lessons.	4.25	0.92	6	I understand the English content.	3.71	1.32
2	I am interested in the content.	4.09	0.91	7	I remember the English words.	4.02	0.99
3	The activities are interesting.	4.15	0.93	8	I can say the content in English.	3.93	1.12
4	I pay attention to learning.	3.97	0.94	9	I can use what they teach in life.	4.07	1.01
5	I use English to reply to questions.	3.83	1.15	10	I hope they can teach us again.	4.17	0.95

Note: Scaled scores for each item (1–10) = 1–5.

felt interested in the content (*M*=4.09, SD=0.91) and the activities (*M*=4.15, SD=0.93) and considered what the student teachers taught helpful in their lives (*M*=4.07, SD=1.01). The children also self-reported that they paid attention to learning (*M*=3.97, SD=0.94), understood the English content (*M*=3.71, SD=1.32), remembered the vocabulary taught (*M*=4.02, SD=0.99), and could use English to talk about the content (*M*=3.93, SD=1.12) in the lessons. Their feedback showed that the pupils thought of the lessons as good ones and the student teachers as effective teachers. Table 6.8 is an overview of the pupil feedback survey, in which the Chinese statements were roughly translated into English.

In the individual interviews with the five English teachers, all of them (*N*=5) spoke highly about their student teachers and mentioned how they made significant progress from their first drafted lessons to their final teaching practices. In their descriptions, the student teachers were "active" and "reflective" learners, such as asking many good questions (BC190607), willing to spend time revising again and again (PL200511), and ready to take suggestions after their practice teaching (FH200220/PL200511/SK200515/CC200512). The student teachers showed progress in different aspects, especially on using simple words and short sentences to guide children (BC191209/FH200220), making clear interdisciplinary objectives (PL200511), focusing on learning rather than merely teaching (BC191209/PL200511), and sequencing activities logically (CC200512/SK200515). Still, according to some teachers (FH200220/CC200512/SK200515/PL200511), many of the student teachers needed more practice on classroom management skills.

The student teachers were asked to reflect on what they had learned in their learning journals. Take one class (*N*=50) as an example: all the student teachers (*N*=50, 100%) agreed on the importance for teachers to reflect on what they do, though few (*N*=8, 16%) stated that they did not always do so. One of the major themes in the journals had to do with what inspired their learning, including "discussions on real teaching experiences" (*N*=49, 98%), "essential questions" (*N*=48, 96%), "practitioner demonstrations" (*N*=48, 96), "practice teaching" (*N*=47, 94%), "real-class observation" (*N*=47, 94%), and "teamwork" or "group members" (*N*=16, 32%). Another major theme had to do with their thoughts about teaching, such as "teaching strategies" (*N*=50, 100%), "lesson or activity designs" (*N*=43, 86%), "motivating children" (*N*=38, 76%), "interdisciplinary" (*N*=37, 74%), "classroom management" (*N*=26, 52%), and reactions or performances of their pupils (*N*=13, 26%). The contents of the journals were consistent with the observation of the English teachers: the student teachers gradually developed the sense of effective teaching and learned to value active and reflective attitudes for teaching.

Feedback about the CBTE courses

To evaluate the CBTE courses, feedback was collected from the children who participated in the practice teaching lessons, the student teachers who took the courses, and the experts in the related fields. According to the pupil feedback survey, as aforementioned, the children were interested in the lessons, engaged in learning, and showed understanding about the content and English in the lessons (*M*>3.5). Based on Table 6.8, the children liked the lessons taught by the student teachers (*M*=4.25, SD=0.92) and hoped to have another chance to take their lessons (*M*=4.17, SD=0.95). Children showed genuine welcome and enthusiasm toward the practice teaching lessons.

In the learning journals of a CBTE course, the student teachers mentioned what inspired them to learn, and more than 90 percent of the student teachers referred to the key features of the CBTE courses mentioned above, including "discussions on real teaching experiences," "essential questions," "practitioner demonstrations," "practice teaching," and "real-class observation." In this class, the student teachers (*N*=39, 78%) responded in the course evaluation system at the university with high satisfaction about this CBTE course (*M*=4.00 on the 5-point scale). In the open-ended course feedback, three student teachers (*N*=3, 6%) indicated their difficulties of not having enough time to prepare the lesson plans, and two student teachers (*N*=2, 4%) expressed their needs for the teacher educator to give a clear lecture on theories rather than finding the answers on their own. Generally, the student teachers considered the practice teaching experience to be "precious," "unforgettable," "fruitful," and "wonderful."

The feedback from the experts in the English education field and teachers at elementary schools was also positive. In different meetings and interviews, the experts in the design review stage (*N*=9, 100%) and the SUP teachers (*N*=19, 100%) in the implementation stage agreed that the design of these teacher education courses met the features of competency-based education and considered them helpful for developing teacher competencies. The experts in the meetings (M191204/M200213) agreed that the curriculum design was interactive and student-driven, attempting to help students construct their understanding. However, there were challenges: one of the experts (AY0113) commented that most student teachers did not have the experience of exploring open-ended essential questions and would require guidance on developing higher-cognitive questioning skills. Another teacher (FH200220) in one of the SUP groups mentioned the time pressure for covering the syllabus at the elementary schools. Many (e.g., FH200220/PL200511/SK200515/SH191204) suggested the CBTE model be officially established so that curricula at elementary school could be flexible for regular practice teaching lessons and specific working time could be set for the elementary school teachers to advise the student teachers. Overall, these participants held a positive attitude toward the CBTE courses.

Conclusion

This chapter starts with the discussion on using a competency-based approach with the support of SUP to develop EFL teacher education courses as a potential CBTE design model. Based on the above findings, this chapter advances the CBTE design as an effective means to develop teacher competencies. The CBTE courses provided a contextual inquiry for understanding with the UbD framework and scaffolding from the real practitioners and real practices with the SUP. The learning cycle set in the CBTE design is a process of gradual release of responsibility for the student teachers to learn to be independent.

The demonstrated competencies of the student teachers before and after the CBTE courses show that they made significant progress on all aspects of the established objectives, especially when they knew clearly what their objectives were. Their self-report results were consistent with the pupil feedback and the English teachers' observation. The EFL-TPACK survey led them to observe their own progress on their PCK, TPCK, and their abilities to teach cognitive skills at different levels, while the guidance of the English teachers at the SUP schools provided them models for their practices.

The evaluations of the CBTE courses from the experts, pupils, English teachers, and student teachers were positive. The practice teaching at the SUP schools as a real-life connection for the CBTE courses was accepted as a crucial element for the effectiveness of the courses. Based on the evidence in the study, it is suggested that the steps taken toward the development of the CBTE courses can be adopted as a model to design a CBTE curriculum. The CBTE design model can be used in other EFL teacher education courses, and the competencies set for the CBTE courses in this study can also serve as a common framework for preparing future EFL teachers.

Nonetheless, some challenges still need to be addressed, such as the pressure of time and the burden to the English teachers at the SUP schools. The pressure of time has also been reported in Kleinsasser and Paradis (1997) as one of the factors that cause resistance to change in the SUP context. NCATE (2010) appeared to have solutions to the challenges and suggested that "specific sites are designated and funded to support embedded clinical preparation" (p. 6). According to NCATE (2010), "to have powerful clinical preparation, it is imperative to develop strategic partnerships among teacher education programs, elementary schools, and policymakers" (p. 6).

It is important to be aware that teacher competencies are never static; they are evolving. Developing a teacher education course in a real class setting helps keep up with the knowledge, skills, attitudes, and values necessary in real settings. As suggested by McLaughlin and Black-Hawkins (2007), although engaging in SUP-related activities is challenging, the benefits still "outweigh the costs" (p. 339).

Acknowledgments

This study was funded by research grants from the Ministry of Science and Technology, Taiwan (MOST 108-2410-H-142-006). Two reviewers provided valuable suggestions. I am grateful to all those who contributed to the research.

References

Adon, N., & Leung, C. (2014). The roles of approaches and methods in second language teacher education. In S. B. Said, & L. J. Zhang (Eds.), *Language teachers and teaching: Global perspective, local initiatives* (pp. 59–73). Routledge.

Blythe & Associates. (1998). *The teaching for understanding guide*. Jossey-Bass.

Bunda, M. A., & & Sanders, J. R. (Eds.) (1979). *Practices and problems in competency-based measurement*. Washington, DC: National Council on Measurement in Education.

CCSS (Common Core State Standards). (2014). Common Core State Standards. http://www.corestandards.org/

Chai, C. S., Koh, J. H. L., & Tsai, C.-C. (2016). A review of the quantitative measures of technological pedagogical content knowledge (TPACK). In M. C. Herring, M. J. Koehler, & P. Mishra (Eds.), *Handbook of technological pedagogical content knowledge (TPACK)* (pp. 87–106). Routledge.

Chang, C.-S. (2017). 素養導向教師教育：理念、挑戰與實踐 [Competency-based teacher education: Ideas, challenges and practices]. *School Administrators*, *112*, 14–27.

Chang, S., & Yen, P. (2009). 大學與中小學教師專業夥伴攜手計畫理念與實踐之研究：以因應課程改革為例 [The research on the concept and implementation of partnership program between college and junior high/elementary school teachers: Take the curriculum reform in Taiwan as example]. *Journal of Educational Research and Development*, *5*(1), 91–130.

Chen, H. S., & Huang, H.-Y. (2017). Advancing 21st century competencies in Taiwan. Asia Society: Center for Global Education. https://asiasociety.org/files/21st-century-competencies-taiwan.pdf

Cydis, S. (2014). Fostering competencies in future teachers: A competency-based approach to teacher education. *Creative Education*, *5*, 1148–1159.

Cydis, S. (2015). Authentic instruction and technology literacy. *Journal of Learning Design*, *8*(1), 68–78.

Darling-Hammond, L. (2006). *Powerful teacher education: Lessons from exemplary programs*. Wiley.

Egbert, J. L., & Shahrokini, S. A. (2019). Balancing old and new: Integrating competency-based learning into CALL teacher education. *JALT CALL Journal*, *15*(1), 3–18.

Egorov, V. V., Jantassova, D. D., & Churchill, N. (2007). Developing pre-service English teachers' competencies for integration of technology in language classrooms in Kazakhstan. *Educational Media International*, *44*(3), 255–265.

Elamin, C., Fordham, N., Hammond, D. R., O'Bannon, B., Vannetta, R., & Gruber, K. (2002). Infusing technology into the elementary classroom: A school/university partnership model. *Computers in the Schools*, *19*(1–2), 149–162.

Fwu, B.-J. (2018). 素養導向國教新課綱的師資培育：國立臺灣大學「探究式—素養導向的師資培育」理想芻議 [Teacher preparation in response to competence-based curriculum reform for K-12 education: National Taiwan University's proposal of inquiry-based and competence-based teacher education]. *Journal of Research in Education Sciences*, *63*(4), 59–87.

Gao, X. (2015). Promoting experiential learning in pre-service teacher education. *Journal of Education for Teaching*, *41*, 435–438. https://doi.org/10.1080/02607476.2015.1080424

Geldens, J. J. M., & Popeijus, H. L. (2014). Teacher education in a workplace learning environment: Distinctive characteristics of powerful workplace learning environments within primary teacher education. *School-University Partnerships*, *7*(2), 62–71.

Gervais, J. (2016). The operational definition of competency-based education. *The Journal of Competency-Based Education*, *1*(2), 98–106.

Green, C. A., Tindall-Ford, S. K., & Eady, M. J. (2020). School-university partnerships in Australia: A systematic literature review. *Asia-Pacific Journal of Teacher Education*, *48*(4), 403–435.

Grossman, P., Hammerness, K., & McDonald, M. (2009). Redefining teaching, re-imagining teacher education. *Teachers and Teaching: Theory and Practice*, *15*, 273–289.

Goodlad, J. I. (1994). *Educational renewal: Better teachers, better schools*. San Francisco, CA: Jossey-Bass.

Hextall, I., Lawn, M., Menter, I., Sidgwick, S., & Walker, S. (1991). *Imaginative projects: Arguments for a new teacher education*. Goldsmith's College.

Jackson, A., & Burch, J. (2019). New directions for teacher education: Investigating school/university partnership in an increasingly school-based context. *Professional Development in Education*, *45*(1), 138–150.

Klebansky, A., & Fraser, S. P. (2013). A strategic approach to curriculum design for information literacy in teacher education—Implementing an information literacy conceptual framework. *Australian Journal of Teacher Education*, *38*(11), 103–125.

Kleinsasser, A. M., & Paradis, E. E. (1997). Changing teacher education in the context of a school-university partnership: Disrupting temporal organization arrangements. *Teacher Education Quarterly*, *24*(2), 63–73.

Koehler, M. J., Shin, T. S., & Mishra, P. (2012). How do we measure TPACK: Let me count the ways. In R. N. Ronau, C. R. Rakes, & M. L. Niess (Eds.), *Educational technology, teacher knowledge, and classroom impact: A research handbook on frameworks and approaches* (pp. 16–31). Information Science Reference (IGI-Global).

Lampert, M. (2010). Learning teaching in, from, and for practice: What do we mean? *Journal of Teacher Education*, *61*, 21–34.

Lieberman, A. (1992). The meaning of scholarly activity and the building of community. *Educational Researcher*, *21*(6), 5–12.

McTighe, J., & Wiggins, G. (2013). *Essential questions: Opening doors to student understanding*. Alexandria, VA: Association for Supervision and Curriculum Development.

McLaughlin, M., & Black-Hawkins, K. (2007). School–university partnerships for educational research—Distinctions, dilemmas and challenges. *The Curriculum Journal*, *18*(3), 327–341.

McLean, C. A., & Rowsell, J. (2013). (Re)designing literacy teacher education: A call for change. *Teaching Education*, *24*(1), 1–26.

Mishra, P., & Koehler, M. J. (2006). Technological pedagogical content knowledge: A framework for teacher knowledge. *Teacher College Record, 108*(6), 1017–1054.

Malan, S. (2000). The 'new paradigm' of outcomes-based education in perspective. *Journal of Family Ecology and Consumer Sciences, 28*, 22–28.

MOE (Ministry of Education, Taiwan). (2014). *Curriculum guidelines of 12-year basic education: General guidelines.* https://cirn.moe.edu.tw/WebContent/index.aspx?sid=11&mid=9900

MOE (Ministry of Education, Taiwan). (2018a). 中華民國教師專業素養指引—師資職前教育階段暨師資職前教育課程基準[Guidelines for teacher professional competencies in the Republic of China: Preservice teacher education stage and pre-service teacher education curriculum benchmarks]. https://edu.law.moe.gov.tw/LawContent.aspx?id=GL001829

MOE (Department of Teacher and Art Education, Ministry of Education, Taiwan). (2018b). 對準新課綱的師資培育課程與教學啟動—與中小學夥伴攜手研發教材教法 [Aligning teacher education with new curriculum: School-university partnerships for developing teaching materials and methods]. *New Curriculum Newsletters, 16*. Retrieved from https://newsletter.edu.tw/2018/10/09

Müller-Hartmann, A. (2016). A task is a task is a task is a task… or is it? Researching telecollaborative teacher competence development – The need for more qualitative research. In S. Jager, M. Kurek, & B. O'Rourke (Eds.), *New directions in telecollaborative research and practice: Selected papers from the second conference on telecollaboration in higher education* (pp. 31–43). Research-publishing.net.

National Curriculum. (2011). *Qualifications and curriculum authority: The aims, values and purposes of the curriculum.* https://www.education.gov.uk/schools/teachingandlearning/curriculum/b00199676/aims-values-and-purposes

NCATE (National Council for the Accreditation of Teacher Education). (2010). Transforming teacher education through clinical practice: A national strategy to prepare effective teachers. (Report of the Blue Ribbon Panel). http://www.highered.nysed.gov/pdf/NCATECR.pdf

Norford, J. S., & Mazano, N. R. (2016). *Personalized competency-based education: Creating a cohesive and coherent system.* Centennial, CO: Marzano Research. http://soltreemrls3.s3-website-us-west-2.amazonaws.com/marzanoresearch.com/media/documents/Personalized_CBE_Whitepaper_September_2016.pdf

OECD. (2013). *Trends shaping education 2013.* OECD.

OECD. (2016). *Global competency for an inclusive world.* OECD.

OECD (Organization for Economic Cooperation and Development). (2018). *The future of education and skills. Education 2030.* Retrieved from https://www.oecd.org/education/2030/E2030%20Position%20Paper%20(05.04.2018).pdf

Pope, C. A. (1999). Technology in language arts teacher education. *Clearing House, 72*(4), 196–197.

Rahimi, M., Zhang, L. J., & Esfahani, N. N. (2016). Advocating school-university partnership for responsive teacher education and classroom-based curricula: Evidence from teachers' cognitions about principles of curriculum design and their own roles. *Australian Journal of Teacher Education*, 41(12).

Ramsaroop, S., & Gravett, S. (2017). The potential of teaching schools in enabling student teacher learning for the teaching profession. *Journal of Curriculum Studies, 49*(6), 848–865.

Richards, J. C. (2017). *Curriculum development in language teaching* (2nd ed.). Cambridge University Press.

Ritchhart, R., Church, M., & Morrison, K. (2011). *Making thinking visible: How to promote engagement, understanding, and independence for all learners.* Jossey-Bass.

Ryan, A. M., Heineken, A. J., & Steindam, C. E. (2014). Preparing globally minded teachers through the incorporation of the international baccalaureate. *Journal of Education, 194*(3), 39–51.

Sharma, U., Grové, C., Laletas, S., Rangarajan, R., & Finkelstein, S. (2021). Bridging gaps between theory and practice of inclusion through an innovative partnership between university academics and school educators in Australia. *International Journal of Inclusive Education.* https://doi.org/10.1080/13603116.2021.1882052

Sturgies, C., Patrick, S., & Pittenger, L. (2011). *It's not a matter of time: Highlights from the 2011 competency-based learning summit.* International Association for K-12 Online Learning. Retrieved from http://www.aurora-institute.org/wp-content/uploads/iNACOL_Its_Not_A_Matter_of_Time_full_report.pdf

Tassinari, M. G. (2012). Evaluating learner autonomy: A dynamic model with descriptors. *Studies in Self-Access Learning Journal, 3*(1), 24–40.

Tucker, J. F. (1982). Developing a global dimension in teacher education: The Florida International University experience. *Theory into Practice, 21*(3), 212–217.

Tuxworth, E. (1989). Competence-based education and training: Background and origins. In J. Bourke (Ed.), *Competency based education and training* (pp. 10–25). Routledge Falmer.

Uusiautti, S., & Määttä, K. (2013). Significant trends in the development of Finnish teacher education programs (1860–2010). *Education Policy Analysis Archives, 21*(59), 1–18.

Vitrella, A. (2015). Reimagining teacher preparation: An invitation to create new programs for changing teacher roles (design ideas). *Education Evolving.* https://files.eric.ed.gov/fulltext/ED605547.pdf

Wang, A. Y. (2019). *Evaluation on TPACK among EFL student teachers: Validation of an EFL-TPACK assessment (MOST 107-2410-h-142-007).* Ministry of Science and Technology.

Whitty, G., & Willmott, E. (1991). Competence-based teacher education: Approaches and issues. *Cambridge Journal of Education, 21*(3), 309–318.

Wiggins, G., & McTighe, J. (2005). *Understanding by design* (2nd ed.). Association for Supervision and Curriculum Development.

Wong, R. M. H. (2008). Competency-based English teaching and learning: Investigating pre-service teachers of Chinese's learning experience. *Porta Linguarum, 9*, 179–198.

Wu, C.-S. (2017). 素養導向教師教育：理念、挑戰與實踐 [Competency-based teacher education: Ideas, challenges and practices]. 學校行政雙月刊 *[School Administrators], 112*, 14–27.

Wu, C.-S. (2018). 素養導向教師教育內涵建構及實踐之研究 [Construction and practice of competency-based teacher education]. *Journal of research in education sciences, 63*(4), 261–293.

Zeichner, K. (2010). Rethinking the connections between campus courses and field experiences in college- and university-based teacher education. *Journal of Teacher Education, 61*(1–2), 89–99.

7 Developing teachers' competencies through intercultural telecollaboration

Martine Derivry-Plard, Paloma Castro-Prieto, Ana Cristina Biondo Salomão, and Sa-hui Fan

Introduction

Teacher competencies need to be reconceptualized to respond to the complexities and demands of an increasingly globalized educational scenario. Intercultural telecollaboration has brought a new dimension to teaching and learning for the past two decades, and especially during the COVID pandemic, it has been a way to maintain and work on social and intercultural links across countries when mobility and face-to-face interaction are limited and borders are closed. It is essential to prepare teachers to support intercultural communication in this global context, by building competencies through which they learn to co-teach and establish the conditions of possible communication across borders as well as develop inward-looking attitudes for openness toward others and their human rights.

This chapter aims at describing and discussing a virtual intercultural exchange environment over three continents designed to support the learning and collaborative activities of student-teachers from Brazil, Spain, France, and Taiwan with the ultimate goal of developing teachers' competencies. Students from four different languages and cultures work together using the medium of English as a Lingua Franca (ELF) to exchange their views on education through collaborative tasks.

This three-continent environment also helps build emerging core educational cultures among future teachers of English or teachers of other disciplines using ELF. In the context of competency-based teacher education, intercultural tele-collaboration is viewed as a challenge and as an opportunity for the development of teachers' repertoires in intercultural communication.

Internationalization of teacher education

Over the last couple of decades, higher education has been deeply affected by globalization (Altbach et al., 2016). The ways in which higher education has responded to globalization have tended to be identified under the themes of "internationalization" and the development of "international strategies" (Altbach & Knight, 2007, p. 290). As Knight (2007) notes, globalization is a

DOI: 10.4324/9781003212805-8

phenomenon impacting internationalization, which she describes as "a process of change through integrating an international, intercultural and global dimension in the goals, functions, and delivery of higher education" (Knight, 2013, p. 81).

Indeed, internationalization has become a key issue for higher education institutions that try to contribute meaningfully to the world and society by responding to the challenges and opportunities of our time. And by critically rethinking their policies and missions as a first step, higher education institutions try to address the question of the role they play in the contemporary world (Castro et al., 2020).

The discourse on internationalization has undergone a transformation in recent years. Stier (2006) has identified three discernible ideological discourses, which in turn lead to different practices. These are: "idealism," "instrumentalism," and "educationalism." The last of these recognizes the personal and societal value of learning itself. Analyzing the actions and perspectives of oneself and others contributes to a person's self-understanding and stimulates meta-reflection. In a recent edited book, Lundgren et al. (2020) adopt the educationalist discourse to internationalization by examining the concept of internationalization from an educational perspective and by giving voice to practitioners to offer accounts to research and practice which address intercultural dialog as an educational approach to the process of internationalization. In their concluding chapter, they state that:

> If universities truly wish to create global-ready graduates who are able to cope with, work with, and change for the better the challenges of our times, then we argue there is no other option than to embrace an educationalist approach in the spirit of intercultural dialogue – however it may be understood in local contexts – through our internationalization policies, operations, teaching and learning, and most fundamentally in our people.
>
> (Woodin et al., 2020, p. 223)

Through internationalizing practices in higher education, there is hope that students will come to develop their "capacity to critique the world they live in, see problems and issues from a range of perspectives, and take action to address them" (Leask, 2015, p. 17). The phenomenon of globalization recognizes the importance of education in understanding and solving global issues. In this regard, it has raised questions about what constitutes meaningful global citizenship. For UNESCO (2015), global citizenship refers to a sense of belonging to a broader community and common humanity. It entails three core conceptual dimensions that serve as the basis for defining goals, learning objectives, competencies, and assessment criteria:

1 Cognitive: To acquire knowledge, understanding and critical thinking about global, regional, national, and local issues and the interconnectedness and interdependency of different countries and populations.

2 Socio-emotional: To have a sense of belonging to a common humanity, to share values and responsibilities, and to nurture empathy, solidarity and respect for differences and diversity.
3 Behavioral: To act effectively and responsibly at local, national, and global levels for a more peaceful and sustainable world (UNESCO, 2015, p. 15).

The role of education is moving toward transformative aims, building on knowledge, skills, values, and attitudes that learners need in order to contribute to a more peaceful and sustainable world.

> The content of such education must be relevant, with a focus on both cognitive and non-cognitive aspects of learning. The knowledge, skills, values and attitudes required by citizens to lead productive lives, make informed decisions and assume active roles locally and globally in facing and resolving global challenges can be acquired through education for sustainable development (ESD) and global citizenship education (GCED), which includes peace and human rights education as well as intercultural education and education for international understanding.
>
> (UNESCO, 2016, p. 49)

UNESCO has stressed the importance of education for international, intercultural, and inter-religious understanding through programs that encourage dialog and make a meaningful contribution to sustainable and tolerant societies.

The discourse on the role of the professional educator is also changing and the importance of teacher competencies has been increasing in the past years (Wiseman & Anderson, 2014). For the European Commission (2013), teacher quality is high on the agenda. High-quality teachers are among the most important factors for achieving high-quality education. According to this document (European Commission, 2013, p. 17), "teaching staff nowadays also need the competences to constantly innovate and adapt; this includes having critical, evidence-based attitudes, enabling them to respond to student´s outcomes, new evidence from inside and outside the classroom, and professional dialogue, in order to adapt their own practices."

Teacher education and professional training are crucial to the successful implementation of global competencies in education. Pre-service teachers and teachers need to be prepared to respond to the complexities and demands within an increasingly globalized educational scenario.

Competency-based language teaching in the international context

Competency-based education (CBE) has been defined in several various ways and translated differently across disciplines. Le et al. (2014) explain that CBE "is an evolving field with no universally shared definition of what makes a model competency-based" (p. 4). However, Gervais (2016) tried to provide it with an operational definition:

> CBE is defined as an outcome-based approach to education that incorporates modes of instructional delivery and assessment efforts designed to evaluate mastery of learning by students through their demonstration of the knowledge, attitudes, values, skills, and behaviors required for the degree sought. (p. 99)

The theoretical roots of CBE can be traced back to several learning theories: behaviorist, functionalist, and humanistic learning theories (Gervais, 2016). Most CBE theorists advocate that education needs to focus less on a traditional classroom-based learning environment; instead, it should be more student-centered and prepare students for their social roles in the future as already mentioned by Riesman (1979). Besides, the curriculum theorist, Tyler (1976) emphasizes the importance for students to learn how to best apply the theories learned to practice. This essential pedagogical reasoning of CBE has been adopted in different disciplines to build practical teaching models.

Generally speaking, applications of CBE in language teaching started to be commonly accepted by educators worldwide in the 1990s. Competency-based language teaching (CBLT) gained its popularity in the United States in the 1990s due to its effectiveness of helping immigrants to acquire survival English (Paul, 2008; Richards & Rodgers, 2001; Wong, 2008). The CBLT reasoning has also been adopted in the multilingual European Union (EU) in the 1990s because of the search for an effective language program to connect the private sectors, academics and employers from different European countries (Tudor, 2013). Furthermore, CBLT gradually caught the attention of foreign language educators in East Asia from the beginning of the 21st century because of their awareness of the negative results brought by traditional credentialism (Jang & Kim, 2004) in language teaching, and some countries, such as Taiwan, would like to replace it with CBLT.

Competency-based language teaching in the United States and in Europe

CBE started in the United States around the beginning of the post-industrial years (1960s) but took off in popularity in the 1990s. Its earliest applications in language teaching were in adult survival-language programs for immigrants and refugees to learn necessary language skills to function (Paul, 2008; Richards & Rodgers, 2001; Wong, 2008). There are several notions emphasized in the CBLT teaching models developed in the United States: (1) a student-centered approach, (2) task-learning for real life, (3) a mastery of learning, (4) self-paced or self-directed learning, and (5) competency of applying theories to practice (Gervais, 2016).

The EU comprises 26 countries with 23 official languages. This makes Europe an intensely multilingual and multicultural area. This situation implies the significant role which a common language and language learning should play. Hence, since 1991, the Council of Europe has actively promoted a competency-based approach for language teaching and learning: the Common European Framework of References for Languages (CEFR). The CEFR is one of the most widely adopted instruments of the Council of Europe in the field of languages. It clearly manifests the "can do" statements of learning a language and its common reference levels (A1 to C2) have been employed by worldwide educational institutions, private sectors as well as testing organizations as a criterion reference of defining language learning outcomes. The prevailing use of the CEFR makes it possible to assess the language competencies of learners in different countries on the same scale (Tudor, 2013).

Traditional and vernacular Confucianism in Asia

Confucianism has undergone a two-thousand-year evolutionary process and its current characteristics have been reshaped and transformed for many times. Its two key characteristics are the method of instruction and examinations (Guthrie, 2011). The original teaching method of Confucius was non-formal and personal in character (Wu, 2011). According to the classical Chinese texts, Analects, Confucius preferred inducing students' reflection and contemplation by answering students with another question. Thus, Confucius actually provided students with student-centered teaching and adaptive learning (Ho, 2018).

Throughout time, more political powers influenced the educational systems and more formalistic and bureaucratic examinations evolved. Gradually, teachers became authoritative, and learning of students was achieved through repetition and imitation. As the imperial examination system (credentialism) became the only possible way for social advancement regardless of birth, it refocused the purpose of Confucian education from inducing students' reflections to passing the examinations through repetitive and imitative learning methods (Guthrie, 2011). These current educational practices in Confucianism have been labeled as "vernacular Confucianism" (Chang, 2000, p. 137).

Many educational phenomena in East Asia, including China, Hong Kong, Japan, Korea, Singapore, and Taiwan, have been attributed to their common heritage, Confucianism and credentialism. Its over-emphasis on rote learning and high-stakes standardized tests has been criticized by many Asian educational scholars (Ho, 2018). The drawbacks of this Confucian educational practice and credentialism might have shaken beliefs of some Asian educators who would like to look for an alternative teaching method, such as the western competency-based teaching (Jang & Kim, 2004). According to Jang and Kim (2004), the criticisms of vernacular Confucianism education and credentialism are listed as follows:

> (1) high private tutoring spending (2) severe competition on the entrance exam for university or more selective universities, (3) mechanical learning, memorization, perfunctory instruction, and lack of creativity, flexibility and self-directed learning; (4) the demise of the classroom. (p. 692)

These criticisms are combined with the emerging problems found by Yi (2001): "(5) weakened teachers' authority, and (6) low academic ability of college students." These drawbacks might have resulted in the East Asian students' inefficiency in applying knowledge in the workplace.

There seems to be a shared reason why CBLT has become popular or been on the rise in the United States, Europe, and East Asia. The policymakers, language teachers and researchers hope that classroom-based teaching should equip students with the competency of applying knowledge in practice. In terms of foreign language education, it means that learners should be able to utilize the learned language in real-life tasks. In the current intensively inter-connected global village, how to communicate well with people from different cultural backgrounds with a common language becomes the major task that a foreign language learner should be equipped with. Accomplishing these intercultural communication tasks requires not only linguistic but also intercultural competencies. Hence, for foreign language teacher training, intercultural communication competencies are essential and should not be neglected.

Intercultural telecollaboration for international teacher education

New contexts of telecollaboration have generated the need for teacher education to review its knowledge base and rethink the role and competencies necessary for teachers to co-teach in intercultural online contexts. Some of the new challenges to be addressed include working together with partners in different places and time zones through the use of communicative tools that enable spoken and written modalities, accommodating diversity in relation to cultural and educational references, dealing with different languages and varied levels of English, as well as engaging in intercultural interaction and learning to co-teach within different educational contexts. We are thus facing a challenge for (language) teacher education with regard to the components of this new role as mediator in digital collaborative spaces, as well as the development of guidelines for initial and continuing training to prepare teachers to understand and negotiate local needs in order to collaboratively plan the activities and co-teach in such contexts.

Our experience in the development of the 3 Continents Intercultural Telecollaboration (3CIT) stems from our understanding of teacher education as a dynamic process of (re)-construction and transformation of practices, which must focus on the development of competencies through action and reflection. The 3CIT started in 2017 aiming at co-constructing a learning/teaching/researching environment designed to support telecollaborative activities of students in the field of teacher education from Brazil, France, Spain, and Taiwan. This learning environment was co-designed by the professors/researchers who jointly made decisions to accommodate specific teaching aims and local conditions, such as schedules, time zones, communication tools, types of tasks, and group settings.

The main objective of the 3CIT is to give students the opportunity to experience intercultural communication through the medium of ELF, by co-constructing the context through their different cultural and language repertoires and by reflecting on their experience. Three tasks to be performed in a period of five weeks were designed to elicit the intercultural process step by step. Two of them involve collaborative group work and one is an individual experience journal. The first collaborative task aims to be the starting point to create a shared and safe space where students will experience intercultural communication. It sets the perspective for students to speak about themselves within an academic context (not something usual in certain cultures) and to reflect on who they are and how similar and different they are from other people. In the second task, students must collaboratively write a text addressing the outcomes of their discussions on educational issues. These discussions are usually guided by input provided in the form of videos and reflective prompts. In the experience journal, each student must write his/her personal reflections on the interactions and exchanges throughout the telecollaboration period.

The groups are planned to have at least one student from each country, but accommodations have to be made taking into consideration the complexity of each local context. For example, decisions have to be made concerning whether or not to integrate the activities in a class, how to schedule synchronous sessions considering the different time zones, as well as strategies to guide students to engage in regular contact to perform the collaborative tasks and comply with the deadlines.

The 3CIT is also a common research environment for the professors/researchers to investigate the intercultural dimension of telecollaborative teaching and learning in order to improve the proposed pedagogy and to explore the potential of interculturality through online interactions in teacher education. In Salomão et al. (in press), we reported on the research we conducted together on the experience journals in order to understand "the different dimensions that emerged from students' experience and to identify if there was a change of perspectives among students through their narratives." The findings show that:

> (…) the experience in the 3CIT project has combined students' individual perceptions on the use of telecollaboration for education with the development of a sense of group built by the bonds established through group dynamics. Communication was both seen as a challenge to meet others through a foreign language but also a meaning-making situation of practice that helped students to gain confidence and explore the emancipatory dimensions of ELF. Above all, it seems that the intercultural experience in the telecollaboration provided by the technological tools and tasks proposed has contributed to the development of students' intercultural awareness, appreciation of diversity and openness to engage with others. By focusing on similarities and differences, participants were able to sense strangeness and familiarity among aspects of their cultures and issues related to their educational systems, which lead to an overall positive attitude and eagerness to overcome fears and idealised expectations.

The experience has helped students to regulate their own learning and develop competencies in relation to metacognitive awareness, reflexivity, and criticality that may aid them to be better equipped to cope with intercultural communication within complex contexts.

An international course for teachers to learn intercultural telecollaboration design

Based on our multilateral experience in intercultural telecollaboration, the notion of third place or space developed by Kramsch as far back as 1994 to characterize the language classroom was definitely the ground on which we reflect and develop our practices:

> Because learning a language is learning to exercise both a social and personal voice, it is both a process of socialization into a given speech community and the acquisition of literacy as a means of expressing personal meanings that may put in question those of the speech community.
>
> (Kramsch, 1994, p. 233)

If the traditional language classroom was limited to the walls of the room in a given time session, and under specific circumstances cast aside linguistic study abroad opportunities, the intercultural experience of the third space was nonetheless dependent on the sole language teacher creating the bridge to another language and culture. With the hyper-connectedness of the world, technology not only enhances and changes our relationship to reading, writing and knowledge but above all allows the language classroom to become a truly balanced third space where at least two language teachers and their learners from different languages and cultures meet and occupy the third space to its full potential.

If virtual online exchanges were not always successful and sometimes counter-productive in terms of language and intercultural competencies (Kern & Develotte, 2020; O'Dowd & Lewis, 2016), it seems that the monolingual paradigm in which generations of language teachers have been brought up and trained is still at work: too much focus on language per se, too much enchantment and fear of Information and Communication Technology, and very little concern of the cultural and intercultural dimension of communication.

In line with the process of internationalization, the language curriculum needs to be expanded taking into account the incredible potential offered by the Internet of linking language teachers and learners from the whole world, and allowing them for the first time in human history to meet the objectives of communication in a second language. The change of scale, from the traditional language classroom within a school located in a country to the updated language classroom of the global age in which language teachers and learners meet equally and co-build their own communicative third space, needs to be fully realized and highlighted by language teachers and language stakeholders.

This unprecedented situation for language teachers means they need to shift from the monolingual/monocultural paradigm they were educated in and in which they brought "otherness" to the margin, to the plurilingual/pluricultural paradigm (Derivry-Plard, 2018, 2019, 2020) in which they need to co-build the intercultural interstices of the specific online exchange. There are therefore with the change of scale, more demands to the language teachers' competencies in order to mitigate power relations that will always resist any co-teaching settings. These new competencies should be addressed with the global agenda of internationalization of higher education and of teachers training. Language teachers should be at the forefront of the global teachers' objectives of a sustainable planet embracing the issues of human beings in relation with all other living bodies and with all other non-animated bodies such as robots and learning machines. Indeed, the traditional role of language teachers has been to offer a bridge to broader world views and perceptions from other learners through a new common language and different cultures. The bridge extension of the traditional language teacher is now a bridge co-designed by language teachers within the context of their educational institutions and co-built by them and their learners in the third space they will work in to develop their intercultural experiences.

What lived and created in the updated third space is:

> The realization of difference, not only between oneself and others, but between one's personal and one's social self, indeed between different perceptions of oneself can be at once an elating and a deeply troubling experience.
>
> (Kramsch, 1994, p. 234)

This is exactly the nexus of competencies from which a common course on intercultural telecollaboration for language teachers and teachers of other disciplines has to delve into. The contexts of teachers and learners need to be first acknowledged, embracing at the same time the specificities of the teachers and their learners in their diverse plurilingual/pluricultural competencies and trajectories (Kramsch, 2009; Kramsch & Zhang, 2018; Liddicoat & Scarino, 2013; Zarate et al., 2011) and then to link them with research in intercultural communication (Zhu, 2016).

Thanks to sociolinguistics, we know the world is multilingual as the majority of speakers are plurilingual. Even among monolinguals, it is quite unlikely not to observe some language variety, hence the notion of language repertoires to better exemplify the language competencies of speakers. These realities have also been put forward by language teachers and researchers who have worked on plurilingualism/pluriculturalism, and interculturality in and outside the classroom, and how the multilingual learner and instructor find their own ways through surrounding monolingual perceptions and settings. Among these monolingual perceptions, the native/non-native divide resists as this is deeply ingrained in either transhistorical or transgeographical discourses and narratives (Derivry-Plard, 2015). Language learners and teachers share the common schemata of allowing different competencies to speakers and teachers. Learners often confuse the speaker of a language to the language teacher. Language teachers often allow different professional competencies to native and non-native language speaker teachers based on the same views as the learners of the native/non-native speaker. These perceptions reifying the speaker and the language teacher to nativism has been coined as nativespeakerism (Holliday, 2006), a form of racism applied to the irreducibility of language. These latent views are deeply rooted in the monolingual/monocultural paradigm in societies, particularly in education and even in international education replicating to a certain extent global geopolitics. However multilingual education (Cenoz & Gorter, 2015; Garcia & Wei, 2014) is emerging and struggling with such rampant monolingual/cultural views[1].

Taking into consideration the digital age and its potential multilingual and multicultural stance for the developments of a democratic and humanist approach to global education, it is necessary to develop an international course for teachers to learn intercultural telecollaboration design that addresses the following competencies (can do):

- Work telecollaboratively with language teachers or teachers from other disciplines and from different countries and languages,
- Design specific intercultural telecollaborations for language or discipline learning in line with the Content and Language Integrated Learning (CLIL) approach,
- Set the intercultural dimension of communication at the core of educational practice, human understanding and democratic principles,
- Approach language and cultural diversity as an inescapable reality worth being nurtured to better understand how similar and different people are from one another,
- Shift from a monolingual/cultural view to a plurilingual/cultural one not as opposing the former but as including it,
- Look at the traditional native/non-native divide as two final or extreme points on a very wide continuum,
- Identify nativespeakerim in discourse,
- Envisage languages and cultures as repertoires as well as pedagogical practices,
- Engage in knowledge and skills as two sides of the same coin and accept the coin to be flawed, repaired or changed when it is no longer useful,
- Trust in human goodwill, empathy, and in suspending judgments and beliefs when not proven,
- Be positively kind, alert and critical of yourself and others to develop curiosity, creativity and imagination.

Conclusion

The global call for teachers is to equip learners not only with linguistic and communicative competencies, but also with an intercultural citizenship agenda within the internationalization of education. The educational milieu for foreign language teaching nowadays has evolved under the use of technology, enabling more cultures to be in contact and create their own third spaces. Foreign language teachers face the challenge to add more competencies on how to perform online intercultural telecollaboration as well as how to design and deliver effective projects and tasks in these complex cultural environments. As exemplified with the CEFR, there is tension between the humanistic approach and the pragmatic operational model. At the same time, if the model of CBE or CBLT is inflated, the educational purpose can be restricted to "market/commodification of qualifications."

Therefore, teacher education plays a key role in preparing language teachers and teachers of other disciplines to enhance the support given to learners in intercultural communication. The philosophical educational purpose of a global curriculum could be developed through intercultural telecollaboration and courses for teachers to develop competencies for successful implementation. In fact, the humanistic, holistic approach of a global curriculum is based both in the original Confucian and Socratic methods for smaller groups of learners and the great philosophers of education such as John Dewey and Paulo Freire, who added the vital dimensions of reflection and democracy in education. The agenda is to develop intercultural citizen's competencies in its broad sense to acknowledge global diversity and communication through languages and cultures within a multicultural world.

Note

1 Bordeaux English/French bilingual Master's program in International Teaching and Training enables English/French-speaking students to deal with such issues. http://pi-learning.inspe-bordeaux.fr/formation-de-formateurs-a-linternational/

References

Altbach, P. G., & Knight, J. (2007). The internationalization of higher education: Motivations and realities. *Journal of Studies in International Education*, *11*(3–4), 290–305. https://doi.org/10.1177/1028315307303542

Altbach, P. G., Reisberg, L., & Rumbley, L. E. (2016). Tracking a global academic revolution. In P. G. Altbach (Ed.), *Global perspectives on higher education* (pp. 15–28). The Johns Hopkins University Press.

Castro, P., Lundgren, U., & Woodin, J. (2020). Intercultural dialogue. An educational approach. In U. Lundgren, P. Castro, & J. Woodin (Eds.), *Educational approaches to internationalisation through intercultural dialogue. Reflections on theory and practice* (pp. 3–14). Routledge.

Cenoz, J., & Gorter, D. (2015). *Multilingual education: Between language learning and translanguaging*. CUP.

Chang, W. C. (2000). In search of the Chinese in all the wrong places! *Journal of Psychology in Chinese Societies*, *1*, 125–142.

Derivry-Plard, M. (2015). *Les enseignants de langues dans la mondialisation. La guerre des représentations dans le champ linguistique de l'enseignement*. Éditions des Archives Contemporaines/PLID. Postface de C. Kramsch. http://pub.lucidpress.com/EnseignantsMondialisation/

Derivry-Plard, M. (2018). A multilingual paradigm in language education: What it means for language teachers. In S. A. Houghton & K. Hashimoto (Eds.), *Towards post-native-speakerism: Dynamics and shifts* (pp. 131–148). Springer.

Derivry-Plard, M. (2019). Un paradigme plurilingue et pluriculturel pour la formation des enseignants. *Voces y Silencios Revista Latinoamericana de Educación, Open Access Journal, 10*(1), 63–79. https://revistas.uniandes.edu.co/doi/full/10.18175/vys10.1.2019.06

Derivry-Plard, M. (2020). A multilingual paradigm: Bridging theory and practice. In S. A. Houghton & J. Bouchard (Eds.), *Native-speakerism: Its resilience and undoing*. Springer.

European Commission. (2013). *Supporting teacher competence development for better learning outcomes*. http://ec.europa.eu/education/policy/school/doc/teachercomp_en.pdf

Garcia, O., & Wei, L. (2014). *Translanguaging: Language, bilingualism and education*. Palgrave Macmillan.

Gervais, J. (2016). The operational definition of competency-based education. *The Journal of Competency-Based Education, 1*(2), 98–106.

Guthrie, G. (2011). Formalistic traditions in China. In G. Guthrie (Ed.), *The progressive education fallacy in developing countries: In favour of formalism* (pp. 173–193). Springer.

Ho, F. M. (2018). Reforms in pedagogy and the Confucian tradition: Looking below the surface. *Cultural Studies of Science Education, 13*(1), 133–145.

Holliday, A. (2006). Native-speakerism. *ELT, 60*(4), 385–387.

Jang, S., & Kim, N. (2004). Transition from high school to higher education and work in Korea, from the competency-based education perspective. *International Journal of Educational Development, 24*(6), 691–703.

Kern, R., & Develotte, C. (2020). *Screens and scenes, multimodal communication in online intercultural encounters*. Routledge.

Knight, J. (2007). Internationalisation: Concepts, complexities and challenges. In J. K. Forest, & P. G. Altbach (Eds.), *International handbook of higher education* (pp. 207–227). Springer.

Knight, J. (2013). Probable and preferable futures of internationalisation. In H. De Wit, F. Hunter, L. Johnson, & H.-G. Van Liempd (Eds.), *Possible futures: The next 25 years of the internationalisation of higher education* (pp. 80–84). European Association for International Education (EAIE).

Kramsch, C. (1994). *Context and culture in language teaching*. OUP.

Kramsch, C. (2009). *The multilingual subject*. OUP.

Kramsch, C., & Zhang, L. (2018). *The multilingual instructor*. OUP.

Le, C., Wolfe, R. E., & Steinberg, A. (2014). *The past and the promise: Today's competency education movement*. Students at the Center: Competency Education Research Series. Jobs For the Future.

Leask, B. (2015). *Internationalizing the curriculum*. Routledge.

Liddicoat, J. A., & Scarino, A. (2013). *Intercultural language teaching and learning*. Wiley-Blackwell.

Lundgren, U., Castro, P. Woodin, J. (Eds.). (2020). *Educational approaches to internationalisation through intercultural dialogue: Reflections on theory and practice*. Routledge.

O'Dowd, R., & Lewis, T. (2016). *Online intercultural exchange: Policy, pedagogy, practice*. Routledge.

Paul, G. (2008, December 16). Competency-based language teaching report [Web log comment]. http://glendapaul62.blogspot.com/2008/12/competency-based-language-teaching.html

Richards, J., & Rodgers, T. (2001). *Approaches and methods in language teaching*. Cambridge University Press.

Riesman, D. (1979). Society's demands for competence. In G. Grant, P. Elbow, T. Ewens, Z. Gamson, W. Kohli, W. Neumann, V. Olesen, & D. Riesman (Eds.), *On competence: A critical analysis of competence-based reforms in higher education* (pp. 18–65). Jossey-Bass, Inc.

Salomão, A. C. B., Castro, P., Fan, S., & Derivry-Plard, M. (in press). Intercultural telecollaboration for teacher education through three continents: Insights from experience journals. In A. Potolia, & M. Derivry-Plard (Eds.), *Virtual exchange for intercultural language learning and teaching: Fostering communication for the digital age*. Routledge.

Stier, J. (2006). Internationalisation, intercultural communication and intercultural competence. *Journal of Intercultural Communication, 11*, 1–11.

Tudor, I. (2013). From content to competency: Challenges facing higher education language teaching in Europe. In P. Cañado, & M. Luisa (Eds.), *Competency-based language teaching in higher education* (pp. 21–32). Springer.

Tyler, R. W. (1976). *Perspectives on American education: Reflections on the past...Challenges for the future*. Science Research Associates INC.

UNESCO. (2015). *Global citizenship education: Topics and learning objectives*. UNESCO.

UNESCO. (2016). *Education 2030: Incheon declaration and framework for action for the implementation of sustainable development Goal 4: Ensure inclusive and equitable quality education and promote lifelong learning opportunities for all*. https://unesdoc.unesco.org/ark:/48223/pf0000245656

Wiseman, A. W., & Anderson, E. (2014). Introduction to the annual review: The reciprocal effects of teacher education on comparative and international education. *Annual Review of Comparative and International Education, 25*, 3–11.

Wong, R. M. H. (2008). Competency-based English teaching and learning: Investigating pre-service teachers of Chinese's learning experience. *Porta Linguarum, 9*, 179–198. http://www.ugr.es/~portalin/articulos/PL_numero9/13%20Ruth%20Ming.pdf

Woodin, J., Castro, P., & Lundgren, U. (2020). Internationalisation and higher education. Questions from an educationalist/intercultural dialogue perspective. In U. Lundgren, P. Castro, & J. Woodin (Eds.), *Educational approaches to internationalisation through intercultural dialogue. Reflections on theory and practice* (pp. 211–226). Routledge.

Wu, Z. (2011). Interpretation, autonomy, and transformation: Chinese pedagogic discourse in a crosscultural perspective. *Journal of Curriculum Studies, 43*, 569–590. https://doi.org/10.1080/00220272.2011.577812

Yi, J. T. (2001). An inquiry into the implications of "the Crisis of Schooling". *The Journal of Korean Education, 82*(2), 229–249 (in Korean).

Zarate, G., Levy, D., & Kramsch, C. (2011). *Handbook of multilingualism and multiculturalism*. Éditions des Archives Contemporaines.

Zhu, H. (Ed.). (2016). *Research methods in intercultural communication*. Wiley Blackwell.

Section III

Practice

8 Impact of different intercultural telecollaborative environments on Taiwanese ELF learner's communicative competencies

Sa-hui Fan and Martine Derivry-Plard

Introduction

Globalization has profoundly influenced human interactions since the last decade of the previous century. Due to the frequent moves of people, commodities, and money, the need for everyone to interact with people from different language/culture backgrounds has been increasing. Thus, in this era of globalization, enhancing intercultural communicative competence (ICC) has become fundamental when acquiring a foreign language.

Competency-based language teaching (CBLT) follows the outcome-based and pragmatic spirit of competency-based education (CBE) that has been widely adopted in Europe and the United States since the 1990s (Paul, 2008; Tudor, 2013) and is now gaining popularity in Asian countries (Jang & Kim, 2004). In terms of practicality in the era of globalization, ICC is a skill that teachers/learners cannot overlook in CBLT. Regarding the pedagogical options for ICC, telecollaboration is considered to be one with abundant potentials (Dooly, 2011; Dooly & O'Dowd, 2012; Kern, 2006; Ware & Kessler, 2016). Hence, this study focused on how five Taiwanese graduate students developed their intercultural competencies through two different telecollaborative environments with the same task organization.

Competency-based education and competency-based language teaching

According to curriculum theorists, such as D. Riesman (1979) and J. Gervais (2016), CBE is distinguished by its emphasis on outcome-based education and the importance it places on students being able to apply the learned material into practice in real life. Its instructional philosophies are rooted in behaviorist, functionalist, and humanistic learning theories (Gervais, 2016). When CBE takes form in foreign language teaching, the pragmatic nature of CBLT has influenced the American Council on the Teaching of Foreign Languages (ACTFL) proficiency guidelines and the Common European Framework of Reference (CEFR) for language proficiency. It is now commonly accepted by foreign language educators worldwide that knowing how to use a learned language pragmatically to

DOI: 10.4324/9781003212805-9

communicate with people from different language/cultural backgrounds is essential. Thus, the pedagogical concerns of CBLT should also include how to teach ICC.

Intercultural communicative competence and telecollaboration

Byram (1997) defines ICC as a series of five "*savoirs*" (knowledge-abilities), and this notion has caught the attention of many researchers and practitioners in foreign language education since then. ICC is generally regarded as "the ability to interact effectively with individuals from different cultures in a variety of contexts" (Godwin-Jones, 2013, p. 1). Both the ACTFL in the United States and the CEFR in Europe include ICC in their proficiency standards. However, teaching ICC is still absent from most foreign language classrooms nowadays because ICC is sometimes categorized as non-linguistic by applied linguists, and there is no room to accommodate culture-specific but non-linguistic topics in classes (Godwin-Jones, 2013).

However, telecollaboration has been found to be a useful method for including the intercultural dimension of foreign language learning in foreign language classrooms. O'Dowd (2005) specifically defines telecollaboration as "the use of online communication tools to connect language learners in different countries for the development of collaborative project work and intercultural exchange" (p. 144). In the past 30 years, telecollaboration has been reported to be widely employed by foreign language teachers as a useful pedagogical option for increasing students' language exposure and ICC (Belz, 2003; Belz & Müller-Hartmann, 2003; Belz & Thorne, 2006; Castro et al., 2021; Dooly, 2011; Dooly & O'Dowd, 2012; Kern, 2006; Ware & Kessler, 2016; Ware & O'Dowd, 2008; Warschauer, 2000). Thus, it is essential for teachers to understand the nature of practicing telecollaboration before adopting it in the foreign language classroom to enhance learners' interculturality.

Telecollaboration 2.0

The notions of contemporary fracturing space (Lankshear & Knobel, 2007; Thorne & Reinhardt, 2008) and ubiquitous presence (Thorne & Reinhardt, 2008) in cyber practices have evolved with the changing interactive nature from Web 1.0 to 2.0 and have created transformations in telecollaborative projects. A new generation of telecollaboration has appeared in recent years by following the technological evolution from Web 1.0 to 2.0. This new telecollaborative model (Telecollaboration 2.0) reflects in many ways a more flexible (in terms of time and space), as well as an adaptable teaching approach for intercultural exchanges (O'Dowd, 2016). Several features of the online environments of Telecollaboration 2.0 are categorized based on notions of past studies (Hauck, 2010; Helm & Guth, 2010; Thorne, 2010) into the following: (1) multilateral, multilingual, and multimodal; and (2) undoing native-spea kerism.

The current study

This study explores how five Taiwanese graduate students have developed their intercultural competencies in different virtual environments. The ages of the five Taiwanese students ranged from 25 to 32 and included two males and three females. They were all studying for their master's degrees in teaching English as a foreign language, and their English proficiencies were all above CEFR B2. The research was carried out in two consecutive semesters from 2017 to 2018. The first semester (or stage 1) was designed as class-embedded activities between the bilateral ends in Taiwan and France (in two continents), while the second semester (or stage 2) consisted of voluntary activities with the trilateral ends, Taiwan, France, and Brazil (spanning three continents). Qualitative data were collected through the learners' experience journals (both stages) and written task homework (first stage only). All homework, journals, and notes were written in English.

The first-stage telecollaboration was implemented in a graduate-level course. The telecollaborative activity included three tasks (described in more detail below). It was a bilateral activity between 5 Taiwanese graduate students and 12 French graduate students. In this stage, the telecollaborative project was carried out in an online environment consistent with Telecollaboration 1.0 (Helm & Guth, 2010). Each Taiwanese student was assigned to interact with two to three French students during the class periods inside the computer lab. The pairings were randomly assigned in the Taiwanese end.

The second stage telecollaborative activity was conducted on a voluntary basis without being implemented in or framed by any traditional courses. The telecollaborative activity included the same three tasks as the first stage. The telecollaborative project in the second stage was carried out in an online environment consistent with Telecollaboration 2.0, due to its features of (1) the trilateral ends (including the Taiwanese, French, and Brazilian learners), (2) the use of English as a *lingua franca*, and (3) the unrestricted timeframe and activity venue. The time and place of conducting the telecollaborative activities were commonly determined by all the group participants. In the second stage, the same five Taiwanese students were randomly assigned to different groups with different French and new Brazilian learners..

Time and space

Time and space options for these two stages were different. In the first stage, all telecollaborative activities were carried out in class, but participants wrote their task and journal logs after class. In the second stage, the participants as a group had to find a solution to overcome the time differences of the three continents and choose a common time to conduct the telecollaborative activities.

In the first stage, all telecollaborative activities were conducted in the designated computer lab and supervised by the instructors on both ends. The Taiwanese participants shared the university facilities and Internet. In the second stage, the Taiwanese participants were allowed to use their own computers or tablets and choose any convenient place.

Telecollaborative tasks

Task-based language teaching has long been regarded by many researchers as a useful teaching approach (Long, 1985; Nunan, 2004; Skehan, 1998). Ellis (2009) offers comprehensive criteria of language tasks as: (1) focusing on meaning; (2) addressing the information "gap"; (3) relying on linguistic or non-linguistic resources to complete the activity; and (4) clearly defining the outcome other than the use of language. Task assignments and telecollaborations were a suitable match because of their shared focuses on authenticity and practical ends.

Three similar tasks were adopted in both stages with the topics of self-introduction, comparisons of university life, and comparisons of educational systems. Each Taiwanese participant was required to submit a four-page individual task report and a two-page reflection log (experience journal) after every task in the first stage. However, during the second stage, only two-page experience journals after each task and a final four-page comparison paper of the two stages required. The minimum meeting time for each task was 60 minutes. Different online communication tools, such as Skype and Google Hangout, were also options available to each group. The participants chose Skype as the main communication tool (Table 8.1).

Data collection and analysis

The primary mode used in this study to gather data was qualitative, and the inquiry methods included: (1) experience journals of the participants (both stages), (2) the four-page task report for each task (the first stage only), (3) the comparison papers of the two telecollaborations (the second stage only), and (4) discussion records of the instructors (both stages).

Table 8.1 Comparison of the two telecollaborations

	1st stage telecollaboration	*2nd stage telecollaboration*
Three same tasks	Four-page assignments after every task	No assignments to turn in
Space	All in the computer lab	At any convenient place
Time	During class time	Chosen by the group members
Internet	Shared the Internet connections	Individual Internet connections
Participants	Bilateral	Trilateral:
	Taiwan: 5 participants	Taiwan: 5 same participants from the previous stage
	France: 12 participants	France: 10 different participants from the previous stage
		Brazil: 5 participants

The qualitative data were collected, coded, and assigned to the emergent categories and themes through a content thematic analysis (Bardin, 1993; Krippendorff & Bock, 2008; Roberts, 1997). Interpretations and findings were derived after coding.

Findings

In this study, the results indicated that different group atmospheres were fostered in the two distinctive virtual environments. Nevertheless, the cultural reflexivity of the Taiwanese participants were successfully developed in both stages.

Group atmosphere

The two stages of telecollaborative activities presented quite distinctive atmospheres and dialogic intentions in spite of their similar time lengths and tasks. According to the Taiwanese participants, the atmosphere in the first stage was formal and serious. Furthermore, the dialogic intentions were task-oriented and goal-focused. These group dynamics were projected in their communication styles. In the first stage of telecollaboration, the Taiwanese participants seemed to focus on the assignments and rarely showed interest in developing companionship with their distant partners. In contrast, in the second stage, they expressed tremendous reciprocal eagerness to create group bonding with their distant partners in France and Brazil. This finding implies that different telecollaborative settings might create varied group atmospheres.

The first telecollaboration: Task-oriented and formal

The participants' journals at the first stage showed that most of the telecollaborative communications were in a serious and task-oriented mood similar to question-and-answer time. All the Taiwanese participants expressed a practical desire of getting answers quickly from their French partners for the homework. Excerpts from the participants' journals are highlighted below:

> Lu: *The process was more of a formal discussion of education. And sometimes it feels like it is a mission-oriented telecollaboration. We ask questions and get answers so that we could finish the assignment soon.*
>
> *the way of the first group carried out the telecollaboration was somehow tiresome for me, because there were three of them, and there was only me to answer all of their questions.*

The second telecollaboration: Relationship-oriented and relaxing

In the second stage of telecollaborative activities, in which the same group of students from stage one volunteered for, quite contrasting group dynamics had appeared. Even though the Taiwanese participants worked in bigger groups than in the first stage with partners from two other locations, it was described in their journals as a welcoming, open, and relaxing atmosphere in most of the online conversations. Their dialogues seemed to be reciprocal and warm. The conversation topics were diverse and the group bonding seemed to have been built.

> Lu: *I found that this time is more dialogic and interactive. The interactions like smiling, exclaiming or confirming are all making the conversation dynamic…*
>
> Hsu: *Therefore, during the gap, we had a free talk and I thought it would be interesting to introduce to them the Mid-Autumn Festival, which I happened to bring one mooncake and showed it to them. My partners were curious and seemed intrigued.*

In the second stage, the Taiwanese students no longer being pressured by the tasks to be done with this voluntary telecollaboration, showed engagement in the different topics presented and felt free to add or present other topics. Moreover, the fact the groups were bigger but with students from different countries added to better group dynamics.

Strategies adopted for telecollaborative activities

Data showed that the strategies employed were varied in the two telecollaborations. In the first stage of telecollaboration, the strategies included (1) using the partners' native language, and (2) making more linguistic and technical preparations. In the second stage telecollaboration, the atmosphere and interactions seemed to be spontaneous, casual, and pleasant, so more social bonding among the trilateral ends had been naturally built. The Taiwanese participants seemed to use "going with the flow" as their main strategy. This study shows that different telecollaborative environments had obvious impacts on the atmosphere and strategies employed.

Strategies for the 1st telecollaboration

Due to the fact that the first stage telecollaboration was restricted to the frame of a formal class, the Taiwanese seemed to attempt to choose certain strategies that could trigger their French partners to respond easily and immediately. Their strategies included using simple French, spending more time on preparing PowerPoint presentations, photos, and outlines as well as using other alternative online contact tools, such as email and Facebook.

Using partners' native language

> Hsu: *On a side note, during the discussion, we went astrayed and talked about "la bise" (a French way to greet by kissing on the cheeks) just to make the conversation more energetic. This shall be effective strategy to keep the conversation going.*

Yang: *For the last discussion, one of the group members who is not good at English raised some questions in French to me on facebook previously. I really enjoyed replying in French with her because it was a chance of language exchange.*

These Taiwanese participants were able to use simple French in order to maintain the communication flow and avoid some breaks in English communication. It might indicate that even though English was the *lingua franca*, once people from different backgrounds use ELF, they are also interested in knowing about their respective cultural backgrounds other than the native-speaking culture of English.

Preparations

According to the experience journals, the Taiwanese students had made preparations in different forms to facilitate the telecollaborative activities. Their preparations included making PowerPoint presentations for their partners, emailing the partners beforehand, making a layout for online discussions, as well as searching for online photos.

Chen: *Regarding to the topic that we talked about, I prepared a simple PPT file with the map of Taiwan to describe the location of our university so that they can have more idea about the specific place of our school in Taiwan.*

Yang: *I prepared a lot of photos and picture to illustrate my descriptions to make it more vivid.*

The second telecollaboration strategy: "Going with the flow!"

In the second stage of telecollaborative activities, the online environment seemed to be quite friendly, supportive, and relaxing. The Taiwanese participants soon bonded with their distant partners. The bonding process was reciprocal in this online environment, and few communication breakdowns seemed to occur. Therefore, the Taiwanese participants only needed to engage in the group conversations and activities. They enjoyed the relaxing group atmosphere and naturally bonded with their partners in France and Brazil. The main strategy they used was "Going with the flow!"

Hong: *I also learnt to respect that people had different pace in talking. There's no need to rush or being afraid of not completing assigned topics, just enjoy it.*

When we were having conversations, we patiently wait for each other to share, allowed pauses and silent moments existing, moved on to the next topic when everyone's ready to do so. It turns out we were quite relaxing and were able to seek for supports from our classmates to add more information or express more clearly.

Despite the fact that the second stage telecollaborative activities were trilateral and there were more group members, it appeared to be much easier for the Taiwanese participants to bond with their distant partners from the two distant locations. Summarizing from the Taiwanese participants' experience journals, there were several reasons for the easiness of in-group bonding in this stage: (1) the telecollaborative activities of the three locations seemed to co-create an exotic dynamic which enhanced the Taiwanese participants' curiosity of understanding their distant partners; (2) without the stress of meeting task deadlines, the Taiwanese participants were able to feel less tense and more patient and flexible.

> Lu: *During the call, I think all of us got deeper understandings about each other's backgrounds and countries. This telecollaboration was going well and we all took a picture together in the end. It was very different from the last time. I can feel the friendship bonding among us.*
>
> Hong: *When talking with them, the topic assigned was just considered as a beginning and common topic to open a conversation instead of an assignment. It kind of reminded me that we could relax and simply enjoy our meetings then complete tasks instead of taking the meeting as a tunnel to get information from others only.*

Dimensions of intercultural competence and reflexivity

As described in the previous sections, the distinct telecollaborative environments had an apparent influence on the atmosphere created and the strategies adopted. The reflexive outcomes of the two telecollaborations, however, seem to be quite similar. The first-stage telecollaborative communications looked rough and exhausting, but there was a great amount of cultural and intercultural reflections shown in the participants' assignments. The second telecollaboration looked relaxing and loose, but cultural and intercultural reflexivities had also been derived. In both cases, the development of meaning-making was not only fostered by the common tasks to be carried out but by the individual writings of an experience journal (EJ) that supported reflexivity and cultural/intercultural comments on these intercultural exchanges.

In the first stage of telecollaboration, the restricted online environment and assigned requirements reduced the pleasure of participating in the telecollaborative activities. However, the Taiwanese participants still had gained abundant cultural and intercultural knowledge from their French partners. For instance, they learned about the unfamiliar position of "librarian teacher" in French schools as Lu wrote:

> The other question was "Do we have a library in school?" I wasn't aware of this question was connecting with what (librarian teachers) they are studying right now. I understand why they ask the question. And I am amazed by this new concept of education, because we don't' have this in Taiwan.

They also learned about different life priorities in the two societies as Hsu reflected:

> In Taiwan, as a graduate student myself, I have been incredibly busy than ever as I am still working part-time while studying for master's courses. It appears to me that, the way I am raised, we value work very much and probably not taking too much time in doing leisure activities. Many students I know of, especially those who have a job and study as a part-time student, they would always put work first before recreation. We believe that working can lead to a wealthy life, whilst in France, a quality life means balance, both having fun and working hard. This is a very different mindset.

By completing the assignment of comparisons, most Taiwanese participants had developed in-depth reflexivity regarding the Taiwanese culture and "the otherness," e.g., the different emphasis on autonomy, the comparable focus on the pragmatic subjects, and the similar evolutionary respect toward teachers in both societies. It also showed that the cultural and intercultural reflexivity of Taiwanese participants gradually evolved during and after the telecollaboration thanks to the completion of tasks and of the writing of an experience journal.

Lu, for example, reflects about her Taiwanese education regarding what she has perceived from a French education:

> For example, for a college student in Taiwan, they may need to go through the process to be trained or develop independence with themselves. The reason why we need this is that, we don't have the opportunities to develop independence or autonomy, even critical thinking before college, due to the test-oriented educational style and the cultural setting as we were taught to be good or subservient to the teachers or parents and lack of individual growth... On the contrary, students in France are developing independence, critical thinking and confidence in an early stage. As for them, their college lives would be conceived differently as we did, it means that they have a clear and specific goal to attend college, and they want to achieve the goal, which could be influential in pursuing their career, like the students we contact in the class.

Chen also reflects on common educative attitudes that Taiwan and France have about mathematics and sciences:

> In the society of France, people think studying science, technology or math will be more successful in the future careers than studying other majors at schools, like arts or education, which is similar to the value in Taiwan. Therefore, mathematics and sciences are regarded as important subjects at school... However, it may cause the curriculum or training at schools are too narrow focus on certain subjects to help the development of children with different intelligences.

The Taiwanese participants were able to compare French and Taiwanese attitudes toward teachers and find out common points as Hsu wrote:

> My French partner and I spoke about how teachers are valued in the society. According to my partner, teachers need more respect in the country. Many teachers find it is difficult to teach because of managing students' behavior… In Taiwan, teachers used to be a respectable and stable job, on the management level, they had a dense control and higher power over students and parents. However, in the recent decade, the dynamic has changed. Teachers now are hard to find a long-term job due to the dysfunctional education policy, and parents tend to have more say in how their children should be educated.

They were also able to question their own prejudices or stereotypes about their French partners as Hong said:

> It's quite surprising to know that the one I meet is different from the stereotype I have or what teachers introduce to us for French.

Even though communication was not as positive in the first telecollaboration than in the second one due to the overall settings of the different telecollaborations, the first one being class-embedded and the second one voluntarily, the intercultural dimension of the telecollaborations was not missed in the two telecollaborations. This is an important result showing that the settings of a telecollaboration can affect communication and communicative development when too class-guided but can be nonetheless beneficial to reflexivity and intercultural meaning-making through tasks designed with a comparative element and with the specific task of an experience journal.

The second-stage telecollaborative activities were conducted in a cordial, dialogic, and relaxing atmosphere and the intercultural dimension seemed even more enhanced. We cannot say if this was due to the fact the second telecollaboration was voluntary or because, the first telecollaboration helped understand the potential or interest of this pedagogy for the students. Compared with the first stage of telecollaboration, the assigned topics for group conversations were seen more as a conversation opening rather than a task or assignment that had a deadline to meet. In regard to intercultural learning, Taiwanese participants' pre-conceived ideas of the French and Brazilian people were resolved in a friendly atmosphere. Hence, the Taiwanese participants seem to gain abundant intercultural retrospection through the loose and relaxing telecollaborative dialogues.

All the Taiwanese participants expressed in their journals that they had gained tremendous cultural knowledge, including the differences of school schedules as mentioned by Lu:

> One thing I found to be interesting was that the students' school time table in Brazil is arranged quite differently from Taiwan. They explained that they

> can choose whether you want to take the class in the morning, afternoon or evening. And they have classes everyday of that class period. This is different from us in Taiwan. In Taiwan, students could arrange their own school timetable, except for the required classes. In this way, it gives the students space and freedom to learn to arrange their own time.

They also compared tuition policies in the three countries as reported in Lu's journal:

> The other thing that we talked about is tuition of university in different countries. In Brazil, students do not pay tuition to the school, the government would defray the expenses for the students. We explained that college tuition in Taiwan would be different depends on the school and department that students go to. Educational supports or policies in different countries are offered and set differently, but every country has its own investment on their education.

They were able to reflect on the various viewpoints toward "a strike" in the three societies as Hsu expressed:

> In French, even teachers can go on strikes, not only officers who work for the government but employees who work for the private corporation also would take action to voice for their laborious rights. The Taiwan group and Brazilian group shared that we have a similar situation that if employees go on strike, then we might lose their job.

And they also were able to discuss the unfamiliar obligations of school advisors in French high schools as reported by Chen:

> They (the French students) are studying the program for training them to be advisors for children in their future career. According to their information, the advisor who is like a consulter or a facilitator for helping children's study and homework. Different with a teacher, the advisor doesn't teach certain subjects. There is no similar position in formal schools in Taiwan.

In the second stage, the Taiwanese participants did not stop at asking about factual knowledge but joined actively in and contributed to the explanations of cultural reasoning. Engagements in exploring cultural reasoning helped the participants to construct their cultural and intercultural reflexivity. The Taiwanese participants confessed in their experience journals that they had held biases toward their distant partners, but the stereotypes were critically examined in the telecollaborative conversations as Lu wrote:

> Through the conversation, there are some new facts learner about France and Brazil, and there are some deeper understandings about other countries

> gained. Such as the stereotype we might have of other countries, however, when we get a deeper understanding, we realized that not all the French or Brazilian would fit stereotypes.

They were able to overcome some clichés or prejudices as Hong reflected in her experience journal:

> This tele-collaboration changed my view a little bit towards French and Brazilian from the image we got from social media or previous experience meeting French students. They were still hardworking when studying, they were friendly to Asian, and they are willing to share their ideas. It's a fun experience and a great chance to peek how others live, how their education systems different from ours and most importantly, we had fun time to exchange and communicate.

The organized setting of the telecollaboration has had a strong impact on how the Taiwanese students responded to the tasks: at stage1 the weight of context and formal education in Taiwan was far too evident for Taiwanese students to fully engaged in the innovative intercultural practice within the language classroom, whereas at stage 2 the practice being voluntary and aside from any formal foreign language class helped the Taiwanese students to benefit more from the open space created.

Conclusion

Online environments continue to evolve because of the fast-changing technology. There is a high public anticipation that technology will put forth new and efficient types of learning for many different leaners. This study in telecollaboration can only provide partial evidence with regard to this high expectation. The telecollaborative participants seemed to be more restricted to the structures of the institutions and the communication styles of their inherited cultures in Telecollaboration 1.0 so that the first telecollaborative atmosphere fostered was awkward and tiring; in the second stage telecollaboration, the atmosphere was in contrast friendly, cordial and enjoyable due to its voluntary and less restricted nature. These results indicate that the different environments indeed impacted the telecollaborative atmosphere. Some might see this result and then believe that the outcomes of intercultural learning of the second stage would have exceeded those of the first stage. However, the results showed similar intercultural reflexive outcomes appearing in both stages but seemed even more enhanced with the second one. This might imply that the more structured scaffolding of intercultural teaching (particularly with the on-going process of the writing of an experience journal) compensated for the negative effects brought by the tiring and unenjoyable group atmosphere in telecollaboration.

Moreover, the different outcomes of the two telecollaborations are understood by knowing that the Taiwanese participants had expressed different dialogic intentions. In the first stage, with an online environment similar to Telecollaboration 1.0, their dialogic intentions were more passive and low, as the tasks were embedded in a strictly instrumental and functional environment, e.g., have the tasks done to meet precise deadlines. However, in the second stage with a Telecollaboration 2.0 environment, they appeared eager and active to carry on the intercultural conversations. As they were given an open space for intercultural exchange in which communication was no longer constrained by the instrumental and functional objective of the language classroom, and in which they could explore the pleasure of non-instrumental/functional communication to get authentic, human exchanges from which they could learn and experience different learning goals.

From the perspective of CBLT practitioners, the pragmatic outcomes of learning foreign languages should include not only communicating with people from other language/culture backgrounds in person, but also with people online in different environments since technologies have been fast developed and kept changing. Institutions and their educational cultures need to take into account these fast changing technologies that learners adopt easily without thinking and sometimes without reflecting on their affordances and drawbacks. This is time for language educators and teachers to grasp these technologies (not for themselves but for what they are, means to a human purpose) for their own language and intercultural communicative purposes. In that way, teachers would help their learners deal with languages, communication and the intercultural dimension attached to them: they would help learners evolve and communicate better in this global and more diverse world as shown with these two intercultural telecollaborations. Intercultural telecollaboration is at the beginnings of the "intercultural" part of telecollaboration, while a lot has been said about technologies and telecollaboration. We have shown using a qualitative content analysis of task productions that the intercultural dimension is really developed in terms of communicative reflexivity, meaning-making and intercultural and educational awareness. As the world becoming smaller needs to find out diverse ways of communicating with diverse topics and people, and with numerous ways of doing, the intercultural dimension of telecollaboration is definitely one of the challenges faced by language teachers of the 21st century.

References

Bardin, L. (1993). *L'analyse de contenu* (7ème éd. corrigée, 291 p.). PUF.

Belz, J. A. (2003). Linguistic perspectives on the development of intercultural competence in telecollaboration. *Language Learning & Technology*, *7*(2), 68–117.

Belz, J. A., & Müller-Hartmann, A. (2003). Teachers as intercultural learners: Negotiating German–American telecollaboration along the institutional fault line. *The Modern Language Journal*, *87*(1), 71–89.

Belz, J. A., & Thorne, S. L. (Eds.). (2006). *Internet-mediated intercultural foreign language education*. Heinle.

Byram, M. (1997). *Teaching and assessing intercultural communicative competence*. Multilingual Matters.

Castro, P., Biondo Salomão, A. C., Fan, S.-H., & Plard, M. D. (2021). *Intercultural virtual exchange for teacher education through three continents: Insights from experience journals. Virtual exchange for intercultural language learning and teaching: Fostering communication for the digital age.* Routledge – Taylor and Francis Group.

Dooly, M., & O'Dowd, R. (2012). *Researching online foreign language interaction and exchange: Theories, methods and challenges. Telecollaboration in Education* (Vol. 3) (ERIC Document, ED534262).

Dooly, M. A. (2011). Crossing the intercultural borders into 3rd space culture (s): Implications for teacher education in the twenty-first century. *Language and Intercultural Communication, 11*(4), 319–337.

Ellis, R. (2009). Corrective feedback and teacher development. *L2 Journal, 1*(1), 3–8.

Gervais, J. (2016). The operational definition of competency-based education. *The Journal of Competency-Based Education, 1*(2), 98–106.

Godwin-Jones, R. (2013). Integrating intercultural competence into language learning through technology. *Language Learning & Technology, 17*(2), 1–11.

Hauck, M. (2010). The enactment of task design in Telecollaboration 2.0. In M. Thomas, & H. Reinders (Eds.), *Task-based language learning and teaching with technology* (pp. 197–217). Bloomsbury.

Helm, F., & Guth, S. (2010). The multifarious goals of Telecollaboration 2.0: Theoretical and practical implications. In S. Guth, & F. Helm (Eds.), *Telecollaboration* (Vol. 2, pp. 69–106). Perter Lang.

Jang, S., & Kim, N. (2004). Transition from high school to higher education and work in Korea, from the competency-based education perspective. *International Journal of Educational Development, 24*(6), 691–703.

Kern, R. (2006). Perspectives of technology in learning and teaching languages. *TESOL Quarterly, 40*(1), 183–210.

Krippendorff, K., & Bock, M. A. (Eds.). (2008). *The content analysis reader.* Sage.

Lankshear, C., & Knobel, M. (2007). Researching new literacies: Web 2.0 practices and insider perspectives. *E-learning and Digital Media, 4*(3), 224–240.

Long, M. H. (1985). A role for instruction in second language acquisition: Task-based language teaching. *Modelling and Assessing Second Language Acquisition, 18*, 77–99.

Nunan, D. (2004). *Task-based language teaching* (Cambridge Language Teaching Library). Cambridge University Press.

O'Dowd, R. (2005). Negotiating sociocultural and institutional contexts: The case of Spanish–American telecollaboration. *Language and Intercultural Communication, 5*(1), 40–56.

O'Dowd, R. (2016). Learning from the past and looking to the future of online intercultural exchange. In R. O'Dowd, & T. Lewis (Eds.), *Online intercultural exchange: Policy, pedagogy, practice* (pp. 273–294). Routledge.

Paul, G. (2008, December 16). Competency-Based Language Teaching Report. [Web log comment]. http://glendapaul62.blogspot.com/2008/12/competency-based-language-teaching.html

Riesman, D. (1979). Society's demands for competence. In G. Grant, P. Elbow, T. Ewens, Z. Gamson, W. Kohli, W. Neumann, V. Olesen, & D. Riesman (Eds.), *On competence: A critical analysis of competence-based reforms in higher education* (pp. 18–65). Jossey-Bass Inc.

Roberts, C. W. (1997). *Text analysis for the social sciences: Methods for drawing inferences from texts and transcripts.* Lawrence Erlbaum.

Skehan, P. (1998). *A cognitive approach to language learning.* Oxford University Press.

Thorne, S. L. (2010). The "intercultural turn" and language learning in the crucible of new media. *Telecollaboration*, *2*, 139–164.

Thorne, S. L., & Reinhardt, J. (2008). "Bridging activities," new media literacies, and advanced foreign language proficiency. *CALICO Journal*, *25*(3), 558–572.

Tudor, I. (2013). From content to competency: Challenges facing higher education language teaching in Europe. In *Competency-based language teaching in higher education* (pp. 21–32). Springer.

Ware, P., & Kessler, G. (2016). Telecollaboration in the secondary language classroom: Case study of adolescent interaction and pedagogical integration. *Computer Assisted Language Learning*, *29*(3), 427–450.

Ware, P., & O'Dowd, R. (2008). Peer feedback on language form in telecollaboration. *Language Learning & Technology*, *12*(1), 43–63.

Warschauer, M. (2000). The changing global economy and the future of English teaching. *TESOL Quarterly*, *34*(3), 511.

9 Preparing pre-service EFL teachers to design issue-centered English instruction

I-An Chen

Competency-based education and the changing role of EFL teachers

Competency-based education has been widely adopted as a holistic model of education in the recent educational reforms trend (Bristow & Patrick, 2014; Cheng, 2017; Mulder et al., 2011). This trend recognizes that students in the 21st century need to develop a broad set of knowledge, skills, and attitudes to meet the demands of a global world (OECD, 2016). Competency-based education focuses on identifying the key competencies necessary for students to participate in an ever-changing society and offering relevant learning opportunities that foster competence development and workplace readiness (Sturgis & Casey, 2018). A review of the literature reveals a set of characteristics of competency-based education (see Colby, 2017; Cydis, 2014; Sturgis & Casey, 2018). Competency-based curricular activities emphasize real-world connection and discipline integration so that students learn to solve increasingly complex problems in future work. Instructional strategies engage students as active participants and self-directed learners who can scaffold their learning to meet their goals. Assessment is considered to be an integral part of the learning process rather than merely for accountability. At each instructional stage along the way, students receive feedback about their progress toward mastering the competencies.

Educational reforms drawing on competency-based education have changed the role and responsibilities of English as a foreign language (EFL) teachers. EFL teachers are now responsible for teaching in fundamentally new ways that go beyond drilling decontextualized language forms and instructing students to participate in oral dialogues as idealized tourists visiting idealized English-speaking countries (Griffith & Lim, 2014; Kramsch, 2014). EFL instruction must focus on supporting students for meeting the demands of global communities where English is used for various social, academic, professional, and civic purposes (Warschauer, 2000). These demands may involve using English to learn knowledge of different disciplines, solve real-world problems, engage in cross-cultural communication, and carry out tasks in a wide range of situations where English is used to negotiate the goals. As such, EFL teachers are

DOI: 10.4324/9781003212805-10

expected to redefine their role as the "designer" of instruction (Sharif & Cho, 2015), who are able to identify the language demands of tasks that students are likely to encounter in the real world and design a meaningful set of lessons that help students master the competencies necessary for performing their life roles successfully.

However, research has demonstrated that most language educators are not prepared for the changing role of their profession because teacher education programs have not kept step with the shifting landscape of language education (Scarino, 2014). This chapter argues that revitalizing language teacher education requires a competency-based curriculum reform that addresses high standards for performance-based teacher professional development, links theory and practice in an interdisciplinary way, and emphasizes the cultivation of integrated competencies for the complex design work that teachers frequently encounter in the educational settings.

This chapter reports an English language teacher education course that draws on competency-based education as a conceptual framework for curriculum development. That is, competency-based education informs three areas of the curriculum: (1) the content of the curriculum, or what teachers need to know; (2) the pedagogies that are taught in the course, or how teachers should teach; and (3) the ways in which both the content and pedagogies are delivered, or how teachers learn to teach (Johnson, 2009). This report begins by describing the context where this course is offered. Next, it outlines the process of designing the course curriculum, instruction, and assessment projects. Last, it analyzes the impact of this course on pre-service teachers' learning and discusses the implications for future teacher education practice.

The competency-based English language teacher education course

This course, titled *Designing Activities for Teaching English*, was part of a 26-credit EFL teacher endorsement program offered by a teacher education university located in the central region of Taiwan. A total of 44 pre-service teachers enrolled in this course. The majority of them were pursuing an elementary school teacher license and wanted to be able to teach English in a public-school setting. The instructor, also the author of this chapter, is a faculty member in this university, who taught EFL for several years and then received her Ph.D. in Teacher Education and Curriculum Studies. Having taught this course twice, the instructor attempted to revitalize the course curriculum to address the new sets of goals and standards for pre-service teacher education in the context of curriculum reform in Taiwan.

Taiwan's new national K-12 curriculum was developed based on the principles of competency-based education and has been officially implemented since 2019. The curriculum guidelines suggest using core competencies as the basis of curriculum development within and across subject areas. These core competencies, broadly identified as "taking the initiative," "engaging in interaction," and "seeking the common good," are seen as higher-level competencies that enable learners to successfully perform their life roles and meet the challenges of the future (Ministry of Education, 2014, p. 5). Each of the three higher-level competencies involves common constructs shared by all disciplines and the constructs that differ among disciplines to reflect the educational essence of each discipline. The ultimate goals of the new national K-12 curriculum are to cultivate self-directed learners and socially responsible citizens (Ministry of Education, 2014).

To equip pre-service teachers with the knowledge and skills to implement the new national curriculum, this teacher education course drew on competency-based education as an overarching framework for determining the instructional goals, curriculum content, and assessment forms. In addition, the instructor adopted the backward design model (Wiggins & McTighe, 2011) for curriculum mapping and sequencing. In contrast to traditional curriculum design that begins the planning process with a focus on activities, textbooks, or predetermined assignments, the backward design model takes student learning goals as the point of departure and builds a course around the knowledge and skills necessary to achieve the goals (Wiggins & McTighe, 2011). This model emphasizes the teacher's role as a designer of student learning, helping teachers clarify learning goals, devise revealing assessments of learning, and create effective instructional activities. By modeling how to use backward design, the instructor intended to apprentice the pre-service teachers to become the designer of competency-based English instruction.

Curriculum development process

The planning of this course involved three phases. It began with an identification of the desired learning outcomes. These outcomes embodied the enduring understandings and skills that the instructor expected the pre-service teachers to have developed when they complete the course. Next, the instructor designed performance assessment tasks, which emphasized the manner in which the pre-service teachers could demonstrate translation of knowledge into practice. Last, modules, lessons, and learning activities were developed to support the pre-service teachers in achieving the learning goals and success on the assessments. Table 9.1 summarizes the phases of the course development process.

Phase 1 focused on identifying the desired learning outcomes of this course. Table 9.2 lists the enduring understandings and performance-based skills that the pre-service teachers were expected to have developed upon completion of this course. This outcome identification was derived from an investigation of the core competencies that EFL teachers are expected to possess in today's language teaching profession. These core competencies include knowing English as a meaning-making tool and the ability to engage students in learning English while at the same time using English for critical thinking, problem-solving, and cross-culture interaction (Kuhlman & Knezevic, 2013). Moreover, the

Table 9.1 Phases of course curriculum development

Phase 1 *Identify desired outcomes*	*Phase 2* *Determine assessment evidence*	*Phase 3* *Plan instruction*
• Define EFL teaching competencies from the perspective of competency-based education; • Examine standards for teacher education in the context of the new curriculum reform in Taiwan; • Establish course goals that reflect the EFL teacher competencies and the standards.	• Design performance tasks that will demonstrate pre-service teachers' ability to plan, implement, and reflect on competency-based English teaching; • Create task guidelines and assessment rubrics to assist learning and task preparation; • Establish a partnership with local elementary schools to allow opportunities for lesson implementation.	• Form essential questions to provoke inquiry and guide learning; • Plan instructional modules, lessons, and activities that will support pre-service teachers in gaining the knowledge and ability to perform the design work; • Create lecture slides and instructional materials.

instructor examined the national standards for teacher education programs in Taiwan. These standards played an essential role in the development of this course, as they specified what qualified teachers are supposed to know and able to do in the areas of learner development, learning environment, curriculum and planning, instruction and assessment, and responsibilities for professional

Table 9.2 Course desired learning outcomes

Enduring understandings	Upon completion of the course, pre-service teachers will understand: 1 English is not only a medium of communication but also a tool for learning new knowledge; 2 English language teaching is more than developing linguistic knowledge and daily communication skills; it also cultivates cultural responsiveness, information literacy, and civic engagement.
Performance-based skills	Upon completion of the course, pre-service teachers will be able to: 3 design learning experiences that enable students to learn English while simultaneously using English to explore topics that contain important social or global issues; 4 apply principles of competency-based education to develop instructional units that meet the national curriculum standards; 5 collaborate with colleagues to plan and facilitate learning; 6 identify and solve problems regarding curriculum and instruction; 7 identify and plan professional learning needs.

development (Ministry of Education, 2018). This course aimed to meet some of these standards that were most relevant to the nature of the course to prepare the pre-service teachers for their future work. Last, the instructor reviewed the English language standards for elementary students in Taiwan. Content standards significantly influence teachers' work as teachers must constantly design instruction that addresses the standards. It is important to integrate the content standards in teacher education curricula to equip pre-service teachers with the ability to use, analyze, and reflect on those standards.

Phase 2 focuses on determining assessment evidence for knowing if and how the pre-service teachers have achieved the desired learning outcomes. This phase consisted of designing the midterm and the final performance assessment tasks that could demonstrate the pre-service teachers' translation of competency-based pedagogical principles into practice. The midterm performance task required the pre-service teachers to design a 40-minute lesson that included pre-reading, during-reading, and post-reading activities for a picture book that addresses specific issues. The final performance task extended the scope of the midterm, requiring the pre-service teachers to design a unit of instruction aimed at helping EFL students learn English while simultaneously using English to explore important issues. Assignment guides and assessment rubrics were created and made public to the pre-service teachers from the beginning of each project (see Table 9.3). This teaching practice allowed the pre-service teachers to know the desired outcomes of performance and monitor their learning processes. In this sense, the performance tasks served both as opportunities for learning and as evidence of learning.

Both performance tasks required the pre-service teachers to implement their lessons in real elementary classrooms. The purpose of this requirement was to link teacher training curriculum to real-world situations. Pre-service teachers were given opportunities to experience whether their written lesson plans worked in the actual classroom setting and learn to solve problems. Besides, both performance tasks required the pre-service teachers to reflect on their lesson planning and implementation processes (see Table 9.4). The pre-service teachers were guided to practice a reflective cycle that consisted of describing what they have done in a lesson, evaluating their experience of teaching the lesson, and forming new actions for improving their subsequent planning and teaching (Markkanen et al., 2020).

Phase 3 of the course development focused on planning modules and lessons that supported the pre-service teachers in achieving the desired learning outcomes identified in Phase 1 and helped them complete the performance assessment tasks. A total of five modules and sixteen lessons were developed (see Table 9.5). Each lesson lasted two hours and occurred weekly. The modules were built around the competencies that the pre-service teachers were expected to develop. These competencies corresponded to the enduring understanding and performance-based skills. Each lesson addressed specific topics and essential questions. The instructor created these essential questions to stimulate the pre-service teachers' inquiry and guide their learning.

Table 9.3 Performance task guides

Midterm assignment guide	*Final assignment guide*
This project aims to equip you with the ability to design instructional activities that engage students in learning English and exploring important issues through children's literature. You are expected to: 1 Select a picture book that addresses a specific social or global issue (e.g., gender stereotypes, water pollution, waste, cyber addiction, etc.). 2 Design a 40-minute lesson that engages students in reading, discussing, and reflecting on the picture book that your group has selected. Your lesson should include the following three types of activities: a *Pre-reading:* Activate students' prior knowledge and arouse their interest in the topic under discussion. b *During-reading*: Engage students actively with the text for better comprehension and language skills. c *Post-reading*: Provide students with the opportunities to analyze and respond to the issue discussed in the text. 3 Implement your lesson in a classroom, and observe how students interact and participate in learning activities. 4 Take and analyze class observation notes in ways that inform your next design task. 5 Reflect on your lesson planning and implementation.	This project aims to support you in designing a unit of instruction that is based on the spirit of competency-based language teaching and aligned with the national curriculum standards for elementary education. You are expected to: 1 Integrate a real-world issue in English language instruction. 2 Provide an analysis of learners, including their needs, interests, and levels of English proficiency in ways that inform your unit design. 3 Apply the principles of competency-based teaching to plan your unit. These principles, as specified in the national curriculum guidelines, include: a Promoting holistic learning that integrates knowledge, skills, and attitudes b Connecting instructional tasks with real-world situations that students experience c Emphasizing the process and strategies of learning to develop self-directed learners d Providing opportunities for students to apply what they have learned to real-life situations or in a new context 4 Draw on the "Backward Design" approach to plan a unit that links desired outcomes, assessment methods, and learning activities tightly and logically. 5 Implement one lesson from your unit with the same group of students you taught for the midterm, and then reflect on your planning and teaching processes.

The impact of the competency-based curriculum on teacher learning

An analysis of the pre-service teachers' lesson plans, teaching performance, and written reflections reveals a number of achieved learning outcomes and some areas for improvement. First, this course appeared to have developed the

Table 9.4 Guiding questions for teacher reflection

Lesson plan self-reflection and evaluation

1. Preparation for the lesson
   - a Was I well prepared? In what ways?
   - b Did the written lesson plan work, or not? In what ways?
2. Presentation of the lesson
   - a Was I clear in my presentation?
   - b How was the pacing?
   - c Were the students engaged?
3. Strengths and areas for improvement
   - a What went well in this lesson?
   - b What problems did I experience?
   - c What could I have done differently?
   - d What did I learn from this experience that will help me in the future?

Table 9.5 Course curriculum map

Module	*Lesson*	*Topic*	*Essential questions*
Re-thinking English language teaching from the perspective of competency-based education.	1	Trend and issues in today's English language teaching	• How are competencies defined? • What core competencies does Taiwan's new national K-12 curriculum promote? • What competencies in relation to the English language do students of the 21st century need to develop?
	2	Competency-based language teaching	• What characterizes competency-based language teaching? • How does competency-based language teaching change the role of teachers?
Integrating real-world issues into English language Teaching	3	Integrated instruction	• Why has integrating language and issue learning been considered supportive of foreign language development?
	4	Issued-based picture books in English teaching	• How do teachers use picture books to help EFL students learn English and simultaneously use English to explore important issues?
	5	Pre- and during-reading strategies	• What can teachers do to facilitate language and issue learning before and during reading a children's picture book?
	6	Post-reading strategies	• What can teachers do to facilitate language and issue learning after reading a children's picture book?

(*continued*)

Table 9.5 Course curriculum map (*Continued*)

Module	*Lesson*	*Topic*	*Essential questions*
Midterm lesson implementation and reflection	7	Lesson co-planning	• How do co-planning and co-teaching support teachers' professional development?
	8	Implementation and reflection	• How do teachers improve their planning and teaching skills through reflection?
Designing competency-based, standards-aligned English instruction	9	Principles for designing competency-based instruction	• How do teachers translate the principles of competency-based education into instructional design?
	10	Need analysis & Backward design	• What does it mean to design a unit "backward"? • What is the meaning of curriculum standards and how do they guide instructional planning? • How do teachers identify the language demands of the unit?
	11	Identifying desired learning outcomes	• How do teachers define the desired outcomes of both learning English and using English to learn? • What makes an effective learning objective?
	12	Determining Performance tasks	• How do teachers collect evidence for knowing whether students have achieved the desired learning outcomes?
	13, 14	Planning learning activities	• How do teachers design activities that have meaning beyond the school setting and connect to the larger social context where students live?
Final lesson implementation and reflection	15	Lesson co-planning and co-teaching	• How do co-planning and co-teaching support teachers' professional development?
	16	Teaching reflection	• How do teachers improve their planning and teaching skills through reflection?

pre-service teachers' ability to design instruction that integrates English and issue learning through children's literature. Moreover, the pre-service teachers demonstrated the ability to solve and reflect on instructional problems in ways that help them self-direct their professional learning. However, the pre-service teachers experienced difficulties in designing authentic performance tasks that offered students opportunities to apply their learning to real-life situations. The following section discusses the three impacts of the competency-based teacher education course on teacher learning.

Gaining the ability to design issue-centered English instruction

Integrating real-world issues in English instruction was new to most of the pre-service teachers at the beginning of the course. In their written reflections, many pre-service teachers mentioned that this integration, especially through the use of children's picture books, had expanded their perspectives of and approaches to English teaching. For example, Jia-Wen, who was in the third year of her teacher education program, stated that "I used to rely on textbooks. This is a fresh experience for me to design lesson plans based on important issues."

The issue of environmental sustainability received the most attention from the pre-service teachers, followed by the issues regarding gender equality, excessive phone use, and self-esteem. These issues were considered relevant to students' life experiences and therefore were selected for instruction. For example, one group of pre-service teachers designed a unit of instruction on 3R (reduce, recycle, reuse). They chose the book *Joseph Had a Little Overcoat* by Simms Taback as the primary learning material. This book depicts a farmer, who makes an old, worn overcoat into a little jacket and so on until he makes it into a button.

To help learners understand and apply the concepts of 3R, these pre-service teachers designed a series of learning activities that included (a) interactive read-aloud of the picture book, (b) post-reading discussion about what 3R means and how to do them, (c) songs and games for vocabulary word study, and (d) brainstorming of ideas for reusing old things. These activities aimed to help students carry out a performance task that asked them to turn old or broken household items into new products and then make a presentation. This unit was partially implemented with eighteen fourth-grade EFL students. In reflecting on lesson implementation, Yi-Ling, one member of the design group, stated that student engagement was both the most successful part of the lesson and the area for improvement. Since she didn't expect students to be highly motivated to talk about environmental issues, she only allocated a small amount of time for class discussion. She said that she would reduce the time for songs and games in the future and provide more opportunities for students to share their thoughts about real-world issues.

It is noteworthy that many pre-service teachers articulated that they were impressed by students' thoughtfulness and creativity in response to the issues under discussion. For example, in a unit on excessive phone use, Pei-Yun read to a group of sixth-grade students the book *If You Give a Mouse an iPhone* by Ann Droyd, and asked them to role play either parents or children in proposing solutions for reducing phone use. Then, students commented on each other's solutions using the targeted vocabulary words and sentence patterns. Pei-Yun noticed that "students were very creative in problem-solving." She added, "We should give students more time to think and express their thoughts. Teachers should not provide answers right away."

Mei-Hua, who designed a unit on gender equality based on *William's Doll* by Charlotte Zolotow, summarized very well students' capability of using English for issue-based inquiry.

> I think teachers should have more faith in students. At first, my team was worried that 4th grade students might have difficulty answering questions in English or understanding the content of this picture book. However, students could speak more English and understand the content better than we thought. I think as long as teachers are encouraging and know how to guide them, they can do things very well.
>
> (Mei-Hua, written reflection)

Developing reflective problem-solving skills

This course successfully provided the pre-service teachers with the firsthand experience of solving and reflecting on curriculum and instruction problems. The reflective problem-solving experiences enabled the pre-service teachers to identify their own learning needs and take the initiative to improve teaching practices. For example, Yu-Ting, who was in her first year of the teacher education program and had no experience of English teaching, designed a lesson based on the picture book *Around the World Piggy Wiggy* by Christyan and Diane Fox. Yu-Ting intended to arouse third-grade EFL students' interests in different cultures and enhance their cultural appreciation. During lesson implementation, she experienced a gap between lesson plans and actual teaching. She recognized that she "planned too many activities for one lesson." This resulted in her rushing through every activity in her lesson plan and losing interaction with students. This experience made her aware of the issue of time management in lesson planning. Besides, she wanted to learn strategies to "encourage students to speak more English" in class. In planning her subsequent issue-centered instruction, she strategically reduced the number of learning activities in each lesson and designed a few guiding questions for class discussion. Yu-Ting gave her second lesson implementation a positive comment, "It was wise to have fewer focuses in one class instead of trying to teach students a lot. If we teach too much, they cannot learn well."

In addition to time management, planning learning activities suitable for students' English proficiency and cognitive abilities also posed challenges for many pre-service teachers. Jia-Ming and her team, for instance, intended to engage fifth-grade students in discussing solutions for climate change through deliberation, a discussion approach commonly used for policy-making and civic engagement. Deliberative practices involve a set of strategies for expressing an individual's stance toward a topic, justifying arguments with reasons, and reaching an actionable decision on how to move forward. Jia-Ming intended to teach students the idea and strategies of deliberation and develop their civic responsibility. However, while Jia-Ming's students might be cognitively able to participate in deliberation under teacher guidance, their level of English proficiency constrained their engagement in the discussion. As a result, Jia-Ming's first lesson went poorly. To facilitate student participation, Jia-Ming made some changes in her second lesson, which continued using deliberation for tackling environmental issues. Jia-Ming's strategies for improvement included "cutting down the number of questions" to allow time for deeper discussion, using "more gestures and pictures" to facilitate comprehension, giving directions in "easier words," and pre-teaching a set of key phrases and sentence patterns necessary for deliberation. These changes resulted in a class that involved less Chinese-English translation and better student engagement. In reflecting on her two lesson implementation experiences, Jia-Ming reiterated that her major takeaway was learning to design and continuously modify activities that adjust to students' levels of English proficiency.

Korthagen (2001) has advocated a "realistic approach" to teacher education. He argued that teacher education must start from having pre-service teachers experience real-world problems, especially the problems teachers frequently encounter in classrooms. Through trial-and-error, pre-service teachers learn to bridge the gap between theory and practice and develop their conceptual framework of teaching and learning. This course, to some degree, reflects realistic teacher education in that it provided the pre-service teachers with the opportunity to implement and reflect on their lessons in real classroom settings. Many pre-service teachers commented on this aspect of the course in their reflections. For example, Chen-Lin, who was in her first semester of teacher preparation program, remarked:

> I think teaching a lesson in a real classroom is very different from demonstrating a lesson in a teacher education program. In a real classroom, there are many unexpected situations to be dealt with, and we can interact with students to understand their language and thoughts. This experience made me more aware of what I will face in my future teaching career.
>
> (Chen-Lin, written reflection)

Having difficulty designing authentic performance tasks

Despite several achieved competencies the pre-service teachers had demonstrated at the end of the course, they remained unfamiliar with authentic performance tasks. An authentic performance task provides opportunities for learners to apply what they learn to solve real-world problems or carry out projects that have meaning beyond the classroom. A well-designed authentic performance task serves both as a learning activity and as a form of assessment. By contrast, the kinds of performance tasks that most of the pre-service teachers designed for their units were relatively classroom-based and looked more like the practice of language than the application of integrated competencies for problem-solving. The tasks that the pre-service teachers designed were, for example, role-playing a given scenario about gender stereotypes, completing a worksheet about personal strengths and weaknesses, and making a group presentation of how to protect the environment. What students were expected to accomplish in these tasks was mainly to report what they had learned in English.

Only a couple of the pre-service teachers developed the performance tasks that allowed students to construct their knowledge through self-directed inquiry and problem-solving in real-world contexts. For instance, in a fifth-grade environmental education unit, Pei-Chin designed a performance task that asked students to create environmental posters for their communities. Pei-Chin divided this task into several sub-tasks. Students were required to (a) identify the major environmental problems facing their communities, (b) analyze the problems using the 5W techniques (i.e., *what is the problem, why is it important, how do I solve the problems, where can I start, who can help*), (c) create a poster proposing specific problem-solving actions, and (d) persuade a shop owner in a community to put up the poster inside the store. In reflecting on her unit plan, Pei-Chin said that competency-based language teaching significantly differed from the ways she was taught, which focused mainly on discrete linguistic knowledge and usage. While she did not have the chance to implement her entire unit and see how students performed in the tasks, this unit planning experience had helped her "learn how to make English teaching meaningful."

The fact that few pre-service teachers demonstrated an ability to design authentic performance tasks reveals that contextualizing English instruction is challenging for novice teachers. To connect English instruction with real-world issues requires teachers to have subject knowledge related to an issue under discussion and know how English is used to construct and convey the information about the issue. One pre-service teacher articulated this challenge in her end-of-semester reflection.

> Many issues contain information and language that are both difficult for me, let alone the students. So I think the teacher should learn (about an issue) first, take the time to digest it, and then use examples that children can understand. This way, they will be more interested in learning.
>
> (Pei-Chin, written reflection)

Conclusion

The primary benefit of a competency-based approach to teacher education is that it allows pre-service teachers to construct knowledge, skills, and professional dispositions through engaging in problem-solving and reflection in authentic contexts. Pre-service teachers are empowered to become the leader of their learning, who take the initiative to identify their individual learning needs and plan strategies for improvement. Another benefit of this approach is that pre-service teachers are apprenticed to become the instructional designers, who can create relevant and engaging learning experiences that help students use English to tackle real-world problems. In particular, issue-centered children's literature has proven to be valuable resources for novice teachers to begin the design journey, as they convey meaningful information through the use of simple, sometimes repetitive, language structure. This feature enables novice teachers to design activities for focused language learning and thought-provoking discussions.

However, the results of the course implementation have shown that pre-service teachers need more systematic support in learning to design performance assessment tasks that allow students to apply a broad, integrated set of skills in authentic contexts. Teacher education courses need to create more opportunities for pre-service teachers to explore how English can be used as a meaning-making tool to facilitate a wide variety of cognitive activities (e.g., discussion, explanation, synthesis, analysis, evaluation). It also requires teacher education courses to guide pre-service teachers through the process of exploring, practicing, and applying a set of teaching practices for contextualized instruction. Last, giving ongoing feedback is essential to effective teacher learning and helps demonstrate the reciprocal relationship between assessment and instruction.

References

Bristow, S. F., & Patrick, S. (2014). *An international study in competency education: Postcards from abroad.* International Association for K-12 Online Learning.

Cheng, K. (2017). *Advancing 21st century competencies in East Asian education systems.* Asia Society.

Colby, R. L. (2017). *Competency-based education: A new architecture for k-12 schooling.* Harvard Education Press.

Cydis, S. (2014). Fostering competencies in future teachers: A competency-based approach to teacher education. *Creative Education, 5*(13), 1148–1159.

Griffith, W. I., & Lim, H. (2014). Introduction to competency-based language teaching. *MEXTESOL Journal, 38*(2), 1–8.

Johnson, K. (2009). *Second language teacher education: A sociocultural perspective.* Routledge.

Korthagen, F. (2001). Building a realistic teacher education program. In F. Korthagen, J. Kessels, B. Koster, B. Lagerwerf, & T. Wubbels (Eds.), *Linking practice and theory: The pedagogy of realistic education* (pp. 69–87). Lawrence Erlbaum Associates.

Kramsch, C. (2014). Teaching foreign languages in an era of globalization: Introduction. *The Modern Language Journal, 98*(1), 296–311.

Kuhlman, N., & Knezevic, B. (2013). *The TESOL guidelines for developing EFL standards.* TESOL International Association.

Markkanen, P., Välimäki, M., Anttila, M., & Kuuskorpi, M. (2020). A reflective cycle: Understanding challenging situations in a school setting. *Educational Research, 62*(1), 46–62.

Ministry of Education. (2014). *Curriculum guidelines for 12-year basic education.* Ministry of Education.

Ministry of Education. (2018). *Guidelines for ROC's teacher professional competence: Standards for pre-service teacher education curriculum.* Ministry of Education.

Mulder, M., Eppink, H. J., & Akkermans, L. (2011, September). Competence-based education as an innovation in East Africa [Paper presentation]. ECER VETNET Conference 2011 Urban Education, Berlin. https://edepot.wur.nl/193717

OECD (Organization for Economic Co-Operation and Development). (2016). *Global competency for an inclusive world.* OECD.

Scarino, A. (2014). Learning as reciprocal, interpretive meaning-making: A view from collaborative research into the professional learning of teachers of languages. *The Modern Language Journal, 98*(1), 386–401.

Sharif, A., & Cho, S. (2015). 21st-century instructional designers: Bridging the perceptual gaps between identity, practice, impact and professional development. *RUSC. Universities and Knowledge Society Journal, 12*(3), 72–85.

Sturgis, C., & Casey, K. (2018). *Quality principles for competency-based education.* iNACOL.

Warschauer, M. (2000). The changing global economy and the future of English teaching. *Teacher Quarterly, 34*(3), 511–535.

Wiggins, G., & McTighe, J. (2011). *Understanding by design: Guide to creating high-quality units.* Association for Supervision and Curriculum Development ASCD.

References for issue-centered children's literature

Droyd, A. (2014). *If you give a mouse an iPhone.* Penguin Putnam Inc.

Fox, C., & Fox, D. (2002). *Around the world Piggy Wiggy.* Magi Publications.

Taback, S. (1999). *Joseph had a little overcoat.* Penguin Books Australia.

Zolotow, C. (1991). *William's doll.* Harper Collins Publishers.

10 Integrating global competence into elementary school pre-service teacher education of English language in Taiwan

Yilin Chen and Rae Ping Lin

Introduction

To cultivate students to be critical-thinkers, independent and lifelong learners, the Ministry of Education (MOE) in Taiwan has launched an education reform in 2019—the 12-Year Basic Education. Competency is the buzzword in this pedagogical transition. According to National Academy for Educational Research (NAER, 2014) competency refers to "all information, ability, and attitude that a person should possess to equip him or her for daily life and for tackling future challenges" (p. 5). Accordingly, the new curriculum of English language education emphasizes that in addition to developing students' linguistic knowledge of the English language, English education should also aim at establishing students' global competence. This encompasses the knowledge of cultural diversity, critical thinking, and ability to reflect global issues and participate in global sustainable development (NAER, 2018). The new English language curriculum that emphasizes students' competence to respond to current and future global issues resonates with the international framework of cultivating global competence assessment proposed by the Organization for Economic Co-operation and Development (OECD) in 2018. OECD defines global competence as:

> The capacity to examine local, global and intercultural issues, to understand and appreciate the perspectives and the world views of others, to engage in open, appropriate and effective interactions with others from different cultures, and to act for collective well-being and sustainable development.
>
> (OECD, 2018a, p. 7)

Given the growing national and international attention in the realm of global competence education, this paper reviews the current trends of global competence education with a focus on the knowledge domain of global competence for pre-service teachers' training. We then offer a course design to prepare elementary school pre-teachers to develop global-competent English courses within the framework of OECD PISA Global Competence.

DOI: 10.4324/9781003212805-11

Defining global competence

While global competence has only recently become a hot topic in academic circles and policymaking, it is not a new concept but an extension of multiple research traditions, such as intercultural competence (Deardorff, 2006), intercultural communication (Fantini et al., 2001) and global citizenship (UNESCO, 2014). First, intercultural competence focuses on effective and appropriate communication and behavior in cross-cultural settings. Though similar but slightly different, intercultural communication focuses more on an individual's aptitude to communicate in an acceptable and intelligible manner within a specific context across cultures (Fantini et al., 2001). Lastly, global citizenship is defined as the knowledge, skills, values, and attitudes that students need to be able to engage in their own well-being and to contribute to that of others (UNESCO, 2014). Rooted in such multifaceted research traditions and influenced by the rapidly changing world, the definitions of global competence remain open and inconsistent. For example, Reimers (2009), one of the influential educators and scholars of global competence, defines global competence as "the knowledge and skills that help people understand the flat world in which they live, the skills to integrate across disciplinary domains to comprehend global affairs and events and to create possibilities to address them" (p. 183). According to Reimers, global competence encompasses three dimensions necessary to prepare students to engage in this fast-paced, inter-connected world. They are as follows: (1) morality that allows students to be positive and open-minded to cultural differences; (2) skills that prepare students to have efficient communication and critical thinking skills; and (3) cross-disciplinary knowledge that enable students to understand, reflect and face global issues such as health, climate, and economics. On the other hand, Boix Mansilla and Jacoson (2011), the leading educators of Asia Society, define global competence as "the capacity and disposition to understand and act upon issues of global significance" (xiii). They point out three major global issues that students need to know to become globally competent citizens: (1) the changing global economic and demands of work; (2) unprecedented global migration; and (3) climate instability and environmental stewardship. Although somehow different in definitions, these approaches to global competence share a similar core objective: to cultivate students into more agile individuals competent to face and respond to current and future challenges brought on by this fast-shifting society and world.

To respond to the increasing attention to global competence, many countries have integrated global competence into their curriculum development. In the United Kingdom, the Department for International Development has tried to integrate global development issues into the formal curriculum through the Global Partnership Schools program, linking British schools to schools in Africa, Asia, Latin America, and the Caribbean (Sizmur et al., 2011). In the United States, the National Education Association (2010) proposed that global competence is a 21st century imperative and tried to infuse global competence education into their K-12 curriculum. As stated in the *Teacher Guide: K-12*

Global Competence Grade-level Indicators (Partnership for 21st century skills, 2014), "global competence is the fuel students need to develop sensibilities for advancing local and global solutions with concern for all people and generations" (p. 1). Significant indicators mentioned in the teacher guide are to "develop students' understanding of themselves as integral parts of the world community" and to make "students become aware of the world as a dynamic, interconnected system that often requires sophisticated interventions to equitably promote human interests" (p. 1). Despite the great effort to improve global competence education worldwide, experts in the fields of education (Reimers, 2009) argue that more acts are desperately needed to prepare children and adolescents to understand and tackle global issues and challenges.

Building on different models and theories of global competence and the education mentioned above, OECD (2018a) has recently developed a new framework in the Program for International Student Assessment (PISA) that offers comprehensive indicators to assess students' understanding of the world. This empowers them to express their views and encourages them to participate in social changes. PISA defines global competence as:

> Global competence is the capacity to examine local, global and intercultural issues, to understand and appreciate the perspectives and worldviews of others, to engage in open, appropriate and effective interactions with people from different cultures, and to act for collective well-being and sustainable development. (p. 7)

To reach this goal, PISA lists four target dimensions for becoming globally competent students and citizens by successfully applying knowledge, skills, attitudes, and values (OECD, 2018a, pp. 8–12) to daily life:

Dimension 1: The capacity to examine issues and situations of local, global, and cultural significance (e.g., poverty, economic interdependence, migration, inequality, environmental risks, conflicts, cultural differences, and stereotypes).

This dimension refers to students being able to effectively combine disciplinary knowledge about the world and develop critical reasoning whenever they form their own opinions about a global issue. Students are expected to be able to apply higher-order thinking skills, such as selecting and weighing appropriate evidence to ask questions, analyze data and arguments, explain phenomena, and develop a position concerning a local, global or cultural issue (Boix Mansilla and Jackson, 2011). Also, globally competent students are effective users and creators of both traditional and digital media. Therefore, global competence also requires media literacy, the ability to access, analyze and critically evaluate media messages, as well as to create new media content (Buckingham, 2007).

Dimension 2: The capacity to understand and appreciate different perspectives and worldviews.

This dimension highlights the capacity of considering global issues from other people's viewpoints influenced by diverse historical and cultural values as well as different communication styles and behaviors. Recognizing and appreciating another's values or beliefs is not necessarily to accept that position. Instead, it helps see through "another cultural filter" and provides opportunities to question and deepen one's own perspectives, and thus helps students make more mature decisions when it comes to dealing with others (Fennes & Hapgood, 1997). Individuals with this competence are able to bridge differences and create common ground for the global issues at hand.

Dimension 3: The ability to establish positive interactions with people of different national, ethnic, religious, social or cultural backgrounds, or gender.

This dimension requires students to be able to interact with people across different cultures in ways that are open, appropriate and effective. First, open interaction refers to all participants demonstrating sensitivity toward, curiosity about and willingness to engage with others and their perspectives. Appropriate interactions require respect to the cultural norms of all involved parties. As for an effective interaction, all participants are able to make themselves understood and make effort to understand the other (Barrett et al., 2014).

Dimension 4: The capacity and disposition to take constructive action toward sustainable development and collective well-being.

This dimension focuses on young people's active and responsible role in society to respond to a given local, global or intercultural issue or situation. This dimension recognizes that young people have multiple realms of influence ranging from personal and local to digital and global. Competent people are able to create opportunities to take informed, reflective action and have their voices heard. Globally competent people are engaged to improve living conditions in their own communities and also to build a more just, peaceful, inclusive and environmentally sustainable world. Figure 10.1 demonstrates specific knowledge, skills, attitudes, and values built in each dimension and the combination of the four dimensions as global competence.

The framework created by OECD/PISA as a quantitative tool to measure students' global competence is not without critiques (please see Engel et al., 2019 for details). However, its clear and comprehensive indicators indeed provide a helpful guide for educators to design a global-competent sensitive curriculum necessary in this fast-changing society and world to prepare students to better tackle both current and unknown challenges.

More recently, the United Nations (UN) (UNESCO, 2016) view 17 Sustainable Development Goals (SDGs) and global competence education as two sides of the same coin, and has been actively integrated the SDGs into global competence education (Chou et al., 2019). To respond the current and future challenges faced by human beings and the planet, in the 2015 annual meeting, UN proposed 17 SDGs with an aim to create a sustainable global with peace and prosperity for people and the planet by 2030. The 17 SDGs include: (1) no poverty; (2) zero hunger; (3) good health and well-being; (4) quality education; (5) gender equality; (6) clean water and sanitation; (7) affordable and clean energy; (8) decent work and economic growth; (9) industry, innovation

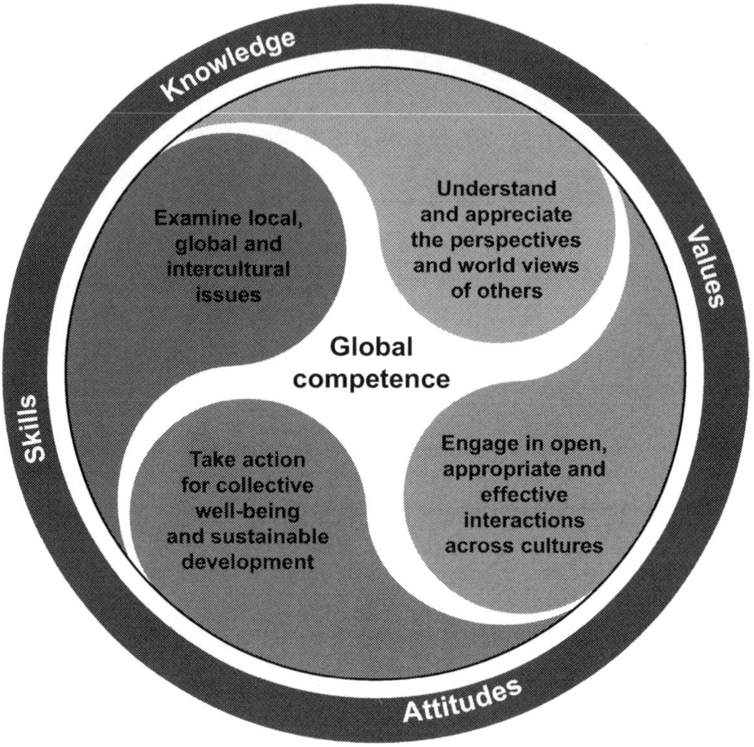

Figure 10.1 PISA: Four dimensions of global competence.

Source: OECD. (2018a). Preparing our youth for an inclusive and sustainable world, p. 11 (http://www.oecd.org/pisa/Handbook-PISA-2018-Global-Competence.pdf).

and infrastructure; (10) reduced inequality; (11) sustainable cities and communities; (12) responsible consumption and production; (13) climate change; (14) life below water; (15) life on land; (16) peace, justice, and strong institutions; and (17) partnership for the goals. These 17 SDGs offer a substantive guideline of *what the global issues and challenges are* for educators to design effective courses to cultivate students into globally competent members of the society when dealing with these global issues mentioned.

As the UN's SDGs were announced in 2015, the OECD positioned itself as an agency responsible for tracking progress on the SDGs. The updated OECD Education 2030 (OECD, 2018b) was particularly dedicated to the UN 2030 Global Goals for Sustainable Development (SDGs), aiming to ensure the sustainability of people, profit, planet and peace, through partnership. Emphasized by the OECD, many countries have integrated the UN's 17 SDGs into their formal education curriculum. It is also important for Taiwan to design a globally-competent and locally-sensitive curriculum in this fast-changing society and world to prepare our students to better tackle both current and unknown challenges.

Global competence education in Taiwan

Seeing that globalization has increased at a rapid pace in society, primary and secondary education urgently needs to jump out of the traditional curriculum framework and cultivate the talent of global competence. To this end, in August 2019, the MOE in Taiwan launched the 12-Year Basic Education Curriculum. A year later in May 2020, a new version of International Education Program, A White Paper on International Education for Primary and Secondary Schools 2.0 (MOE, 2020) was also released. Both of the national education reforms emphasized the importance of cultivating our students into competent citizens aware of local values and global issues, from which they grow global competitiveness and global responsibility (NAER, 2014). Particularly, the UN's 17 SDGs are taken as one of the priority objectives in both national education policies. As clearly stated in 12-Year Basic Education Curriculum (NAER, 2014), the new curriculum should aim at educating our students to be able to seek the common good for all human beings, including actively put SDGs into actions. It is also mentioned in A White Paper on International Education for Primary and Secondary Schools 2.0 (MOE, 2020) that the SDGs determine human being's lives and development. They are crucial concepts for every global citizen to learn, and should be integrated into students' learning and everyday life.

Teacher education and global competence

Teachers are considered to be the most influential agents of global competence education, because they determine both the way and the extent to which global competence is implemented in classrooms. (Yemini et al., 2019). Although global competence and its education has gained much attention in the fields of student learning and policy making, teacher education and the professional development of both pre- and in-service teachers in the realm of global competence remains under-examined (Kerkhoff & Cloud, 2020; Yemini et al., 2019). To have globally competent citizens, teachers should be educated for global competence by providing "students with the skills, knowledge, and attitudes necessary to understand how the world works and preparing them to participate in an interconnected society" (Moss et al., 2012, p. 2). With an aim to fill this scholarly and pedagogical gap, we developed a SDGs-informed curriculum, following the imperative pedagogical goal for global competence, and demonstrated one course design to share how an ocean issue (SDG 14) is incorporated into training for developing pre-service teachers' global competence.

The ocean is selected as our focus in developing the demonstrated training course because Taiwan is surrounded by the ocean and students on the island can easily relate their lives to it. According to OECD, global competence "is the capacity to examine local, global and intercultural issues, to understand and appreciate the perspectives and worldviews of others, to engage in open, appropriate and effective interactions with people from different cultures, and to act for collective well-being and sustainable development" (2018a, p. 7). By paying attention to an easy-to-access local issue like the ocean, students could better understand the values of their own cultures and environment, from which they could develop knowledge and confidence to contribute to the "collective well-being and sustainable development" for all human beings. Through SDGs-informed pre-service teacher training, we hope to cultivate our student teachers into globally competent English teachers, capable not only to develop and design a competence-driven English curriculum just recently launched in Taiwan, but also to guide their future students to establish "a body of knowledge about world regions, cultures, and global issues, and the skills and dispositions to engage responsibly and effectively in a global environment" (Longview Foundation, 2008, p. 7).

Course design

The following course design demonstrates how to guide pre-service teachers to develop a lesson plan for building students' global competence through SDG-informed curriculum. The course design will stimulate pre-service teachers to explore SDG 14 from a local perspective in a global context. In class, they are guided to explore ocean issues in SDG 14, which is concerned with marine environment and resources, such as marine pollution, the marine ecosystem, ocean acidification, sustainable fishing, etc. On the Internet, there are several teaching materials concerning ocean education, e.g., *Ocean Curriculum Catalogue* (World Ocean Observatory, n.d.), *Educational Resources Library* (Canadian Network for Education, n.d.), and *Explorers Planning Guide for Primary School Teachers: Marine Projects Environmental Awareness and Care* (Explorers Education Program, n.d.). These websites provide useful lesson plans for primary school students, and yet, global competence is not included in their learning objectives. Pre-service teachers will be asked to classify which ocean issues are explored in these lesson plans and how the issues are related to SDG 14. By examining these lesson plans, pre-service teachers will be aware of how ocean issues are taught in western countries and eventually lead them to consider what local ocean issues could be integrated into a primary school class in Taiwan.

Second, after pre-service teachers are acquainted with the ocean issues, they will be instructed to examine a lesson plan developed by the Marine Institute in Ireland for primary school students. For instance, a lesson plan called, "Keeping our Beaches Clean from Litter," aims to help students recognize the beach as a place where people can play and suggests ways that the beach could be kept clean and safe. The OECD PISA Global Competence Framework (see Figure 10.1) will then be introduced to the pre-service teachers. The student teachers will be asked to integrate at least one of the four knowledge domains of the OECD PISA global competence into the lesson plan. After they decide which knowledge domain(s) they will explore in their lesson plan, their third task is to examine the learning objectives in the lesson plan of "Keeping our Beaches Clean from Litter" and map out what ocean issues are brought into discussion through the learning activities. The learning objectives and learning activities are listed in Table 10.1.

Table 10.1 Learning objectives and learning activities

Learning objectives	*Learning activities*
The child will be enabled to: Identify local recreational areas.	**Talk and discussion:** Discuss with the class places where we can play in our community. Elicit answers such as green areas, playgrounds and beaches from the pupils. These could be identified on an aerial map of the locality.
Examine pictorial evidence that shows how badly beaches are being polluted.	**Photos and artifacts:** In an effort to generate awareness amongst the pupils, show photographs of seashores and beaches littered with rubbish and animals that are affected by marine litter. • Explain to the pupils the grim fact that people are far more likely to litter at the beach. • Allow the children some individual think time to consider whether this litter hampers our enjoyment at the beach. • Allow the children to come forward with their opinions, e.g., it makes it dangerous to play on the beach as we may cut our fingers on some broken glass. • Discuss how animals at the seashore and in the ocean (such as seagulls, dolphins, and turtles, etc.) get sick when they feast on these unhealthy snacks – such as fast food wrappers and plastic bags left behind by people. Also rubbish from landfills or even from our homes and communities can get caught in the wind and blow out to sea. This can also affect animals in the ocean who get caught up in the rubbish or eat it.
Consider how the litter affects them.	**Active learning/collaborative learning:** Divide children into groups of 3 or 4. In a hat, have a number of beach litter scenarios written on index cards. • A family having a picnic on the beach leaves all the wrappers on the sand. • A little child making a sandcastle leaves a plastic bag in the moat of his castle. • Plastic used to hold cans and bottles is left on the beach by a grown-up. • Someone sunbathing on the beach forgets to take their plastic bottle of suntan lotion with them and leaves it on the beach. • People litter the street and the rubbish washes down the drain into the ocean – which then gets washed up on the seashore. • The rubbish bins near the seashore are all overflowing with rubbish. Each group comes forward and selects an index card. The teacher goes to each group and tells them what their card says. The groups must then divide themselves into the problem and the solution. Some children in the group act out the litter crime and then the others in the group help them see the error of their ways and give them an alternative way of dealing with their waste. These little dramas can be performed in front of the whole class.
Put into action	**Active learning:** An extension activity for this lesson could be a yard clean up with the class to increase awareness about how easily areas that are there to be enjoyed are being destroyed by litter bugs in our community!

The fourth task is to integrate knowledge domains of global competence into the learning objectives. For example, as far as culture and intercultural relations is concerned, the littering problem that happened in Ireland can be seen in Taiwan. By showing pictures of how the beach is badly polluted in Taiwan, students will become aware of the littering problem on the local beach. Furthermore, to show photos of the litter on the beach in Ireland, students will realize that the littering problem is a global issue. The next step is to discuss the impact of this littering problem on marine animals and their ecosystems around the globe. The learning objectives could be also be related to the other three knowledge domains, and it is up to the pre-service teachers to determine which domains they would like to include in their lesson plans.

Facilitated with knowledge, the last task is to have the pre-service teachers to create activities that engage students to connect the local and global issues, establishing students the awareness that littering is happening in every corner of the world so it requires every global citizen to get involved to solve this problem. In the lesson plan of "Keeping our Beaches Clean from Litter" Irish students are asked to identify local recreational areas through an aerial map. Pre-service teachers can work as a team and explore how local beaches are used or abused in Taiwan. From there they are asked to design appropriate activities to have their future students to recognize these local issues. Moreover, in the Irish lesson plan, when students are asked to examine pictorial evidence that shows how badly beaches are being polluted, the activity is to identify what types of litter are found in the photos of beaches in Ireland. Similarly, the pre-service teachers will be asked to develop an activity that relates what happened in Ireland to the local context. For example, after showing them about the pollution in Ireland, the activity could be an outdoor field trip, such as a one-day event of cleaning the beach. By participating in the event to solve a pollution problem, students will hopefully develop a close tie to the local beach and eventually grow responsibility to deal with the ocean pollution locally and globally. Pre-service teachers will then present and share their designed activities with their peers and will receive feedback from both their peers and the course instructor for revising their activities for preparing their future students to become more aware of their own culture and environment, helping them understand differences and similarities in dealing with the global issue among different countries and cultures.

By the end of this teacher training course, pre-service teachers need to complete a lesson plan containing subject, class level, time required, unit, title, contents, learning objectives, learning activities, global competence, SDGs integrated into the class, and assessment. The assessment can be formative to evaluate what students have learned during the class. Table 10.2 is an example of a lesson plan that pre-service teachers need to fulfill in class.

Pre-service teachers may need assistance to design the activities if they do not have background knowledge of teaching methods and strategies, and it may be necessary to introduce how to conduct classroom discussion, pair work, and group work for collaborative learning.

Table 10.2 An example of a lesson design

Subject	*Class level*	*Time*
Science & English	4th grade	50 minutes

Unit Marine Animal **Contents**	**Title** Keeping our Beaches **Clean** from Litter **Science** Litter problem and marine ecosystem **Language** Vocabulary related to marine animals and environment
Global competence Students will become aware of their own culture and environment and their role in sustaining clean and safe ocean, both locally and globally.	**SDGs integrated into class** Marine pollution and marine ecosystem
Learning objectives 1 The aims of the lesson plan are to Identify the beach as a place where people can play in Taiwan and suggest ways that the beach could be kept clean and safe. 2 Recognize how litter affects the habitats of marine animals in Taiwan and across the globe.	**Learning activities** 1 (a) Sorting game Give pictures of trash items and ask students to sort trash into different recycle categories (e.g., plastic, organic, glass, metal or paper). (b) Talk and discussion Discuss with the class places where we can play in our community and identify locations on an aerial map. 2 (a) Matching game Match names with pictures of the marine animals (b) Talk and discussion Discuss with the class how the trash and litter will affect animals at the seashore and in the ocean. (c) Concept check List items that might endanger animals and how they might get sick at the seashore and in the ocean.
Assessment A quiz to check whether students developed a sense of local and global awareness in response to the littering problem at the beach or not.	

Conclusion

This chapter examines definitions of global competence from different perspectives, including the framework of global competence proposed by OECD/PISA. The OECD's assessment of global competence aligns with the SDGs to call students to action for the purpose of social, economic and environmental sustainability. However, due to the conceptual idea of global competence remaining divisive across the world, its assessment has not been universally accepted. Consequently, we propose to customize the education of global competence in response to two newly-launched national education policies in Taiwan: 12-Year Basic Education Curriculum and International Education 2.0. Both policies emphasize the importance of cultivating our students into competent citizens aware of local values and global issues, from which they grow global competitiveness and global responsibility (NAER, 2014). Particularly, the UN's 17 SGDs are taken as one of the priority objectives in the policies. To reach these goals, we created and demonstrated a course for pre-service English teachers of primary schools, aiming at training them into global competent agents. By doing so we hope that they are able to pass on the global competence to their students and provide them with the skills, knowledge, and attitudes necessary to understand and deal with the challenges faced in the local and global contexts. The designed course could guide primary school pre-service teachers to develop a lesson plan with an aim to cultivate their students' awareness of the local and global marine issues. When pre-service teachers are equipped with the knowledge of local, global, and intercultural issues and are aware of differences and conflicts around the world, they would be able to guide students to respect cultural differences and take action for social, economic, and environmental challenges across the globe.

References

Barrett, M., Byram, M., Lázár, I., Mompoint-Gaillard, P., & Philippou, S. (2014). *Developing intercultural competence through education*. Council of Europe Publishing.

Boix Mansilla, V., & Jackson, A. (2011). *Educating for global competence: Preparing our youth to engage the world*. Asia Society. Online. https://asiasociety.org/files/book-globalcompetence.pdf (accessed 25 March 2018).

Buckingham, D. (2007). Digital media literacies: Rethinking media education in the age of the Internet. *Research in Comparative and International Education*, *2*(1), 43–55.

Canadian Network for Education. (n.d.). *Educational Resources Library*. http://oceanliteracy.ca/resources-for-educators/

Chou, P., Wang, Y., & Wu, S. (2019) [周珮儀, 王雅婷, & 吳舒婷, 2019]. 國民中學英語教科書全球素養概念內容分析—以 PISA 2018 全球素養評量認知 測驗內容領域為參照架構. *Journal of Textbook Research*, *12*(1), 1–38.

Deardorff, D. K. (2006). Identification and assessment of intercultural competence as a student outcome of internationalization. *Journal of Studies in International Education*, *10*(3), 241–266.

Engel, L. C., Rutkowski, D., & Thompson, G. (2019). Toward an international measure of global competence? A critical look at the PISA 2018 framework. *Globalisation, Societies and Education*, *17*(2), 117–131.

Explorers Education Program. (n.d.). *Explorers Planning Guide for Primary School Teachers: Marine Projects Environmental Awareness and Care*. https://oar.marine.ie/bitstream/handle/10793/1316/Explorers%20Planning%20Guide%20for%20Primary%20School%20Teachers_Marine%20Projects_Environmental%20Awareness%20and%20Care.pdf?sequence=1&isAllowed=y

Fantini, A. E., Arias-Galicia, F., & Guay, D. (2001). *Globalization and 21st century competencies: Challenges for North American higher education* (Consortium for North

American Higher Education Collaboration 'Understanding the Differences' Working Paper 11). Boulder, CO: Western Interstate Commission for Higher Education.

Fennes, H., & Hapgood, K. (1997). *Intercultural learning in the classroom: Crossing borders.* Cassell.

Kerkhoff, S. N., & Cloud, M. E. (2020). Equipping teachers with globally competent practices: A mixed methods study on integrating global competence and teacher education. *International Journal of Educational Research, 103*, 101629.

Longview Foundation. (2008). *Teacher preparation for the global age: The imperative for change*. Silver Spring, MD: Author.

Moss, D. M., Manise, J., & Soppelsa, B. (2012). *Preparing globally competent teachers.* NAFSA.

MOE (Ministry of Education, Taiwan). (2020). *A White Paper on International Education for Primary and Secondary Schools 2.0.* https://www.edu.tw/News_Content.aspx?n=9E7AC85F1954DDA8&sms=169B8E91BB75571F&s=C56B0FF1E7E21B45

NAER (National Academy for Educational Research 國家教育研究院). (2014). 十二年國民基本教育課程綱要總綱。國家教育研究院.

NAER (National Academy for Educational Research 國家教育研究院). (2018). 十二年國民基本教育課程綱要國民中小學暨普通型高級中等學校語文領域-英語文課程手冊。國家教育研究院.

National Education Association. (2010). *Global competence is a 21st century imperative: A NEA policy brief.* Washington, DC: Author.

OECD. (2018a). *Preparing our youth for an inclusive and sustainable world: The OECD PISA global competence framework.* OECD website: http://www.oecd.org/pisa/Handbook-PISA-2018-Global-Competence.pdf.

OECD. (2018b). *The future of education and skills: Education 2030.* https://www.oecd.org/education/2030/E2030%20Position%20Paper%20(05.04.2018).pdf

Partnership for 21st century skills. (2014). *Teacher guide: K-12 global competence grade-level indicators.* Washington, DC: Author.

Reimers, F. (2009). Educating for global competency. In J. E. Cohen, & M. B. Malin (Eds.), *International perspectives on the goals of universal basic and secondary education* (pp. 183–202). Routledge.

Sizmur, J., Brzyska, B., Cooper, L., Morrison, J., Wilkinson, K., & Kerr, D. (2011). *Global school partnerships programme impact evaluation report.* NFER.

UNESCO. (2016). *Education for people and planet: Creating sustainable futures for all.* http://unesdoc.unesco.org/images/0024/002457/245752e.pdf

UNESCO. (2014). *Global citizenship education: Preparing learners for the challenges of the twenty-first century.* UNESCO.

World Ocean Observatory. (n.d.). *Ocean Curriculum Catalogue.* http://worldoceanobservatory.org/content/ocean-curriculum-catalogue

Yemini, M., Tibbitts, F., & Goren, H. (2019). Trends and caveats: Review of literature on global citizenship education in teacher training. *Teaching and Teacher Education, 77*(1), 77–89.

11 Developing competency-based teacher training through mind mapping for interdisciplinary school-based curricula

Ai Chun Yen and Jeffrey Gamble

Introduction and background

The transition from pre-service teacher training to in-service classroom teaching can be difficult, with novice teachers often experiencing challenges related to hard skills, including subject matter knowledge teaching and assessment, soft skills, such as relationships with colleagues and parents and classroom management, as well as a lack of support and materials (Sali & Kecik, 2018). This resulting "reality shock" is characterized by a shift from teachers' "imagined identity" in the pre-service stage of their career, to a "practiced identity," with an increased emphasis on the structures and guidelines in a professional teaching context (Xu, 2013). Given the amount of linguistic content and pedagogic knowledge required by language teachers, competency-based teacher training, emphasizing mastery learning, apprenticeship learning, meaning-focused instruction, and demonstration of curricular standards, has been suggested by scholars (Egbert & Shahrokini, 2019). As such, the optimal goal of teacher training is to develop not only effective teachers but also "curriculum-developers" or "curriculum-makers," a task that, according to Shawer (2017) requires the acquisition of both hard skills (such as pedagogical, design, and assessment skills) as well as soft skills (which include self-efficacy, strategy use, and motivation).

The urgency of enhancing the competencies of local English as a foreign language (EFL) teachers has been accelerated by the recent "Blueprint for developing Taiwan into a bilingual nation by 2030" (Ministry of Education, 2018a), a policy that challenges in-service and pre-service EFL teachers' competencies in various areas, including teaching English in other subjects, increased emphasis on internationalization, developing individualized learning, and enhancing teaching in rural and remote schools, among others. Thus, the competencies required for contemporary teaching and learning are continuing to evolve and apply increasingly to both teachers and students. As an example, the most recent curriculum reform undertaken by Taiwanese Ministry of Education (2018b) highlights five major competencies for K-12 learners in the English domain: an emphasis on daily-life language skills; promotion of student interest and positive attitudes toward English through interdisciplinary learning; enhanced

DOI: 10.4324/9781003212805-12

self-learning skills and life-long learning; respect for multiculturalism and an international vision; and students' logical thinking, analytical skills, and innovation through use of the English language. The above outcomes fall under the umbrella of competency-based language teaching, in that they emphasize awareness of learners' needs, are communicative and student-centered in nature, and emphasize the application to real-life situations in terms of both tasks and assessments (Boillos, 2018), factors which have often been neglected by traditional approaches to EFL.

Motivation

The purpose of this chapter is to present how a mind mapping approach used in the "Remote Camps TW" project scaffolded pre-service EFL teachers in developing the competencies required for effective teaching and learning and, in particular, those competencies which have been emphasized by current Taiwanese educational reform. The use of mind maps for course design and assessment had its origins in a project sponsored by the Taiwanese Ministry of Education and was intended to support primary and secondary school student's summer English learning with a specific focus on school-based contexts, particularly in terms of the local discourse that spans globalization and localization (glocalization). Given the expectations of EFL teachers highlighted in the above section, this chapter will focus on the promotion of four target competencies: (a) awareness and skillful application of national curricular objectives, (b) integration of school-based curricula, (c) interdisciplinary lesson design, and (d) inter-cultural competence.

Specific procedures utilized for teacher training in the development of mind mapping will be discussed. The goal of this chapter is to provide a replicable model for pre-service teacher volunteer training that emphasizes the co-construction of a mind map for a five-day unit. The examples provided in this chapter are from teams of pre-service teacher volunteers who prepared and implemented five-day Remote Camps TW English summer camps.

Target teacher trainee competencies

The selection of target teacher trainee competencies was largely based on the current K-12 curriculum guidelines of Taiwan's Ministry of Education. In fact, the first competency discussed is the teacher trainee's ability to understand and apply the K-12 curricular objectives, particularly in terms of the core competencies. Competency in terms of school-based curriculum (SBC) development and the design of interdisciplinary lessons was selected due to its growing importance and prominence in the literature and in educational policy in Taiwan. Finally, inter-cultural competence was emphasized in part due to the government's goal of developing Taiwan into a bilingual nation by 2030, and the role of English as a lingua franca or tool for communication across cultures.

Awareness and skillful application of curricular objectives

Along with the five major outcomes emphasized by the 2018 K-12 curricular guidelines published based on years of educational reform in Taiwan, core competencies have been gradually introduced for all subjects. These core competencies are summarized by dimension in Table 11.1. As is evident from the descriptions in the table, these skills (A: Spontaneity, B: Communication and Interaction, and C: Social Participation) are largely "soft skills" which are to be integrated with subject matter content, which focuses more on "hard skills" in order to develop learners into lifelong learners. As such, these core competencies are just as relevant to pre-service and in-service teachers as they are to students in primary, secondary, and post-secondary contexts. According to the guidelines (Ministry of Education, 2014, p. 5), the concept of the core competencies is to "ensure continuity between educational stages, bridging between domains, and integration between subjects," and encompass the "information, ability, and attitude" necessary for both daily life and future success. Research has shown that many novice EFL teachers have failed to successfully adopt curricular standards, but for those who did, greater professional confidence and collaboration with colleagues were evidenced (Yuan, 2017). As such, understanding of these core competencies and their inclusion in the pre-service teacher volunteers' mind maps (application) were the primary goals of the intervention outlined in this chapter.

Integration of school-based curricula

The concept of a SBC was introduced to Taiwan's basic curriculum in 1998, with aims of decentralizing or sharing governance of the curriculum with schools by sharing resources and authority, motivating administrators and teachers, enhancing ownership of curricular decisions and, empowering teachers with professional autonomy (Chen & Chung, 2000). Some evidence has indicated that principals have been largely responsible for encouraging the development of SBC in Taiwan, encouraging holistic programs for student development, opportunities for teacher autonomy, interaction with the community, and promotion of teacher professional development regarding SBC (Pan et al., 2017).

Table 11.1 Core competencies by dimension

Dimension	*Item*
A. Autonomous action	A1. Physical and mental wellness and self-advancement
	A2. Logical thinking and problem-solving
	A3. Planning, execution, innovation, and adaptation
B. Interactive communication	B1. Semiotics and expression
	B2. Information and technology literacy and media literacy
	B3. Artistic appreciation and aesthetic literacy
C. Social participation	C1. Moral praxis and citizenship
	C2. Interpersonal relationships and teamwork
	C3. Cultural and global understanding

Source: Ministry of Education (2014).

However, when language teachers are active in implementing such curricular change, they can serve as "change agents" and attain greater autonomy, innovation, and courage (Yuan, 2017), soft skills which are essential teaching competencies. In fact, recent research from Hong Kong suggests that a shift toward greater teacher autonomy and increased collaboration are critical factors in the integration of SBC reform (Lee et al., 2018). Thus, given the ongoing state of educational reform, pre-service teacher volunteers' future needs, and benefits for collaboration and co-development of SBC, this was included as one competency to be integrated into the mind map design intervention.

Design of interdisciplinary instruction

Interdisciplinary learning is a central emphasis of the 2018 curriculum guidelines in Taiwan (Ministry of Education, 2018b), and is suggested as a contributing factor in developing student engagement and interest in English. In fact, when pre-service teacher volunteers are properly prepared, there is evidence that the time spent in various non-linguistic domains can be used to connect to and enhance literacy activities (Akerson & Flanigan, 2000). Fostering interdisciplinary programs for EFL has even been suggested as a means toward achieving sustainable social and economic development (Syahril, 2019), which fits with policies emphasizing international competitiveness (Ministry of Education, 2018a). Since the integration of other disciplines with authentic content and opportunities for hands-on interaction provides a motivating context for learning, there is potential for EFL learners to improve in terms of language, content, and motivational outcomes when interdisciplinary topics are presented (Chen, 2020). Thus, during this intervention, pre-service teacher volunteers were encouraged to explore different disciplines based on their background and interests, including science, technology, drama, and visual arts.

Development of inter-cultural competence

While the SBC may include elements of the school's local culture or environment (such as famous temples, foods, or historical elements), the factor of inter-cultural competence is more in response to (a) a balance between localization and globalization/internationalization, as well as (b) the respectful and sensitive manner in which a foreign language (and culture) is integrated into the instructional design. In this manner, inter-cultural competence constitutes elements of knowledge (including cultural self-awareness), skills (including perspective-taking), and attitudes (including respect) about one's own culture and other cultures (Deardorff, 2006). As the pre-service volunteers most likely come from similar cultural contexts as their students, opportunities to "teach culture through language" and open up opportunities for dialogue and exploration (Kramsch, 1995) must be created. Thus, culture was a common thread throughout pre-service teacher volunteers' mind maps, including both local and foreign cultures. For related instructional activities, pre-service teacher volunteers took on the role of eliciting intercultural communicative competence (Sercu, 2006), as teachers of both the foreign language and culture, and as models of individuals who are able to position themselves between cultures. In order to provide opportunities for intercultural experiences, pre-service teacher volunteers designed unit plans with the assistance of mind maps to visualize where cultural and linguistic issues could be introduced.

Competency-based mind-maps as scaffolds for pre-service teacher volunteers

Mind mapping, which Buzan (1974) describes as a note taking technique, is a method for eliciting and structuring the information, thoughts, concepts, cognitive schema, and conceptual relations of students for the development of deeper conceptual understanding (Brinkmann, 2003). In the relevant literature, from both educational and neurological fields, mind maps have been associated with benefits such as improved memory and concentration, the ability to more clearly execute problem solving and decision making and, furthermore, empowerment in breaking down barriers to free thinking and discovering a wide range of solutions and ideas (Wycoff, 1991).

Mind maps can serve to more effectively communicate the essence of a curriculum to key stakeholders, and avoid overwhelming them with details. In their systematic literature review of knowledge maps, Balaid et al. (2016) highlighted several benefits that mind maps can provide in terms of the acquisition of both hard skills (including accessing expert knowledge and restructuring knowledge) as well as soft skills (including team-building, identifying knowledge gaps, and identifying existing knowledge resources). The following section will illustrate the fundamental procedures for supporting pre-service teacher volunteers in the development of SBC-based, interdisciplinary curriculum mind maps and the role these mind maps play in scaffolding teachers' competencies.

Mind-map design procedures

This section covers the procedures related to teacher trainee's design of mind maps for interdisciplinary SBC design. The mind maps are based on the overall structure of the camp (hereafter referred to as the GREAT-Cycle framework). In supporting recruited pre-service teacher volunteers, several supports were provided, including face-to-face and online tutoring in the months preceding the camps and microteaching modules during a five-day intensive preparatory camp, in which expert mentors provided feedback on specific aspects of volunteers' curriculum design and also demonstrated how to implement it. Finally, this section discusses the implementation of the designed courses following the mind maps. This will illustrate how the mind maps served as a "road map" for conducting the designed lessons and how the teacher-trainee competencies discussed in the previous section were observed.

Overall model (GREAT)

In order to illustrate the process of mind map design for interdisciplinary, competency-based EFL lesson plan design, a five-stage GREAT-Cycle framework was developed and included the following stages (see Figure 11.1): **G**et to know the school (SBC-based background); **R**esearch and background assessment (developing themes, selecting interdisciplinary topics, and exploring the K-12 curriculum guidelines); **E**valuate language and content (with mentors and during microteaching); **A**ctivity design and refinement (with mentors and during microteaching); **T**each and touch students' hearts (successfully implementing the designed instructional intervention).

Pre-service teacher volunteers and in-service teachers, along with experienced teacher trainers, worked collaboratively in co-constructing knowledge related to interdisciplinary school-based camp curricula following the five-stage GREAT-Cycle framework. Both informal (weekend tutoring and online mentoring) and formal (five-day micro-teaching) strategies were adopted to develop both hard and soft skills related to the design, implementation, and assessment of curricular interventions. These interventions took advantage of the strategies of weekend tutoring and mentoring in designing mind maps with five days of intensive microteaching, feedback, and revisions. Within this process, mind maps served as a scaffold for representing competency-based, school-based, interdisciplinary, and intercultural instructional activities and expected outcomes. Pre-service teacher volunteers were encouraged to become more active and responsible for their own teaching, to begin practicing analysis of the instructional content for all levels of the mind map in detail, and to think more deeply about how core concepts could be represented in SBC learning activities.

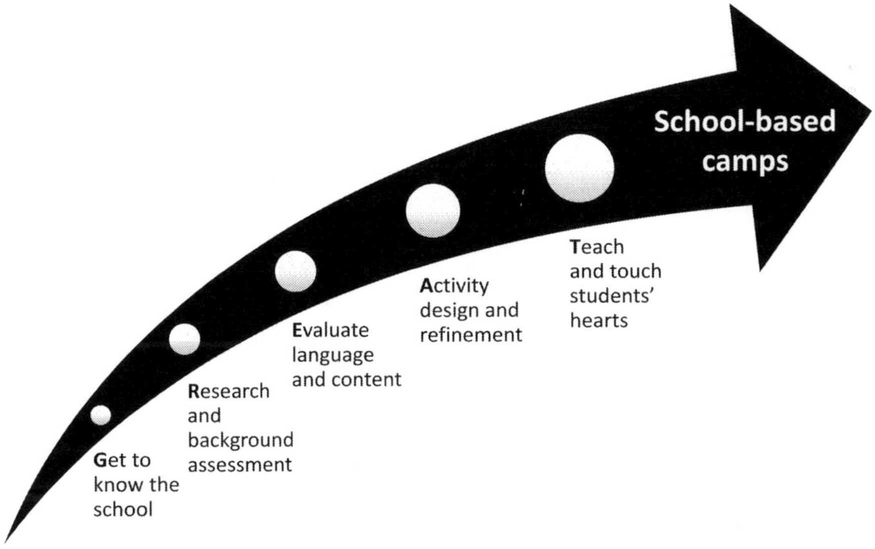

Figure 11.1 Five-stage GREAT-cycle framework.

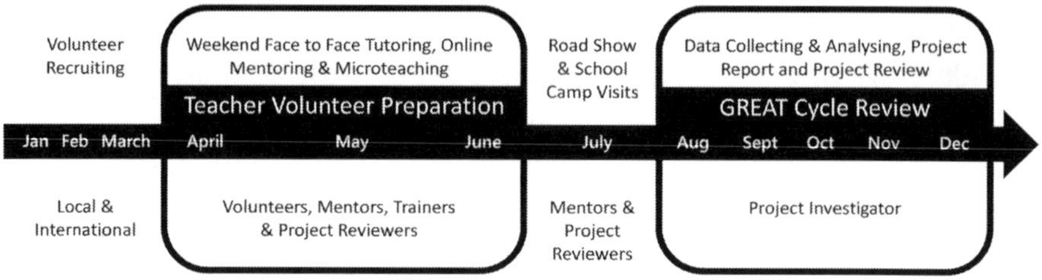

Figure 11.2 Project timeline.

Procedures for supporting pre-service teacher volunteers

After an island-wide volunteer team recruitment, which including team video submissions, potential pre-service teacher volunteers were selected (*N*=135). Selected pre-service teacher volunteer teams were paired with expert Taiwanese in-service English teacher mentors from Y1-12 (*N*=27). Following recruitment, pre-service teacher volunteer preparation was provided (online discussions, regular face-to-face supervision, and a five-day microteaching workshop). Following these preparatory measures, camp visits were conducted with relevant data collected, analyzed, and provided as feedback (see Figure 11.2). Analysis of the teams' observed teaching competencies through camp visits and interviews, and feedback from all participants was utilized in order to ensure the fidelity of implementation (including the development of pre-service teacher competencies) and to evaluate the success of the project overall.

In-person mentorship and online tutoring

Mentoring is a proven approach for achieving mutual learning and development for both mentees and mentors in terms of both hard skills (such as content-area expertise) and soft skills (such as support and collaboration) in the context of language teacher competency development programs (Kissau & King, 2015). From the view of apprenticeship, mentorship is enabled when individuals engage in real-life tasks in authentic contexts through hands-on activities. Mentors initially provide more modeling of tasks before taking on the supportive role of a coach and then "fade" in order to allow mentees to develop independence in their teaching competencies (Hockly, 2000). As camp "curriculum-makers," pre-service teacher volunteers are doing more than developing knowledge and skill-related competencies. Mentorship which empowers pre-service teachers as "curriculum-makers" requires the transformation of identity through which participants adopt the beliefs, perceptions, language, and practice of a professional teacher, a process that is social and experiential in nature (Timoštšuk & Ugaste, 2010).

Since the pre-service teacher volunteers and their mentors are from different schools, weekend in-person tutoring and online discussions were a good fit for mentorship. In addition, to address students' "hard skills" and knowledge needs, such as those related to Taiwan's K-12 core competencies, tutoring was fundamental to the teacher preparation process. Participants adopted a constructivist definition of teaching that emphasizes the role of a teacher's values and beliefs in guiding instructional decisions which, over time, lead to the development of teaching competencies (Pratt, 2002). Later, volunteer teams worked to co-construct preliminary mind maps including elements of the four key competencies described above.

From this constructivist perspective, volunteer teams applied existing knowledge to evaluate and clarify the new content provided by their mentors (Pratt, 2002). As an iterative process either in person or online, relying upon participants' problem-solving skills, the mind maps took form through the mentoring process in the months preceding the five-day microteaching camp.

Microteaching modules

Microteaching involves small groups of participant teachers first planning a short section of a unit, then presenting the content to peers and/or expert teachers, before engaging in reflection on their teaching and required revisions to their teaching content (Karlström & Hamza, 2019). This is a process which takes advantage of connecting theory to practice, providing relevant critique, and offering follow-up support. Subject-matter competencies and self-regulation have both been highlighted as fundamental goals of microteaching programs (Sumantri et al., 2018). Moreover, despite the fact that pre-service teachers' existing mastery of content knowledge is critical in the development of their self-efficacy, a soft skill necessary for the development of "curriculum-makers," effective use of microteaching in a controlled and collaborative environment has been found to further benefit teachers' self-efficacy (d'Alessio, 2018).

In the week before the camps commenced, teams of pre-service teacher volunteers along with their in-service teacher mentors, experienced teacher trainers, and project reviewers met for a five-day-long preparatory camp. Throughout the camp, expert teacher trainers and in-service teacher mentors co-led microteaching sessions focused on various elements of the mind maps and how to improve the lesson plans designed based on their competency-based mind maps. Seven microteaching themes were adopted: "classroom English" and language use during camps; teaching aids and outdoor game design analysis; vocabulary, sentence patterns and grammar for intercultural competence; teaching aid and indoor game design analysis; story/picture book reading related to SBC or glocalization; camp song and cheers; and teaching demonstrations of selected portions of the lesson.

These hands-on activities involved the participation of four different teams, led by expert micro-teaching reviewers. Both expert and peer feedback were provided during the sessions and were uploaded as notes and comments following each session. In addition, both in-service teacher mentors and advising professors spent time after the micro-teaching sessions in order to guide the pre-service volunteers explicitly in the optimization and adaptation of their mind maps to meet students' learning needs, address specific elements of the school-based curricula, and ensure the integration of core competencies. In many cases this involved changes to the types of activities adopted, the level and content of language used, or the timing and sequence of activities. Furthermore, feedback from other groups was reported as very useful to participants, as groups were asked to perform a short segment of their lesson plan during the microteaching sessions in front of both the reviewers and their peers.

Unit design: Course implementation

During the instructional design of camp activities, the mind map served as a "road map" to ensure that the lesson designs covered the four key elements: awareness and skillful application of curricular objectives, integration of school-based curricula, design of interdisciplinary instruction, and development of inter-cultural competence. With the mind map as a guide, students designed a time table and complete lesson plans for each of the sub-topics. As with the example provided above, each lesson plan (generally 40 minutes) included which teacher(s) would lead each part, the relevant section of the mind map (which was highlighted), the core competencies covered (as described above), learning objectives, learning strategies, a schedule for completion of tasks related to preparing the lesson (in the draft version), necessary materials, the instructional procedures (with specific steps and their allocated time), learning performance indicators (from the English domain handbook of the K-12 curricular guidelines), and assessment methods.

At the core of the intervention was an over-arching theme. This topic itself was discussed among stakeholders, including the pre-service teacher volunteers, experienced in-service teacher mentors, and local school-based teachers (N=43). The topics were selected in order to take advantage of both SBC and opportunities for exploring culture and language, while still addressing the national curriculum and offering interdisciplinary instruction.

During consultation with in-service teacher mentors and school-based teacher consultants, the design of the mind map or the content of the lesson plans were revised as needed. In some cases, schools requested additional interdisciplinary topics (including the integration of more technology, such as drones), more school-based curricular content (such as a tour of a local temple), or further emphasis on certain elements of language (such as increased use of songs and chants) or culture (including deeper explanation of foreign mythology). During the camps, in-service teachers or advising professors visited each of the teams and interviewed the campers, the pre-service teacher volunteers, and the administrative team. The results of the visit and subsequent assessment were used to provide valuable feedback to the teams on their teaching. Once the theme was determined, this served as the "central topic." For example, in the mind map shown in Figure 11.3, the central topic is "Inside the Green Corner." This topic was selected due to the abundance of greenery near the school, and the thriving local agricultural-based economy.

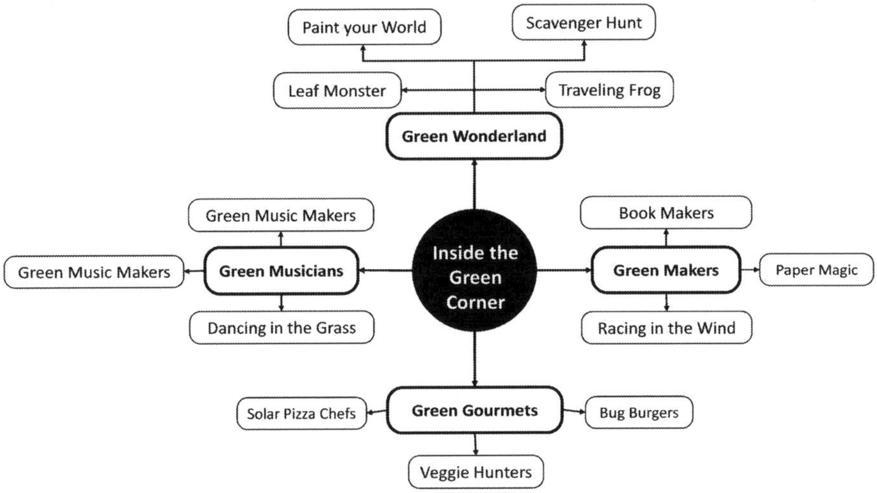

Figure 11.3 Sample mind map (with central theme, main topics, and sub-topics).

Based on the central theme, several "main topics" were selected. These topics could be related to the school's SBC, to cultural elements, to different disciplines, or arranged thematically. Although each group designed their mind map using different criteria, the goal was to organize instructional activities to address each of the four core teaching competencies (curricular objectives, SBC, interdisciplinary teaching, and inter-cultural competence). In the example below, the main topics include "Green Wonderland" (which included most of the SBC content related to the local area), "Green Makers" (which emphasized arts and aesthetics, including the English and art interdisciplinary activities), "Green Gourmet" (which included activities integrating science, environmental protection, and cooking), and "Green Musicians" (which focused on dance and music, utilizing English songs and games from other cultures). As evident from the examples above, the SBC, interdisciplinary instruction, and intercultural activities were integrated throughout the lesson plans.

Under each of the "main topics" were several "sub-topics." Examples of these include "Travelling Frog" under "Green Wonderland." This topic focused on the school's local ecology, which included a pond, integrated reading (using library resources) and a survey of the local habitat (integrating science and math). This activity was labeled by students as including the following Taiwanese K-12 core competencies: A2 (Logical thinking and problem-solving: Conducting a field survey), A3 (Planning, execution, innovation, and adaptation: Use of library resources to plan the ecological trip), B3 (Artistic appreciation and aesthetic literacy: Appreciating the beauty of the pond environment and completing some simple sketches), and C1 (Moral praxis and citizenship: Understanding how to take care and protect the environment of the pond). From the example of the "Travelling Frog" lesson mentioned above, the volunteers ensured coverage of:

(a) the required core competencies (A2, A3, B3, C1), (b) the SBC (by adopting the school's library resources to engage in a discovery unit based on the local ecology), (c) interdisciplinary learning opportunities (science, math, art, music, and dance), and (d) inter-cultural competence development (through introducing English picture books from the library, which were related to Chinese stories the children had already learned, and teaching simple English chants and songs related to the topic).

Analysis of pre-service teacher competencies

While the effectiveness of the mind maps in assisting teacher trainees by scaffolding the design and implementation of interdisciplinary school-based curricula in terms of teacher trainee competencies can be observed in the example provided in the previous section, empirical evaluation of these competencies is required. This section provides the results of teacher trainee self-evaluated competencies, through a pre-test/post-test questionnaire, based on items related to the national K-12 core competencies. Additionally, to support these quantitative findings, the results of school visit reports written by expert observers were also analyzed. They included measures addressing competencies related to (a) instructional preparation and implementation, (b) in-class teaching performance, and (c) inter-personal factors.

Self-review and self-reflection

After obtaining pre-service teachers volunteers' consent for voluntary participation, the volunteers completed a pretest (Cronbach's α=.95), containing 17 items related to Taiwanese K-12 core competencies prior to the 5-day microteaching program. Each question included a Likert-type response, ranging from 1 (strongly disagree) to 4 (strongly agree). The questionnaire also served as a posttest questionnaire to assess the effectiveness of the training, including mentorship and microteaching, and was also utilized to assess how perceptive participants were to the competency-based knowledge and practical skills emphasized by the training. Paired-sample *t*-tests were conducted to compare the pre-service teacher volunteers' confidence in performing core competencies based on Taiwan's national curriculum standards. As such, items were related to the dimensions shown in Table 11.1, which includes Spontaneity (A), Communication and Interaction (B), and Social Participation (C) (see Table 11.2).

Significant differences were found between pre-test and post-test scores for each dimension of teacher competency. In terms of spontaneity, a significant increase was found between the pre-test and post-test, $t(134)=35.26$, $p<.001$ (see Table 11.3). These results suggest that the training process using mind maps truly did have an effect on pre-service teacher volunteers' spontaneity teaching competence. An increase on this dimension is expected due to the nature of the mentorship provided by the in-service teacher mentors gradually developing

Table 11.2 Paired samples statistics for core competencies by dimension

Dimension	*Occasion*	*Mean*	*N*	*Standard deviation*	*Standard error of the mean*
Autonomous action	Pre-test	1.70	135	.50	.04
	Post-test	3.53	135	.39	.03
Interactive communication	Pre-test	1.61	135	.48	.04
	Post-test	3.46	135	.46	.04
Social participation	Pre-test	1.55	135	.55	.05
	Post-test	3.55	135	.41	.04

independence in using the mind maps to design courses (Hockly, 2000), as well as the effectiveness of microteaching in developing self-efficacy (d'Alessio, 2018).

Similar results were found for pre-service teachers' communication and interaction skills competency, with a significant increase from the pre-test to the post-test; $t(134)=-36.19$, $p<.001$ and social participation competency, with significant increases between the pre-test and post-test; $t(134)=35.99$, $p<.001$. These findings can be explained by the mentorship program, emphasizing a social and experiential context for developing "curriculum-maker" competencies (Timoštšuk & Ugaste, 2010). The microteaching training also provided pre-service teacher volunteers with assurance in their teaching abilities through interactive communication and community engagement, as different groups and instructors provided guidance on mind map development and application in a collaborative manner (Karlström & Hamza, 2019).

School visit reports

To further evaluate the fidelity of implementation for the training program, in terms of pre-service teacher competencies, and to provide explicit feedback to volunteer teams based on an observation of their actual teaching, experienced teachers and mentor professors visited each of the schools and evaluated the volunteers as a team. Bearing in mind each team's mind maps and designed lesson plans, the teams were evaluated in terms of the appropriateness and professionalism competencies, including A: instructional preparation and implementation

Table 11.3 Paired samples *T*-test results for core competencies (microteaching)

			95% Confidence interval			
Dimension	*Mean difference*	*Standard deviation*	*Lower*	*Upper*	*t*	*p (2-tailed)*
Autonomous action	−1.83	.60	−1.93	−1.72	−35.26	.00
Interactive communication	−1.85	.60	−1.95	−1.75	−36.20	.00
Social participation	−2.00	.65	−2.11	−1.89	−35.99	.00

(including material, teaching aid, and activity design), B: in-class teaching performance (including use of voice, time management, and effective teaching techniques), and C: inter-personal factors (including student-teacher interactions, team management, and group cohesion). A total of 22 items, adopting a five-point Likert-type scale, ranging from 1 (strongly disagree) to 5 (strongly agree), were used to evaluate pre-service teacher volunteers' teaching competencies. The average overall score for instructional preparation and implementation (six items) was 4.55, while the average score for in-class teaching performance (nine items) was 4.43, and the average score for inter-personal factors (seven items) was 4.49. The effectiveness of the training, as evaluated by teaching observations, demonstrates high levels of teaching competencies for the pre-service teacher volunteers, as average scores indicate levels between agree (four points) and strongly agree (five points). In terms of fidelity of implementation, the items which evaluate adherence to the designed mind maps and accompanying lesson plans (A: instructional preparation competencies) were the highest on average at 4.55. This suggests that the GREAT-Cycle process for supporting pre-service teachers in designing mind maps was effective in meeting the project goals: fostering competency in integration of K-12 core competencies, inclusion of SBC, use of interdisciplinary teaching, and development of intercultural competence.

Findings and discussion

Mind-maps as scaffolds in developing teaching competencies

Significant improvement in the pre-service teacher volunteers' perceived competencies was observed after training. Mind mapping benefitted the volunteer teams by offering structure and flexibility and, moreover, a sense of mutual contribution to the instructional design by graphically displaying the team's collective integration of core teaching and learning competencies. The structure of the mind maps provided teams a process for engaging in mentorship and was critical in effective and fruitful learning. The resulting co-construction of knowledge became evident as the team collaborated in constructing camp mind maps, which were structured and detailed to address the core teaching and learning competencies. Therefore, the curriculum design focus shifted from "teaching to read mind maps" to "reading mind maps to teach."

When needs arose, mentors and advising professors were available to support pre-service teacher volunteers in dealing with school-based contexts and prompting productive teaching strategies that allowed for hands-on knowledge acquisition and a transformation in teacher self-identity to that of a "curriculum-maker." Proper curriculum planning is crucial in achieving pre-service teacher volunteers' strategic goals through their enhanced core competencies. Visualization of the instructional design for the camp in the form of a mind map helped teachers visualize prior knowledge and transform text into a graphical representation while supporting brainstorming and exchange of information for the attainment of curricular objectives (Mitchell et al., 2016). Also, the process of visualizing key concepts, such as the SBC or interdisciplinary modules, using a mind map encouraged pre-service teacher volunteers to share intellectual control with their colleagues, and eventually their students, which is closely associated with their core teaching competencies.

Volunteering as a form of pre-service teacher training

Volunteer projects for pre-service teachers as an alternative or supplement to formal teacher training courses (including mentoring and microteaching for the development of interdisciplinary, competency-based mind maps) provides several advantages: (a) students can work in teams with an in-service teacher who possesses up-to-date teaching experience and strategies; (b) mind maps can guide students in ensuring that the necessary curricular requirements are covered; (c) microteaching provides both expert and peer feedback on modifying both mind maps and the content/details of individual lesson plans in an authentic, yet relatively stress-free, environment; (d) the opportunity to teach students for five days after sufficient preparation allows volunteers to enhance their practical knowledge of classroom and student-interactive dynamics; and (e) expert guidance and assessment provides valuable feedback on teaching performance and identifies individual competencies.

Volunteering for this project required teams to fulfill three conditions in regards to competency-based learning: (1) the instructional design must be represented clearly, and the language and content adopted must be relevant to the target student's prior SBC learning (factors that were critiqued and honed by the microteaching sessions and ultimately assessed for fidelity of implementation through school visits and observations); (2) the teams must seek out relevant prior SBC knowledge for target students; and (3) the teams must understand and express the essence of SBC and intercultural content rather than simply memorize or translate key terms. The aforementioned challenges led to improvements in pre-service volunteer teams' development of both hard skills (including pedagogic knowledge and lesson plan design concepts) and soft skills (such as self-efficacy and autonomy), yielding successful outcomes in terms of the integration and implementation of core competencies, school-based curricula, interdisciplinary learning, and intercultural competence. Throughout this process, the key design concepts informed the use of strategies for developing both the hard and soft skills necessary for "curriculum-makers" to knowledgably and confidently design interdisciplinary school-based curricular units based on Taiwan's K-12 core competencies.

The heuristic value of mind-maps

A related use of mind maps from this project was to evaluate the fidelity of implementation for the instructional designs of the pre-service teacher volunteers. This was accomplished by discussing the SBC objectives with the mentors for the pre-service teacher volunteers before the five-day microteaching. The camp curriculum reviewers conducting the microteaching found that mind maps improved the ability of teams to identify key issues (including the required interdisciplinary content and SBC-based instruction), as well as related student/camper needs (including meeting Taiwan's K-12 core competencies). The format of the mind maps also allowed groups to share and interact with each other more effectively, given the visual nature of the mind maps, and provided constructive criticism while also learning from the strengths and weaknesses of other groups. During the five-day microteaching camp, groups drew their mind-maps on poster paper and used them during microteaching sessions. These posters were also displayed during a sharing period, which allowed teams to self-assess and compare their designs to those of other groups. As such, these mind maps allowed for a "bigger picture" to emerge. From this big picture, the mind maps made the curriculum more transparent and helped the pre-service teacher volunteers identify areas for improvement, such as missing components or links, inaccurate content, or inconsistencies from their tutoring and online mentoring experiences. When the curriculum needed to be revised, the mind maps allowed for more efficient corrections rather than a complete overhaul with the mind map serving as an underlying template supporting ongoing improvements and revisions.

Conclusions

Research context and aims

In line with international trends, Taiwan's current educational reforms have promoted core competencies for teaching and learning, with increased emphasis on autonomy, life-long learning, higher-order thinking skills, and an inter-disciplinary and cross-cultural instruction. In the face of these reforms, academics, practitioners, and policy-makers require empirically-based practices for competency-based teacher training that will successfully guide teachers in the development and implementation of effective curricula. In order to address the need for research-based design in the area of competency-based teacher training, particularly in addressing the need for guidance in the development of interdisciplinary and school-based curricula, this study proposed a mind map intervention, incorporating elements of mentorship, modeling, and microteaching programs. The design of the project described in this chapter was based on relevant literature regarding apprenticeship learning (Egbert & Shahrokini, 2019) and mentoring (Kissau & King, 2015) for promoting teacher's active and collaborative role in implementing SBC (Lee et al., 2018), interdisciplinary learning experiences (Chen, 2020), and promoting inter-cultural communicative competence (Sercu, 2006). Thus, through the design of mind maps (Balaid et al., 2016) under the guidance of mentors and with the assistance of micro-teaching as a support (d'Alessio, 2018), we hypothesized that teachers would effectively enhance their self-perceptions of their own competencies as "curriculum makers" (based on the K-12 national curriculum core competencies) and demonstrate their proficiency in designing curricula adopting school-based, interdisciplinary curricula. The findings empirically support the proposed mind mapping approach in terms of both teachers' perceived competencies and expert observations of teachers' implementation of curricula based upon these mind maps in authentic instructional context.

Summary of key findings and contributions

This chapter advocates the use of interdisciplinary mind maps for developing the soft skills of pre-service teacher volunteers in designing school-based summer camps based on Taiwan's K-12 curricular objectives. This model of teacher training was designed to empower pre-service teacher volunteers' hard skills in developing their teaching quality through an apprenticeship model of mentorship, a series of preparatory microteaching sessions, and feedback from school visits for camps held in remote areas of Taiwan. A thriving, impactful mentoring scheme was achieved through Remote Camps TW's development of a GREAT-cycle model for planning and sustained commitment to guide pre-service teacher volunteers in the development of mind maps. The findings suggest that the use of mind maps by teams of pre-service teachers, and with the support of mentoring, modeling, and microteaching, can successfully scaffold teachers in the development of key teaching competencies and promote their awareness of the integration of national core competencies in their design and implementation of interdisciplinary, school-based curricula. Furthermore, the heuristic value of mind maps as a tool for assessing the fidelity of implementation of the proposed curricula was reported by experts who participated in both the microteaching workshops and the school visits. In addition, the volunteer experience gained by participants in this intervention offered several unique contributions toward their development of teaching competencies, including collaboration opportunities with in-service expert teachers, peer feedback in a relatively stress-free environment, and the ability to practice their competencies in an authentic camp environment with participating student-campers.

Implications

While there are multiple levels of influence on SBC camp curriculum design, including volunteer team factors, mentoring factors, and school-based factors, competency-based teaching and learning factors were fundamental to the design and success of this project. The design of the intervention tailored to meet these competencies also involved team factors that can be traced and managed though a mentoring scheme, microteaching format, and camp visit follow-up built on the basis of care and trust.

Limitations

While the effectiveness of mind maps in developing teachers' competencies (both perceived and observed) has been supported by the findings of this study, there are some limitations worth consideration. First, the sample may not be representative of teacher trainees in other cultural contexts. The mode of mentoring may not be acceptable or feasible in other context. Likewise, the emphasis of this intervention was on the development of pre-service teachers' competencies, while the impact on student learning (from the perspective of campers) was difficult to evaluate, due to the short duration of the five-day camp. As such, longer term interventions or periods of instruction and observation are recommended to validate the findings of this study.

Directions for future research

Similar models, adopting mind maps for the design, implementation, and assessment of language learning, are recommended in order to simultaneously enhance pre-service or in-service teachers' competencies while providing quality instructional designs for EFL interventions that motivate and inspire language learning. Researchers can evaluate the effectiveness of the mind map approach with differing levels of mentorship, based on the participants' level of experience and proficiency. For example, the efficacy of shorter-term mind mapping workshops with in-service teachers using peer grouping can be evaluating as a form of professional development focusing on the development of school-based, interdisciplinary, and cross-cultural curriculum development. Alternative contexts for the observation of teacher competencies following mind map interventions, such as regular classroom environments, rather than volunteer camps, can also provide further insights into the efficacy and generalizability of the proposed model for pre-service and in-service teachers. Additionally, future studies can evaluate students' learning outcomes, including language and subject-based learning outcomes, particularly if long term implementations are developed and integrated into a SBC. We believe the potential of competency-based teacher training adopting mind maps for guiding teachers in the development of effective instructional can be evaluated and the modes of implementation can be expanded by interested practitioners and researchers in future studies.

Acknowledgments

Remote Camps TW project was supported by grants from Taiwan's Ministry of Education from 2014 to 2018 and was conducted in collaboration with numerous pre-service teacher volunteers, in-service teachers and university trainers.

References

Akerson, V. L., & Flanigan, J. (2000). Preparing pre-service teachers to use an interdisciplinary approach to science and language arts instruction. *Journal of Science Teacher Education*, *11*(4), 345–362.

Balaid, A., Rozan, M. Z. A., Hikmi, S. N., & Memon, J. (2016). Knowledge maps: A systematic literature review and directions for future research. *International Journal of Information Management*, *36*(3), 451–475.

Boillos, M. M. (2018). Competency-based language teaching. *The TESOL Encyclopedia of English Language Teaching*. https://doi.org/10.1002/9781118784235.eelt0158

Brinkmann, A. (2003). Graphical knowledge display – mind mapping and concept mapping as efficient tools in mathematics education. *Mathematics Education Review*, *16*, 35–48.

Buzan, T. (1974). *Use your head*. BBC Books.

Chen, C. H. (2020). AR videos as scaffolding to foster students' learning achievements and motivation in EFL learning. *British Journal of Educational Technology*, *51*(3), 657–672.

Chen, H. L. S., & Chung, J. (2000). The implementation of school-based curriculum development. *School Improvement in Taiwan: Problems and Possibilities*. (ED443159). ERIC. https://files.eric.ed.gov/fulltext/ED443159.pdf

d'Alessio, M. A. (2018). The effect of microteaching on science teaching self-efficacy beliefs in pre-service elementary teachers. *Journal of Science Teacher Education*, *29*(6), 441–467.

Deardorff, D. K. (2006). Identification and assessment of intercultural competence as a student outcome of internationalization. *Journal of Studies in International Education*, *10*(3), 241–266.

Egbert, J. L., & Shahrokini, S. A. (2019). Balancing old and new: Integrating competency-based learning into CALL teacher education. *JALT CALL Journal*, *15*(1), 3–18.

Hockly, N. (2000). Modelling and 'cognitive apprenticeship' in teacher education. *ELT Journal*, *54*(2), 118–125.

Karlström, M., & Hamza, K. (2019). Pre-service science teachers' opportunities for learning through reflection when planning a microteaching unit. *Journal of Science Teacher Education*, *30*(1), 44–62.

Kissau, S. P., & King, E. T. (2015). Peer Mentoring second language teachers: A mutually beneficial experience? *Foreign Language Annals*, *48*(1), 143–160.

Kramsch, C. (1995). The cultural component of language teaching. *Language, Culture and Curriculum*, *8*(2), 83–92.

Lee, T., Cheng, Y. C., & Ko, J. (2018). Curriculum reform with a school-based approach: Intellectual, structural and cultural challenges. *School Leadership & Management*, *38*(3), 278–301.

Ministry of Education. (2014). *Curriculum guidelines of 12-year basic education: General guidelines*. https://www.naer.edu.tw/ezfiles/0/1000/img/52/129488083.pdf

Ministry of Education. (2018a). *Implement in full scale bilingualization of Taiwan's educational system; cultivate bilingual talents to bring Taiwan to the world*. https://english.moe.gov.tw/cp-13-17790-80201-1.html

Ministry of Education. (2018b).十二年國民基本教育課程綱要(國民中小學暨普通型高級中等學校)語文領域-英語文. https://www.naer.edu.tw/ezfiles/0/1000/img/67/122453112.pdf

Mitchell, I., Keast, S., Panizzon, D., & Mitchell, J. (2016). Using 'big ideas' to enhance teaching and student learning. *Teachers and Teaching*, 1–15. https://doi.org/10.1080/13540602.2016.1218328.

Pan, H.-L. W., Nyeu, F.-Y., & Cheng, S.-H. (2017). Leading school for learning: Principal practices in Taiwan. *Journal of Educational Administration*, *55*(2), 168–185. https://doi.org/10.1108/JEA-06-2016-0069

Pratt, D. D. (2002). Good teaching: One size fits all? *New Directions for Adult and Continuing Education*, *2002*(93), 5–16.

Sali, P., & Kecik, I. (2018). Challenges of first years of teaching in Turkey: Voices of novice EFL teachers. *English Language Teaching*, *11*(4), 117–131.

Sercu, L. (2006). The foreign language and intercultural competence teacher: The acquisition of a new professional identity. *Intercultural Education*, *17*(1), 55–72.

Shawer, S. F. (2017). Teacher-driven curriculum development at the classroom level: Implications for curriculum, pedagogy and teacher training. *Teaching and Teacher Education*, *63*, 296–313.

Sumantri, M. S., Prayuningtyas, A. W., Rachmadtullah, R., & Magdalena, I. (2018). The roles of teacher-training programs and student teachers' self-regulation in developing competence in teaching science. *Advanced Science Letters*, *24*(10), 7077–7081.

Syahril, I. (2019). The new generation of high quality ESL/EFL teachers: A proposal for interdisciplinary teacher education. *Journal on Language and Language Teaching*, *22*(1), 33–45.

Timoštšuk, I., & Ugaste, A. (2010). Student teachers' professional identity. *Teaching and Teacher Education*, *26*(8), 1563–1570.

Wycoff, J. (1991). *Mindmapping: Your personal guide to exploring creativity and problem solving*. Berkly Books.

Xu, H. (2013). From the imagined to the practiced: A case study on novice EFL 'teachers' professional identity change in China. *Teaching and Teacher Education*, *31*, 79–86.

Yuan, R. (2017). Appropriating national curriculum standards in classroom teaching: Experiences of novice language teachers in China. *International Journal of Educational Research*, *83*, 55–64.

12 The use of telecollaboration for the development of intercultural competences in CLIL teacher education

Paloma Castro-Prieto

Introduction

Foreign language education plays a key role in most of education policies worldwide. In Europe, the Council of Europe (CoE) has been promoting language learning in the field of education since 1954. In its language education policy, which has been developed ever since, the purpose of the developed actions was to promote language learning and to secure and strengthen human rights, deepen mutual understanding, consolidate democratic citizenship, and contribute to social cohesion. Fleming (2010) in a document prepared for the CoE, acknowledges an integrated approach to language teaching and learning that reinforces the links between language and general aims such as education for active, responsible participatory citizenship and personal growth. From his perspective, "language is seen not only as a tool for communication but as a key focus for the development of thinking, identity and personal growth" (Fleming, 2010, p. 4).

Foreign language education embodies an educational dimension that recognizes the development of intercultural competences (Byram, 1997). Within the field of foreign language learning, intercultural competence is defined as "the ability of a person to behave adequately in a flexible manner when confronted with action, attitudes and expectations of representatives of foreign cultures" (Meyer, 1991, p. 137). This definition adds to the notion of communicative competence a capacity to "stabilize one's self-identity in the process of cross-cultural mediation, and of helping other people to stabilise their self-identity" (Meyer, 1991, p. 137). As Byram (1997) has stated, the success of interaction implies not only an effective interchange of information, as was the goal of communicative language teaching, but also the "ability to decentre and take up the other's perspective on their own culture, anticipating, and where possible, resolving dysfunctions in communication and behaviour" (p. 42).

This change in focus in the conceptualization of foreign language education entails a reconceptualization of teacher education and the development of competences for educating in foreign languages. This chapter presents best practices on how to develop pre-service teachers' content and language integrated learning (CLIL) pedagogical competences by using intercultural telecollaboration

DOI: 10.4324/9781003212805-13

in initial teacher education programs. It describes a 10-week project in which pre-service teachers in two courses at the University of Valladolid (Spain) and at Leuven University (The Netherlands) participate in an intercultural telecollaboration project aiming at upgrading the methodological competences that teachers need for integrating language and content when using the approach of CLIL in primary and secondary education. The course, CLIL Methodology, at the University of Valladolid is at the undergraduate level for pre-service teachers of English as a foreign language, and at Leuven University it is at the graduate level for pre-service subject teachers (geography, math, history, etc.). Through the experience, student teachers gain first-hand experiential knowledge of collaborative work by merging language and content and by planning and designing together CLIL resources that embed the core features of CLIL. As the exchange takes place in English for interacting with their international partners, they also gain intercultural communicative competence, which is at the core of a teacher's CLIL interculturality competence. This chapter concludes with a discussion on the potential of an intercultural teaching and learning online environment for the development of teachers' CLIL competences.

Understanding CLIL

The term CLIL was adopted as curriculum innovation in many European countries in the mid-1990s, mostly in connection with English and is "regarded by some of its practitioners as the ultimate communicative methodology" (Graddol, 2006, p. 86). Since then, the CoE and the European Commission have supported CLIL because it responded to a need in Europe for promoting the learning of other languages which are not native. Although it was originated in Europe, it has rapidly spread to the United States, Asian countries, and Latin America (Garay, 2007). CLIL describes an innovative methodological approach to teaching and learning where subjects such as science, history and/or geography are taught and studied through the use of a non-native language with dual-focused aims, that is, the learning of content and the simultaneous learning of a foreign language (Marsh, 1994; Maljers et al., 2010).

There are a variety of definitions of CLIL, but Coyle et al. (2010, p. 1) refer to it as a "dual-focused educational approach in which an additional language is used for the learning and teaching of both content and language." Although CLIL seems to be a content-driven program where content is taught through a foreign language, Mehisto et al. (2008) insist on the idea that the innovation of CLIL resides in the development of content through a second language integrated within the curricular content of a certain subject. Furthermore, Wolff (2012) considers that CLIL is seen as a change agent that has the potential to innovate our schools and bring about real change into language education and education in general. From this innovative perspective, it not only promotes linguistic competences but also stimulates cognition, which broadens and deepens learners' understanding of subject concepts, their thinking skills, and their creativity. Adopting a constructivist educational perspective, CLIL involves learners as active participants through a process of inquiry and by using complex cognitive processes and means for problem solving. Therefore, CLIL is an approach which is content and not language oriented, meaning that "language learning takes place when learners are involved in the content they are dealing with" (Wolff, 2012, p. 108). Indeed, the conceptualization of CLIL makes explicit the educational perspective as a pedagogical tool (Coyle, 2002) or an innovative methodological approach (Eurydice, 2006).

With the purpose of conceptualizing CLIL and providing teachers with a pedagogical tool for defining teaching aims and learning outcomes in a CLIL classroom, Coyle (2005) developed the 4Cs framework which integrates four connected key building blocks: Content, Communication, Cognition, and Culture.

- Content: the curricular subjects taught in CLIL.
- Communication: the use of language for learning content and for meaningful interaction in the classroom.
- Cognition: the cognitive skills promoted by learning subjects in a non-native language, such as reasoning, creative thinking, and evaluating, as well as thinking processes to meet language demands to express thoughts and ideas.
- Culture: the understanding of oneself and others in a context of diversity.

The integrative nature of CLIL teaching provides an opportunity to simultaneously combine foreign language learning and content subject learning from a student-centered, task-oriented, authentic, and constructivist perspective. According to Coyle (2009) the role of culture in CLIL is a challenging one but fundamental "if we are to achieve intercultural learning and understanding" (p. 105). The cultural dimension is in connection with the formation of the cultural identity of the learner, that is, the process of growing into a culture through the adoption of multiple perspectives. Learning subject content through a language that it is not the native language helps learners to adopt a new perspective from the lenses of a different language. As language and culture are embedded, learners face the existence of a multiplicity of cultures, focusing "on the spaces in-between, that is, on their dialogical interaction, on the elastic nature of cultural identities and on the dynamics of the inter-cultural encounters" (Guilherme, 2004, p. 125). In the context of CLIL, an interactive and dialogic learning is therefore key for learners.

> Intercultural understanding involves competence-building and intercultural learning. It involves the development of attitudes such as curiosity and openness and the capacity to relativise values and beliefs. It is not restricted to the language classroom and is fundamental to realising CLIL.
>
> (Coyle, 2009, p. 109)

The intercultural dimension is central in CLIL although it needs explicit attention (Coyle, 2009). The potential of CLIL with regard to the development of intercultural competences draws our attention in this chapter.

Teachers' competences for implementing CLIL

Research on CLIL has predominantly focused on the language proficiency of learners, bringing to the forefront that receptive language skills, reading, and listening are improved through CLIL programs (Coyle, 2013, 2018; Lasagabaster & Ruiz de Zarobe, 2010). However, there is not yet much CLIL research on pedagogical issues that may offer guidance or pedagogical tools for teachers. Recent studies indicate that many CLIL teachers adopt a traditional and transmission approach (Viebrock, 2010) with a lack of focus on autonomous learning and cognitive skills.

Other research studies show that one of the main challenges that teachers face for implementing CLIL is the integration of the content and the foreign language, as a dual-focused approach, and the integrated assessment of language and content (Cenoz et al., 2014; Coetzee-Lachmann, 2007). The conception of CLIL as education *through* an additional language offers language teachers the opportunity to regenerate their profession (Coyle et al., 2010) and collaborate more with subject teachers. For Dale and Tanner (2012, pp. 14–15)

> CLIL subject teachers need to have a clear understanding of how their subject uses language (…). They also need to learn how to activate their learners' existing knowledge about the topics they are teaching, to provide appropriate, multimodal input and to guide learners to actively understand and process input. Moreover, they need to encourage learners to interact in their classrooms, to use activities which encourage them to think and speak and write. CLIL teachers also need to know how to assess their learners' progress, in both content and language, and give them feedback which will help them to develop both areas.

In this regard, teacher training is viewed as essential for a successful CLIL implementation (Coyle, 2011), which requires a critical reconceptualization of the role teachers play in a CLIL classroom. In the Eurydice report (Eurydice, 2006, p. 46) the "training possibilities are in general fairly limited" and even teachers themselves complain on the lack of training programs to develop the skills needed to provide CLIL. Hui (1997) believes that the pre-service and in-service classes are the most efficient resources through which teachers can gain professional abilities and increase their academic awareness.

With the purpose of guiding the professional development of CLIL teachers, the European Centre for Modern Languages of the CoE published *the European Framework for CLIL Teacher Education* (Marsh et al., 2010). This framework was designed as a conceptual tool and aims to "provide a set of principles and ideas for designing CLIL professional development curricula. Additionally, the Framework seeks to serve as a tool for reflection" (Marsh et al., 2010, p. 3). It identifies the target professional competences for CLIL teachers, it includes the competences necessary to teach content subjects and an additional language in an integrated manner, and it proposes professional development modules to help teachers attain the target professional competences. The overall structure of the framework is determined by two main components: (1) the target professional competences, which the CLIL teacher is expected to acquire or further develop during a training program, and (2) the professional development modules.

The target professional competences are the competences that the CLIL teacher is expected to acquire or further develop during the training program. They comprise:

- Personal reflection: commitment to one's own cognitive, social, and affective development to support the cognitive, social and affective development of students. It is related to the teachers' own professional development as for example, being able to explore their own understanding of content and language learning or being able to define their own pedagogical and content competences.
- CLIL fundamentals: understanding of the core features of CLIL and how these features link with best practices in education, being able to articulate and discuss CLIL with stakeholders and to describe strategies for integrating CLIL.
- Content and language awareness: being able to identify the appropriate content to be taught, to view content through different perspectives, to use strategies to support language learning in content classes, to promote learner awareness of language and the language learning process, to scaffold language learning during content classes, etc.
- Methodology and assessment: being able to support learners in building their capacity, for example to self-motivate, self-assess, etc.; being able to co-operate with other colleagues, being able to use strategies for the co-construction of knowledge to support continuous language growth, s upport students in managing the affective side of learning, or create authentic and meaningful learning environments.
- Research and innovation: competences to conduct action research in collaboration with colleagues, to critically analyze research on CLIL, or to describe strategies and instruments for self, peer and student evaluation of their teaching practices.
- Learning resources and environments: creating criteria for developing CLIL resources that embed the core features of CLIL, or to articulate techniques for developing cooperative networks to help learners build cross-curricular links.
- Classroom management: facilitating the integrated learning of content, language and learning skills. It requires specific knowledge about classroom dynamics and management techniques for learning in CLIL.
- CLIL management: focused on administrative issues of CLIL implementation, calling on stakeholders to build common knowledge about program management and their role in supporting its development.

Another framework is *The CLIL Teacher's Competences Grid* (Bertaux et al., 2010) which is also developed as a tool for teacher education programs. The framework is divided into two sections: (1) underpinning CLIL and (2) setting CLIL in motion. Each area of competence is further divided into competences which are described as can-do statements and are named *indicators of competence.* Under the section "Setting CLIL in Motion," the grid offers the competences which are important to CLIL implementation:

- Integration: merging content, language and learning skills into an integrated approach.
- Implementation: lesson planning, translating plans into action, fostering outcome attainment.
- Second Language Acquisition (SLA): knowing second language attainment levels, applying SLA knowledge in lesson preparation, applying SLA knowledge in the classroom.
- Interculturality: promoting cultural awareness and interculturality.
- Learning environment management: taking into account the affective side of learning, making the CLIL learning process efficient.
- Learner focus in the CLIL environment: applying interactive methodology.
- Learning skills focus in CLIL: having knowledge and awareness of cognition and metacognition in the CLIL environment.
- Learning assessment and evaluation in CLIL: knowledge about and applying assessment and evaluation procedures and tools.
- Lifelong learning and innovative teaching and learning approaches: keeping up with new developments, using ICT as a teaching resource.

Even though the intercultural dimension is not given a central priority when identifying CLIL teachers' competences, there is evidence of the advantage of using CLIL as a pedagogical approach to enhance learners' intercultural competence and understanding for successful intercultural interaction and communication.

Intercultural telecollaboration as a tool in teacher education

In addition to the challenge in the development of CLIL teachers' competences in the context of teacher education, the emergence of communication technologies has allowed digitally mediated learning configurations where students have the means to work together and cooperate with partners from other countries with different cultural and linguistic backgrounds. Research has revealed increases in online intercultural exchange (Belz & Müller-Hartmann, 2003; Belz & Thorne, 2006; Kern et al., 2004) focusing on such areas as the development of intercultural competences (Müller-Hartmann, 2006; O'Dowd, 2003, 2006) or CLIL (O'Dowd, 2018)

One specific kind of online exchange is called telecollaboration, which has evolved as a methodological tool in education the last few years. It has been defined as an "internet-based intercultural exchange between people of different cultural/national backgrounds set up in an institutional context with the aim of developing both language skills and intercultural communicative competence (as defined by Byram, 1997) through structured tasks" (Guth & Helm, 2010, p. 14). Online telecollaboration opens up pathways for teachers to address the cultural and intercultural dimensions of language education (Kramsch, 2009; Liddicoat & Scarino, 2013; O'Dowd, 2007) through the multifaceted dimensions of a telecollaboration practice (Castro & Derivry-Plard, 2016).

This chapter focuses the attention on intercultural telecollaboration as a tool for developing CLIL competences in the context of initial teacher education. Our argument is that intercultural telecollaboration has the potential to engage trainee teachers in a range of intercultural tasks that contribute to the development of professional competences for the CLIL teacher, mainly focused on the intercultural dimension.

In the light of this argument, an intercultural telecollaboration project was set up between the University of Valladolid (Spain) and the University of Leiden (The Netherlands) offering trainee teachers the opportunity to participate in an online exchange in order to experience the tools and processes they will be expected to use in their own teaching in the future. Two classrooms from the mentioned universities were involved having as a common ground the content of the course, which was based on CLIL methodology, in the context of primary teacher education (Spain) and secondary teacher education (The Netherlands).

Telecollaboration provides trainee teachers with a first-hand experience of collaboration with people of different cultural backgrounds. By working together collaboratively through the tasks that the teacher educators designed in the course, the trainee teachers have the chance to reflect more critically on their own cultural perspectives and to be more sensitive to their partners' beliefs and values.

In the next section, we provide a comprehensive description of this intercultural telecollaboration project with a specific focus on the CLIL competence of *Interculturality* (promoting cultural awareness and interculturality), according to the CLIL Teacher's Competences Grid (Bertaux et al., 2010).

The use of intercultural telecollaboration as a tool for developing CLIL pedagogical competences in the context of initial teacher education

Description of the project

During 10 weeks and integrated in a regular course on CLIL methodology[1] for pre-service teachers (primary & secondary education), 35 students in the faculty of education at the University of Valladolid (Spain) and 20 students from Leuven University (The Netherlands) participated in an intercultural telecollaboration virtual exchange organized under the framework of the European project,

Evaluating and Upscaling Telecollaborative Teacher Education (EVALUATE), funded by Erasmus+ Key Action 3 during the academic year 2017–2018.

The approach adopted in the course was based on intercultural telecollaboration. It consisted of bringing together trainee teachers from the field of language (language teachers) and the field of content areas (subject teachers) and teacher trainers from both universities, all working collaboratively in a joint project using a Moodle platform. During 10 consecutive weeks, trainees from the two university classes worked collaboratively online using asynchronous communication to discuss and make agreements on issues related to planning and designing resources and materials for a CLIL classroom, based on their understanding on CLIL methodology principles.

From the teacher educators' perspective, the design and implementation of the course required a joint decision-making process which consisted of designing the aim, content, tasks, and assessment procedures for the course. It required flexibility to make adaptations to their own regular study plans. During the implementation of the course the teacher educators took the role of mediators with their own students when facing conflicting situations that appeared during the process of the collaborative work. They also helped their students in their reflections on the experience.

Aims of the joint course

Based on the 4Cs Framework to CLIL (Coyle, 2005), the aims of the joint course on CLIL methodology were:

- Communication: to use the foreign language to learn about CLIL by negotiating meaning in an international context.
- Content: to develop knowledge, skills, and competences relevant to CLIL approaches.
- Cognition: to foster one's own understanding of CLIL through engagement in a joint decision-making process using inquiry and discussion to design a task sequence for a telecollaborative exchange.
- Culture: to develop intercultural awareness by exploring different cultural perspectives and identities as CLIL teachers and consequently acquire a critical stance.

Tasks

The tasks for the course were designed considering on the one hand the regular contents from the university course, CLIL Methodology, and, on the other hand, the telecollaboration tasks provided by the EVALUATE Project which involved "three interrelated tasks which move from information exchange to comparing and analyzing cultural practices and finally to working on a collaborative product" (O'Dowd, 2017, p. 40). Accordingly, the designed and implemented tasks were:

- Task 1. Information exchange: getting to know each other and sharing background knowledge on CLIL (Weeks 1 and 2)
    - Trainees design a short multimodal presentation about themselves.
- Task 2. CLIL Policy: comparing and analyzing CLIL practices in local contexts (Weeks 3, 4, and 5)
    - Trainees work collaboratively to analyze an intercultural task which was designed for a CLIL classroom and suggest ways to improve it.
    - Trainees jointly design a task for a CLIL classroom based on CLIL criteria, using the CLIL Matrix (https://archive.ecml.at/mtp2/CLILmatrix/EN/qMain.html).
    - Trainees evaluate other group's task on CLIL and give feedback to the group.
- Task 3. Course development: joint decision-making on CLIL (Weeks 6, 7, and 8)
    - Trainees jointly design an online platform for a virtual exchange intended to be used with potential CLIL students.
    - Trainees evaluate other group's online platform and give feedback.

At the end of each week and during the whole process, trainee teachers were invited to reflect on the experience by giving an answer to the following statements: (1) Reflect and comment what you have learned; and (2) Reflect and comment on what you have learned about telecollaboration and the intercultural dimension of communicating in English.

Reflections on the experience

Based on a reflective practice model of teacher education, trainee teachers were asked to reflect on their experience and write their reflections as a Task in Moodle. Each week, they were asked to reflect and comment on what they had learned.

The example below of a Spanish student's reflections, during the 8 weeks they worked collaboratively, illustrates how s/he perceived the learning from the intercultural online environment using intercultural telecollaboration (Table 12.1).

From his/her reflections, the perceptions of what was learned in weeks 1 and 2 are related to his/her own identity and the relationship with others. When the student says, "I have learned to do a short summary of my life and who I am in order to introduce myself," the student is developing his/her own awareness process, but s/he is also learning about others, about his/her partner from The Netherlands, finding out that there are differences but also similarities. The student is trying to find a common nexus between them to create a bond and to find their own group identity. S/he also learned about technological tools such as *About.me* or *Glogster.*

During week 3, s/he started realizing how helpful it is having another trainee working on the same task, and in week 4, in which they are asked to design a

Table 12.1 Excerpts from a pre-service teacher's reflections during the whole process

Week 1:	I have learnt to do a short summary of my life or who I am in order to introduce myself. I think I have never done that in a written way.
Week 2:	I also have learnt more about my Holland partners. I have noticed that we have several differences but also some similarities, not only in what has to do with teaching. For example, I have noticed that one of our Holland partners seems to love Harry Potter movies as much as I do, we just coincide on this in our About.me introductions.
Week 3:	I learnt how helpful is to have another teacher working in the same task with you because it makes easier see mistakes and correct it or develop improvements to any lesson plan.
Week 4:	As in the previous week, I noticed that divide the work make it easier when there is a lot of people working in the same task. If the task that we have designed is right, I think I start to understand what CLIL is now that we practice.
Week 5:	I think this week I have learnt more from the analysis of our classmates task than for ourselves mistakes. I also noticed how easy the table, which we just created based on the CLIL matrix, made a deep analysis of such diverse items that may integrate a CLIL task.
Week 6:	I learned how hard could be empathize some time and how needed it is. Work with people that different subjects, timetables and work systems is really hard. To be concrete is hard to work with people that is different to us in more than the aspects that we are used to. But to overcome those differences have made us great this week, which have been the hardest one to me.
Week 7:	Wait for people work in their proper speed is better than argue.
Week 8:	I learnt how hard is to include all those different items that we have evaluated in the same task, even though you are planning with other five teachers. As in the task 2.3. I realize how easy the table we designed made a deep analysis of such diverse items that may integrate a CLIL task.

task following CLIL criteria, s/he feels supported by other colleagues and feels confident on his/her own learning. It is during week 5 when s/he realizes how important it is to adopt a distance and have the feedback from their own mates with regard to the task the group has designed. S/he also perceives a deeper understanding of the content.

During week 6 the student mentions empathy and how important it is for solving problems. S/he perceives how difficult it is to work with people with a different background although the feeling of success has a very positive impact on him/her.

In week 7, when s/he says that "waiting is better than arguing," s/he is realizing how important is to understand others and not impose his/her own criteria.

In his/her reflection for week 8 we can notice that s/he has adapted to the situation and what was difficult before has now become easy.

In his/her final reflection of the process, s/he was able to express his/her understanding of being a CLIL teacher, giving importance to authentic interactive settings as the one that was created through intercultural telecollaboration and the importance of providing challenging tasks to learners to activate cognition. S/he is also aware of his/her intercultural competence and his/her ability to adopt different perspectives while interacting.

Other voices from pre-service students illustrate many of the key aspects of CLIL competence development as shown in the discussion of data, which have been organized following the 4Cs which are the aims of the course: Content, Communication, Cognition, and Culture.

As regard to "Content," which aimed at knowledge, skills, and competences relevant to CLIL approaches, many of the pre-service teachers highlight the importance of cooperation in CLIL, and the role of CLIL teachers as facilitators. Other knowledge on CLIL is about the concept of scaffolding, the developing of critical thinking, the meaning of a dual-focused approach, etc.

As regard to "Communication," which aimed at the use the foreign language to learn about CLIL by negotiating meaning in an international context, they have used different means of communication that complemented the use of Moodle, which they found very static for interacting. Many of them expressed they wanted to be more immediate in their interactions, so they have opted for the use of Facebook, or WhatsApp, as well as the use of Drive for working on the common word document.

As regard to "Cognition," which aimed at developing own understanding on CLIL through engagement in a joint decision-making process, most of the students have perceived the experience as rich, helping them to understand clearer what they have studied. As one student says "It makes the learning process so significant and teaches us how to design real CLIL tasks and apply CLIL in schools and lessons. Now I understand why CLIL is a dual-focused approach because we have seen it, and we have actually applied it too, promoting both content and language teaching in a balanced way. Thus, we are conscious that we have to pay more attention to the educational process in our practice" (Sp_A12). They have also found useful the task on evaluating another group's work since it helped to go deeper in their analysis of CLIL principles and criteria.

As regard to "Culture," it aimed at developing intercultural awareness by exploring different cultural perspectives and identities as CLIL teachers and consequently acquire a critical stance, pre-service teachers perceive the process of interacting with others as enriching and they perceive the existence of different perspectives. As one student said, "It put us in their shoes. You have to lose your own inhibitions and not judge opinions avoiding prejudices" (Sp_A9).

Conclusions

The experience that has been presented here provides an insight into CLIL methodology competence development in the context of initial teacher education and in an intercultural learning environment. This chapter has specifically addressed the development of intercultural competence using intercultural telecollaboration as a methodological tool. When learners reflect on their experience of intercultural telecollaboration, evidence of CLIL teachers' competences have been identified:

- *The target language competence for teaching CLIL*: learners perceive the importance of fluency rather than accuracy when communicating. They also perceive that during the communication with others there are multiple possibilities of misunderstandings and how important it is to overcome those misunderstandings. From data, we observe that they perceive that it is important to use a variety of strategies for communicating with others and that the experience has contributed to an increased knowledge of grammar and vocabulary, mainly.

- *Competence of integrating CLIL in the curriculum*: learners can articulate key elements of the CLIL approach: they can describe the benefits of CLIL, they can contextualize CLIL teaching regarding the school curriculum, they are able to design and apply evaluation tools, they can integrate or merge language, content and learning, and they can also select appropriate materials and resources.
- *Competence of interculturality*: learners can perceive similarities and differences between people with different cultural background, they are able to perceive the importance of attitudes such as empathy, they perceive the importance of trusting the other in communication, they are able to adopt a distance from one's self, and different perspectives when carrying out a task.

Intercultural telecollaboration changes the social context of learning, involving students from different educational contexts with different cultural and academic perspectives. It requires the teacher trainer to have specific abilities to communicate, negotiate, and mediate. Intercultural telecollaboration initiatives can have an important role to play in achieving the goals of a teacher trainer developing CLIL teachers' competences. Teacher educators are encouraged to create natural environments of interaction where communication breakdowns occur but at the same time these breakdowns are rich learning opportunities for their own students, which can help to explore why members of different cultures interpret behaviors differently, and how different perspectives can find an in-between place. Technology plays an important role too, to facilitate learning, motivation, engagement, and creativity. A challenge-based learning, involving students in solving real-world problems contributes to this endeavor.

Note

1 The course aims to develop awareness of the principles of CLIL methodology and to upgrade communicative competence of English as a foreign language.

References

Belz, J. A., & Müller-Hartmann, A. (2003). Teachers as intercultural learners: Negotiating German-American telecollaboration along the institutional fault line. *The Modern Language Journal*, *87*(1), 71–89.

Belz, J. A., & Thorne, S. L. (2006). *Internet-mediated intercultural foreign language education*. Thomson Heinle.

Bertaux, P., Coonan, C. M., Frigols, M. J., & Mehisto, P. (2010). *The CLIL teacher's competence grid. Common constitution and language learning (CCLL)*. Comenius Network.

Byram, M. (1997). *Teaching and assessing intercultural communicative competence*. Multilingual Matters.

Castro, P., & Derivry-Plard, M. (2016). Multifaceted dimensions of telecollaboration through English as a Lingua Franca (ELF): Paris-Valladolid intercultural telecollaboration project. In Jager, S., Kurek, M., O'Rourke, B. (Eds.), *New directions in telecollaborative research and practice: Selected papers from the second conference on telecollaboration in higher education* (pp. 77–82). Research-publishing.net. https://doi.org/10.14705/rpnet.2016.telecollab2016.492

Cenoz, J., Genesse, F., & Gorter, D. (2014). Critical analysis of CLIL: Taking stock and looking forward. *Applied Linguistics*, *35*(3), 243–262.

Coetzee-Lachmann, D. (2007). *Assessment of subject-specific task performance of bilingual geography learners: Analysing aspects of subject-specific written discourse*. https://repositorium.ub.uni-osnabrueck.de/bitstream/urn:nbn:de:gbv:700-2009030617/2/E-Diss864_thesis.pdf

Coyle, D. (2002). Relevance of CLIL to the European Commission's language learning objectives. In D. Marsh (Ed.), *CLIL/EMILE – The European dimension: Actions, trends, and foresight potential* (pp. 27–28). University of Jyväskylä.

Coyle, D. (2005). *CLIL: Planning tools for teachers*. University of Nottingham. http://www.unifg.it/sites/default/files/allegatiparagrafo/20-01-2014/coyle_clil_planningtool_kit.pdf

Coyle, D. (2009). Promoting cultural diversity through intercultural understanding: A case study of CLIL teacher professional development at in-service and pre-service levels. In M. L. Carrió-Pastor (Ed.), *Content and language integrated learning: Cultural diversity* (pp. 105–124). Peter Lang.

Coyle, D. (2011). Setting the CLIL agenda for successful learning: What pupils have to say. *Plenary conference at the II Congreso Internacional de Enseñanza Bilingüe en Centros Educativos*. Universidad Rey Juan Carlos.

Coyle, D. (2013). Listening to learners: An investigation into 'successful learning' across CLIL contexts. *International Journal of Bilingual Education and Bilingualism*, 16, 244–266. https://doi.org/10.1080/13670050.2013.777384

Coyle, D. (2018). The place of CLIL in (bilingual) education. *Theory into Practice*, *57*(3), 166–176. https://doi.org/10.1080/00405841.2018.1459096

Coyle, D., Hood, P., & Marsh, D. (2010). *CLIL – Content and language integrated learning*. Cambridge University Press.

Dale, L., & Tanner, R. (2012). *CLIL activities: A resource for subject and language teachers*. Cambridge University Press.

Eurydice. (2006). *Content and language integrated learning (CLIL) at school in Europe*. Eurydice.

Fleming, M. (2010). *The aims of language teaching and learning*. Council of Europe.

Garay, O. (2007). CLIL: An innovative new trend in the field of language teaching. *ELT Journal*. https://www.researchgate.net/publication/301291371_CLIL_An_innovative_new_Trend_in_the_Field_of_Language_Teaching

Graddol, D. (2006). *English Next. Why global English may mean the end of "English as a foreign language."* British Council.

Guilherme, M. (2004). The role of intercultural communication and interaction in modern languages departments. *Anglo-Saxonica*, *2*(21), 119–138.

Guth, S., & Helm, F. (2010). *Telecollaboration 2.0*. Peter Lang.

Hui, L. (1997). New bottles, old wine: Communicative language teaching in China. *English Teaching Forum*, *35*(4), 34–41.

Kern, R., Ware, P., & Warschauer, M. (2004). Crossing frontiers: New directions in online pedagogy and research. *Annual Review of Applied Linguistics*, *24*, 243–260.

Kramsch, C. (2009). *The multilingual subject*. Oxford University Press.

Lasagabaster, D., & Ruiz de Zarobe, Y. (Eds.). (2010). *CLIL in Spain: Implementation, results and teacher training*. Cambridge Scholars Publishing.

Liddicoat, A., & Scarino, A. (2013). *Intercultural language teaching and learning*. Wiley-Blackwell.

Maljers, A., Marsh, D., Wolff, D., Genesee, F., Frigols-Martín, M., & Mehisto, Y. (2010). *Diverse contexts-converging goals: CLIL in Europe*. Peter Lang.

Marsh, D. (1994). *Bilingual education & content and language integrated learning*. International Association for Cross-cultural Communication, Language Teaching in the Member States of the European Union, University of Sorbonne.

Marsh, D., Mehisto, P., Wolff, D., & Frigols Martín, M. J. (2010). *European framework for CLIL teacher education*. European Center for Modern Languages.

Mehisto, P., Marsh, D., & Frigols, M. J. (2008). *Uncovering CLIL, content and language integrated learning in bilingual and multilingual education*. MacMillan Publishers Limited.

Meyer, M. (1991). Developing transcultural competence: Case studies of advanced foreign language learners. In D. Buttjes, & M. Byram (Eds.), *Mediating languages and cultures* (pp. 136–158). Multilingual Matters.

Müller-Hartmann, A. (2006). Learning how to teach intercultural communicative competence via telecollaboration: A model for language teacher education. In J. A. Belz, & S. Thorne (Eds.), *Internet-mediated intercultural foreign language education* (pp. 63–84). Heinle & Heinle.

O'Dowd, R. (2003). Understanding "the other side": Intercultural learning in a Spanish-English email exchange. *Language Learning and Technology*, *7*(2), 118–144.

O'Dowd, R. (2006). *Telecollaboration and the development of intercultural communicative competence*. Langenscheidt.

O'Dowd, R. (2007). *Online intercultural exchange: An introduction for foreign language teachers*. Multilingual Matters.

O'Dowd, R. (2017). Exploring the impact of telecollaboration in initial teacher education: The EVALUATE project. *The EUROCALL Review*, *25*(2), 38–41. https://doi.org/10.4995/eurocall.2017.7636

O'Dowd, R. (2018). Innovations and challenges in using online communication technologies in CLIL. *Theory into Practice*, *57*, 1–9. https://doi.org/10.1080/00405841.2018.1484039

Viebrock, B. (2010). Alltagstheorien, methodisches wissen und unterrichtliches handeln. In S. Diff (Ed.), *Bilingualer Sachfachunterricht in der Sekundarstufe. Eine Einführung* (pp. 107–123). Narr.

Wolff, D. (2012). The European framework for CLIL teacher education. *Synergies Italie* (8), 105–116.

Index

Made in the USA
Las Vegas, NV
30 October 2024

d636b912-113f-4a7f-a72a-108210aeaa68R01